The
Pleasure
of the
Play

ALSO BY BERT O. STATES

Dreaming and Storytelling

Great Reckonings in Little Rooms:
  On the Phenomenology of Theater

Hamlet and the Concept of Character

Irony and Drama: A Poetics

The Rhetoric of Dreams

The Shape of Paradox:
  An Essay on "Waiting for Godot"

BERT O. STATES

THE PLEASURE OF THE PLAY

CORNELL UNIVERSITY PRESS

ITHACA AND LONDON

First published 1994 by Cornell University Press.

Printed in the United States of America

⊗ The paper in this book meets the minimum requirements of the American National Standard for Information Sciences—Permanence of Paper for Printed Library Materials, ANSI Z39.48-1984.

Library of Congress Cataloging-in-Publication Data

States, Bert O., b. 1929
  The pleasure of the play / Bert O. States.
     p.   cm.
  Includes bibliographical references and index.
  ISBN 0-8014-3036-4 (cloth). — ISBN 0-8014-8217-8 (paper)
  1. Drama—Technique.   2. Drama—History and criticism.   I. Title.
PN1661.S7   1994
808.2—dc20   94-15630

To
Marvin Carlson,
sui generis

There are things which we see with pain so far as they themselves are concerned but whose images, even when executed
in very great detail, we view with pleasure.

—Aristotle, *Poetics*

Contents

Acknowledgments

The editors of *Modern Drama, Journal of Dramatic Theory and Criticism*, and *Theatre Journal* have kindly permitted me to reprint material that first appeared in their pages: "*Catastrophe:* Beckett's Laboratory Theatre," *Modern Drama* 30 (March 1987); "Tragedy and Tragic Vision: A Darwinian Supplement to Thomas Van Laan," *Journal of Dramatic Theory and Criticism* 6 (Spring 1992); and "The Anatomy of Dramatic Character," *Theatre Journal* 37, no. 1 (1985). These essays appear in substantially revised form in Chapter 12, Chapter 11, and Chapter 9, respectively.

I owe special thanks, as always, to Dan McCall for his invaluable comments on the manuscript and for keeping my "infactual" infractions to a minimum, to Paul Hernadi and Donald Pearce for reading parts of the manuscript with their characteristic care and good advice, and to Stephanie Sandberg for her careful and prompt editorial review. Finally, there is the debt of appreciation any teacher owes to his students, but mine is especially strong to the decade of students who passed through DA 61, the "lab" where many of the ideas were first explored.

B.O.S.

The
Pleasure
of the
Play

Introduction

This book began innocently as an attempt to write an introductory text for a beginning course in dramatic structure. Having taught such a course for many years, I have long thought about writing a book that would deal with basic problems and principles of construction: plot, action, character, reversal, recognition, the relation of dramatic texts to nondramatic, the nature of acting, the actor's presence before an audience, and so on. Indeed, I begin my own course by explaining that "we" will look at plays from three overlapping perspectives: (a) as exercises for realizing the possibilities of the actor and the stage, (b) as artistic vehicles for arousing and satisfying the expectations of the audience, and (c) as carriers of important (or frivolous) ideas about human nature and social experience. And I have generally maintained this orientation here, though the original plan of the book has changed substantially. As it turns out, my "introductory" reader gradually became less and less introductory and was replaced by a hypothetical reader who may already have taken the course or indeed even have thought of teaching such a course. That is, I began assuming more and more acquaintance with world drama and theater, as well as an interest in the most basic perceptual conditions under which we read and view dramatic art. So my elementary text turned into a not-so-elementary text about elementary principles, designed for any reader who is interested in such problems.

I suspect that this shift in orientation has to do partly with my personal inability to write an introductory text and partly with the subject itself. Texts written for elementary-stage learners may be very useful for learning a language or mathematics or physics or electrical wiring, but I doubt that the drama unfolds its mystery in "steps" from simple to complex. Indeed, it turns out that the more elementary the step, the harder the explanation. "Now there would seem to be something a little suspect," Eric Bentley writes in *The Life of the Drama*, "in claiming to solve the advanced problems if you haven't solved the elementary ones. But have you ever solved the elementary ones? The easiest questions are the hardest. And you can only broach them as you broach the hardest: by breaking them down into their component parts, tackling the cruder components, and working your way through to the less crude" (1965, 3–4). Though I agree with this idea, I have doubts that questions ever get any "harder" or more "advanced" than the so-called easy ones, if we take "easy" in the sense of *elementary*, as I think Bentley means it. It depends, I suppose, on what one considers an elementary problem and what an advanced problem. As far as I can see, what Bentley calls a "cruder component" (plot), I am calling an elementary principle. If plot, for example, is a crude component, it would seem to be so only because we tend to use the word in its crude sense of something in fiction that "thickens"; otherwise, it presents a horde of problems, if only because plot is continuously meddling in the business of character, action, thought, and even atmosphere and setting.

So I conclude that even if we can identify the elementary problems, we never solve them to everyone's satisfaction; we simply illustrate different aspects of their elementarity. They endlessly beckon us, and theorists will probably be writing about them as long as poets write about daffodils and death. Indeed, elementary problems demand the most complex consideration because the elementary is what always stands beneath its manifestations, as in elementary particle theory, which never seems to come to an end. All too often, the elementary is what is hidden behind appearances, if not behind other mistakenly elementary problems. The actor is, in one sense, one of these problems for just this reason, being (so to speak) something made of two things that become one thing. But beneath the thing the actor becomes, while acting—a stage figure—there is another elementary problem that goes by the name of mimesis, one of the most complex topics in aesthetic theory. I am not suggesting that this interdependency is hopeless or even frustrating; in fact, it is the most interesting thing about elementary problems, and in my own case it is just what lured me away from writing an introductory text for "beginners": the questions simply became too alluring to put to rest in definitions or categories. Even so, I hope what I have to say about plays and playing can be understood by an intelligent undergraduate coming to the drama for the first time.

My approach to these problems differs from Bentley's in that it is based in Aristotle's *Poetics*, as is my approach in the introductory course itself. And one of my early "Oedipal" difficulties was in not realizing what was in front of my eyes all along—that the real introductory text of the drama had already been written, that I had been using it for years, and that what I wanted to write was a book about *that* book's value as a tool for poking among these so-called elementary problems. As Stephen Booth has cogently put it, the *Poetics* is a "superb container": it is not "a definition, but . . . it gives the things of tragedy definition—definition in the sense of giving them a local habitation" (1983, 87). What I wanted to do, secretly, is to write an addendum to each of "the things" the *Poetics* undertakes to define, both from the standpoint of certain perceptual problems Aristotle simply ignored, for various reasons, and from that of later plays Aristotle couldn't have known, ending with those written yesterday and those to be written tomorrow. I must add that this desire has nothing whatever to do with the *Poetics* needing revision. It has strictly to do with the work's own power of provocation, which probably derives in part from its being acromatic or esoteric, intended for a private audience already familiar with the major terms and principles. As a result, the *Poetics* comes down to us as a virtual manifest text, as Freud might say, whose latent meanings have been obscured in its passage into public life by the circumstances of its origin. One imagines it sitting, apexlike, atop such commentaries as Gerald Else's massive *Aristotle's Poetics: The Argument*, which itself rests on a pyramid of subtexts by Butcher, Bywater, Cooper, and so forth, back through Robertello and Castelvetro, ad infinitum, all painstakingly devoted to explaining what this slender "peak" of notes meant to say.

Indeed, in view of the sacredness of the *Poetics* and the ongoing scholarly concern for the meaning of each syllable and concept, there seemed something vaguely illegal about tampering with it in some other connection than illuminating the text itself, and I have on occasion worried that my classroom practice of adapting Aristotle so liberally would be called to the attention of the classics department and that I would be brought up on a charge of molesting a dead canonical figure. It is, moreover, one thing to do this in a course behind closed doors, another in print, and this gave me some concern. At one point, in the wake of a recent movie, it whimsically occurred to me that one way out of the problem might be to ask my reader to imagine, just for fun, that a group of scientists had found a sample of Aristotle's blood in the body of a mosquito preserved in tree gum in his orchard on the very day he was preparing his lecture for the Lyceum and that they had succeeded in bringing him to life as a clone. Of course, as a citizen of the modern world, Aristotle would be suitably amazed and would want to make many revisions in his philosophy and science, in the light of our achievements. Along the line, we can assume that he might want to revise his *Poetics* to suit modern plays, indeed all plays intervening between his own historical period and his resurrection (for what use is a poetic principle if it doesn't apply to all possible examples of the category?). What would he say? What would he change? What would he retain? Of course, I had ready answers to these questions.

Although I gave up this approach, I confess (having gotten it in anyway) that I am doing something very similar. To put it in a somewhat more responsible light, I am simply extending the ramifications of a text that has dominated my pedagogical life. Kenneth Burke once wrote of Freud, "What I should like most to do would be simply to take representative excerpts from his work, copy them out, and write glosses upon them. Very often these glosses would be straight extensions of his own thinking. At other times they would be attempts to characterize his strategy of presentation with reference to interpretative method in general" (1957, 221). My chapters are not exactly glosses, and some of them ignore Aristotle altogether, but for the most part they are extensions of Aristotle's thinking or attempts to link his thinking to more recent methodologies such as structuralism, semiotics, reader-response theory, and phenomenology. And though I am not hinting that Aristotle would think as I have thought, reaching my conclusions, I found myself continually trying to think as I think he would have thought as the author of the world's first textbook on dramatic art—and probably its best, at least in the sense of posing all the right *elementary* questions and giving, in my opinion at least, *essentially* the right answers. For more often than not, the things you have to change in adapting Aristotle to later drama aren't the principles themselves but the implications his principles carry as a result of being grounded in Greek practice.

What I find surprising is that so many people who write on the drama are reluctant to consider Aristotle as having any elasticity, or of meaning more than he may have meant to mean. For instance, we find Bentley (who is not one of these people) speaking about plot as an element of drama, among others (character, dialogue, thought, and enactment): "In calling plot the 'soul' of tragedy," he writes, "Aristotle is saying, perhaps, that in his view it is the playwright's principal instrument among several. If drama is an art of extreme situations, plot is the means by which the playwright gets us into those situations and (if he wishes) out of them again. Plot is the way in which he creates the necessary collisions—like a perverse traffic policeman, steering the cars, not past, but into each other" (32). I get the impression here, perhaps wrongly, that Bentley thinks of plot as primarily a "plotty" affair, that plot is a certain thick-and-fastness in the unfolding of events leading to "collisions" or to "surprise and suspense." And one could argue that this is what Aristotle thinks about plot, in his sense of something being a "part" of tragedy and in saying that plot is "the arrangement of the events."

But I suspect that Aristotle's use of the word "part" is very different from Bentley's when Bentley says, "The plot imitates an Action, says Aristotle. It imitates a myth, I have imagined Lord Raglan rejoining. In either case it is not the whole play but a part" (23). I don't really know what Aristotle meant by "part," but his notion that it is also "the soul" of the play suggests that he doesn't mean "part" in the sense that there is someplace in a play where there isn't plot, or that plot is a discrete thing separate from, say, character. For it somehow seems to shortchange the soul of anything to claim that it can be located in one part of itself but not in others. The true import of the word "soul" (*psuche*) suggests a spirit inhering in something, or, as in Aristotle's biology, something that is the cause or source of the living body. Even the Greek chorus seems legitimately a part of the plot if you take it not so much as an ode sung *between* episodes of the "plot" but as the community's response to the unfolding of the thickening drama in Thebes, Argos, Troy, or Aulis. This might be stretching Aristotle to the breaking point, but otherwise we would seem to have a problem explaining which "part" of the play we are in when the chorus is interacting directly with the characters and influencing the action. Do they cease to become part of the plot when they sing an ode from which the characters of the play are excluded? And if so, would one want to make the same division of parts in an opera or musical comedy? So I take the word "part" (or element) as meaning something very different from saying that a carburetor is a part of an engine, and if you remove it the motor may cease to run, but the rest of the car is still there. If we don't take it that way, we are in all sorts of trouble when we try to separate plot from character or action or thought, as, for example, when Cyrano is philosophizing and dueling at the same time.

It seems to me that Aristotle is most useful if you grant that he was dealing necessarily with plots as they occur in Greek plays: if Greek dramatists had been in the habit of writing plays about blind old men confined to wheelchairs, tended by irritable servants, he would probably have insisted that plot was *still* the soul of the drama and "the arrangement of the events" (rather than the events arranged), though the events themselves consisted of two men (characters) having an ongoing argument (dialogue), philosophizing (thought), and simply moving the chair from one place to another on the stage (enactment). In other words, *Endgame* can be considered an "Aristotelian" play in every sense that *Oedipus Rex* can. Such a view does not in the least involve a revision of Aristotle's conception of mythos; it involves only our lifting the concept of mythos out of its Greek setting, shaking off the examples that might still cling to it, and allowing it to shape itself to different materials. Plot is like Proteus: it takes many forms and goes by many disguises, but all of them are called by the same name. If you give mythos the benefit of the doubt, it is as valid today *in principle* as Euclid's theorem that you can draw a straight line from any point to any other point—a straight line, in this metaphor, meaning any sequence of events that is set in the best order to get where you want to go—even if that is to an impasse or a return to your starting point. Indeed, if you compare *Endgame* to *Oedipus Rex*, you see that both plays consist of a series of conversations about a father-son relationship; the difference is that there are fewer characters conversing in *Endgame* than in *Oedipus* (though no fewer collisions) and that Hamm is blind at the beginning, whereas Oedipus isn't blind until the end. Nor is this blindness a trivial matter: in the first case blindness is a condition of life, in the second a self-punishment for an act, and that simple difference makes *all* the difference in the nature and quality of the events that compose the plots.

So you can't do justice to Aristotle's conception of plot—as a principle of form—by interpreting it in the shadow of *Oedipus* and Greek tragedy.

Such a practice, altogether common, seems rather like saying that Mendel's principles of heredity are applicable only to the peas growing in his own garden. So it is with Aristotle's other "parts." My approach is not to reinterpret what Aristotle said about the drama but to credit him with having understood, *in principle*, what the principles of drama actually are and to see how such principles might express themselves under other cultural circumstances. In one sense, I am offering a Platonic reading of Aristotle, in that I would convert Aristotle's particulars (designed partly as a polite critique of Plato's critique of imitation) into Platonic universals. But I would do this, as Kenneth Burke has put it, by taking Plato's "universals out of heaven and situat[ing] them in the human mind . . . , making them not metaphysical, but psychological. Instead of divine forms, we now have 'conditions of appeal'" (1953, 48). This book is really about just that: conditions of appeal, or the arousing and satisfying of the expectations of an audience through the complete use of the actor and the stage.

I should add that parts of this book are only loosely connected with Aristotle or the *Poetics*. Aristotle has almost no interest in the actor and very little to say about thought (or theme) or audience psychology beyond some tantalizing remarks on the production of wonder. I spend considerable time on each of these matters, in addition to making some speculations about the possibility of tragedy itself in the modern world (again, Chapter 11) and the problem of the aesthetic enjoyment—what Castelvetro called the "oblique pleasure"—of another's pain (Chapter 12), an issue Aristotle covers in a single sentence.

As for the structure of my argument, I have tried to proceed from the basic principles and to see where they lead in respect to post-Aristotelian playwriting and theory. I suppose there is a sense in which the chapters can be read singly or in almost any order without serious disorientation. My hope is, of course, that my arrangement reflects the relatively non-hierarchical nature of the problems involved, rather than faulty organization of thought. My own ordering of the discussions no doubt reflects my personal Aristotelian view of the primacy of plot and its component parts. Another view might center itself in thought or character, or see plot as the body for a historical soul that inheres in art. I have no interest in advancing a best or universal theory of the drama, or even a definition of drama as a distinct form of *poesis* or making. My simple belief is that Aristotle has been undervalued as a consequence of being overvalued in relation to a particular form of drama, and it seems appropriate to review his poetics in this light.

A note on my title: basically, what interests me is the question of how plays awaken and maintain our interest by imitating a certain structural pattern that is probably imprinted in the human brain at a very early age. In simple terms, this pattern may be expressed as our fascination with the coming about of catastrophe, an oddly versatile word that straddles both the natural and the aesthetic realms and, in the drama, covers everything from comedy to tragedy (as we see, for example, in Edmund's line, in *King Lear*, "Pat he comes like the catastrophe of the old comedy" [1.2.146]).[1] In both instances, catastrophe is the extreme consequence of mutability in things, "an event producing a subversion of the order or system of things" (*OED*), and of all the arts the drama is the one whose special province is the mimesis of change in human affairs. This is a primary assumption throughout the *Poetics*, and a partial synonym for catastrophe might be *peripeteia*, which along with *recognition* and *pathos* are the central elements in Aristotle's conception of plot. Indeed, catastrophe, or some variation on the idea of subversion (overturning, reversal, etc.), belongs in what Kierkegaard calls the category of "the interesting," or more "properly the category of the turning-point," which he defines precisely in relation to Aristotle's principles of plot (1954, 92).

It is not difficult to account for why we find catastrophe so innately interesting a phenomenon. Being what the Greeks called "dying ones" (*brotoi*), we are all unavoidably enmeshed in change; in a thousand daily ways, we are addicted to chronicling change and assessing its effects, and through some apocalyptic longing (in psychoanalysis called the death wish) we are engrossed by the occurrence of extreme events—the more extreme, the more engrossing. For example, as I write, fire engulfs much of southern California. It is unnecessary to say that no one (except the arsonist) wishes such a disaster on other people. But it is equally obvious (if only through the overscrupulous documentation of the event by the television cameras) that few things compel the attention so much as natural rampage, and there is something bordering on satisfaction as the stakes

---

[1] Or, in Samuel Johnson's 1765 preface to the works of Shakespeare: "Plays were written, which, by changing the catastrophe, were tragedies to-day and comedies to-morrow" (1986, 16).

of the rampage run higher. It is my impression, or at least my hope, that this emotion has nothing to do with an absence of fellow feeling for the victims of disaster. It arises rather, I think, from a certain lure of the improbable brought on by the anonymity of distance, the absence of personal risk (the condition, as Kant says, necessary for the terrible sublime), and the possibility for a rare participation in the Absolute, as if relativity might in this instance be overcome by a full development of the possibilities in a given phenomenon. Secretly, we crave the visit of the alien spaceship—which is to say, we crave extremity.

The feeling I am trying to describe has a peculiar kinship with the satisfaction we experience in the plots of plays, particularly tragedy, the form, as I. A. Richards put it, "under which the mind may most clearly and freely contemplate the human situation, its issues unclouded, its possibilities revealed" (1961, 69). Since Aristotle, we have referred to this satisfaction as pleasure, which of course Freud places just beyond the death principle. But it seems safe to assume that if catastrophe were somehow unknown in our world—if we were mercifully exempt from extremity—there would be little reason to invent plays based on such a principle. In sum, find a race of creatures who do not die, and you can bet they do not produce tragedies or comedies. For of what conceivable use would these diversions be to a people who know nothing about beginnings and endings? In any case, I retain the word "pleasure" here as the fundamental feeling produced by the catastrophes of drama. It goes without saying that such pleasure begins at the beginning of the play, for the beginning is nothing more than the origin and onset of the ending.

I must add that this book is not a study of pleasure in the sense that Roland Barthes treats it in *The Pleasure of the Text* ("The text is a fetish object, and *this fetish desires me*" [1975, 27]), or indeed of various kinds of intellectual or moral pleasure aroused by comedy, tragedy, melodrama, farce, and so on, but such a project holds no more interest for me than a book about the various kinds of themes one might find in plays. For my own purposes, I prefer Mikel Dufrenne's approach to the seductive pleasure of art: "One may even say that the virtue of the aesthetic object is largely measured by its ability to seduce the body. If the idea of an aesthetic pleasure has any meaning, it is in terms of a pleasure experienced by the body. . . . It appears that the aesthetic object anticipates the body's desires or gratifies them insofar as it awakens them" (1973, 339–40). The last sentence makes my point: I am interested in how—by what structural means—the play "anticipates" our desires and succeeds in awakening them. In other words, rather than writing an anatomy of erotic pleasures afforded by the drama, I have written (like Aristotle) a manual of seduction.

Finally, I must add that I am not concerned here with the psychological status of the pleasure or emotions experienced by the audience. For example, Kendall L. Walton discusses emotions experienced by spectators and concludes that the spectator does not experience real fear or real pity during a tragic play, but something closer to quasi fear or quasi pity—what he refers to as "fictional" pity and fear (1993, 195–204, 241–49). Granted, this is an interesting problem, but I do not come to grips with it here. I assume that there are very real differences between fearing for Oedipus or Hamlet in the theater and feeling fear while I myself am mounting a scaffold to the guillotine. But I am coming at the idea of pleasure from the standpoint of how plays manage to arouse these feelings in dramaturgic terms. It wouldn't make much difference to my argument, in short, whether the feelings are called real or quasi or fictitious emotions. Whatever they are, we have them, and we do so because plays provoke them in their orchestration of (often) painful emotions.

CHAPTER 1

Mimesis and Pleasure

There is one aspect of pleasure that bears directly on mimesis as a universal practice of making images or representations. It is my sense that our views on pleasure suffer from an implied distinction between pleasure and art. Art produces pleasure (of various kinds) and is therefore the cause of pleasure in roughly the sense that one might say that a machine is the cause of products, or the cause of death was poison, or that love was the cause of marriage. First, there is the art; then the pleasure. We could scarcely have the pleasure if the art weren't there to provide it.

But the notion leads beyond this simple causal necessity to the impression that the pleasure is somehow distinct from the exposure: pleasure is produced by art and goes on to have a certain shelf life. We have similar notions about what goes on in the mind. As Nietzsche puts it in *The Will to Power*, "'There is thinking: therefore there must be something that thinks.'" Or, there is dreaming; therefore there must be something that dreams. But this, he goes on, "is simply a formulation of our grammatical custom that adds a doer to every deed" (1968, 268), or, one might say, an object to every verb. Let us grant that without the physiological foundation of the brain there could be neither thinking nor dreaming (not to mention pleasure). But there isn't something in the brain that thinks the thinking or dreams the dream: there is only thinking and dreaming being done by the brain. The alternative would lead inevitably to the so-called homunculus, or little thinker, within the brain whose thinking is caused (if you follow your own premise) by an even littler thinker—and so on to infinity. So the exposure to art does not produce pleasure, or does so only because grammatical expression must put it that way: pleasure is what occurs (under proper conditions) when human perception confronts an art object, just as pain is what occurs when a human finger confronts a descending hammer.

It would be all right to accept the grammatical way of putting the point, except that we also debate the nature of the pleasure produced by art as if pleasure were something that survives the exposure, like a take-home tune in the musical, usually something of a beneficial kind. It may be true that pleasure does survive; but if something (a play) continues to give us pleasure after it is over, it is probably because we are recalling the pleasure from memory and, reliving the experience, no doubt with increasing weakness of affect, in the mind's eye. Or, it may be that our exposure to art has other benefits, such as refining our sensibility, or (as Aristotle says) our sense of what goes with what, or even the pleasure of knowing that *King Lear* and *War and Peace* are there and available, when we want to reread them, and somehow constitute a permanent monument to human possibilities. But these seem to be forms of pleasure (if that is the word for it) that are different from the pleasure of experiencing artistic works or an ice cream cone in durational time. This may seem a small point, if not a technicality. But I think the cause-effect idea leads us away from the central pleasure we experience in the presence of art, and specifically away from the pleasure that arises from what Aristotle (without further comment: sec. 6) calls its "workmanship."[1] Since almost all of what I say in the following chapters is concerned with the effects and affects of "workmanship"—or the techniques of seduction—this seems a matter to consider before we move to more structural topics.

Aristotle's invocation of the term "mimesis" is usually considered a response to Plato's notion in the *Republic* (book 10) that imitation is "thrice removed from . . . the truth"; the imitator "knows nothing of true existence; he knows appearances only." In this context, Aristotle writes the *Poetics* to show that the tragic poet is imitating not appearances, not kings and generals, but actions and universals. There isn't a word about the aesthetic implications of the term "mimesis" (which of course covers all forms of descriptive representation) or the difference between representa-

[1] I use Gerald Else's translation throughout (Aristotle 1967).

tions and the things of reality. We are told only that "the habit of imitating is congenital to human beings from childhood" and that "all men take [pleasure] in works of imitation" (sec. 6). Moreover, our species differs in this respect from the other animals. Aristotle doesn't claim that animals do not imitate, only that humans are more imitative and learn their first lessons through imitation. My primary concern here centers on how we might account for pleasure in imitation as something grounded in human nature. Since we are also members of the animal kingdom, perhaps that is the best place in nature to begin our inquiry.

I am drawn not to the mating rituals or play habits of animals but to a curious creature from the sea called the anglerfish. My dictionary defines the anglerfish (*Lophius piscatorius*) as "having peculiar filaments projecting from its head, with which it is said to entice the fish on which it feeds." The anglerfish has long fascinated me because it is one of those "dumb" creatures which uses its body to produce a deception, much as a possum "plays dead" or the killdeer lures predators away from its nest by pretending to have a broken wing. These are very sophisticated strategies, and they give rise to strategic questions about art. What, one wonders, is the difference between an anglerfish that (presumably) sets up an imitation prey for other would-be eaters and a theater group that puts on a show and lures an audience to indulge its hunger for imitation? Surely going through the small brain of the anglerfish must be *some* awareness of dangling the lure for fish out there who will (in its experience) become interested enough to drop by to see what's "playing." Does it *know* it's angling? Does it angle only when it is hungry? Does it set up stage at particularly propitious street corners of the sea bottom where traffic is thicker, like the wagon theater of the Renaissance? When it begins to angle (when the curtain rises), does it have even the most rudimentary sense of *pretense*, of using its appendage to perform an impersonation? And, finally, which came first, the filament or the idea of angling? How does nature think these things up?

Obviously this is anthropomorphism of the worst sort. The scientific answer to the question (insofar as we have one) is that the anglerfish isn't imitating anything; it has no such sophisticated concept in mind; it is just carrying out the instructions of a naturally imprinted motor program. A human being comes along, sees a resemblance between what the anglerfish does and what anglers do on dry land in mountain streams, and makes a metaphor about it. Still, say what you will, the anglerfish keeps itself alive by *essentially* theatrical means. All that seems to be different is the motive for imitating, which in our case seems to involve the arousal of a certain pleasure and for the anglerfish the acquisition of food (which is perhaps another kind of pleasure). In any case, if I've incorrectly humanized a fish, it is really my intention to see something fishy in theater—something natural, or naturally selected, that we do, as a species, for absolutely necessary purposes. Why should we leave biology out of account in aesthetic matters? What, after all, *is* the difference between the strutting peacock and the strutting fretting actor? As Edward O. Wilson writes, "The sensuous hues and dark tones [of art] have been produced by the genetic evolution of our nervous and sensory tissues; to treat them as other than objects of biological inquiry is simply to aim too low" (1978, 11). In short, is there not at the bottom of the theater enterprise a level of biological insistence that is, as Aristotle puts it, "rooted in human nature," something that we do naturally, even if for other reasons than the rest of the animal kingdom performs its so-called imitations. We are assured from Aristotle forward that this naturalness involves our pleasure and instruction. But what then is it that binds pleasure, instruction, and mimesis? What is it about the production of images that is pleasurable and instructive? Not that they are representations of human experience, because many pleasurable imitations have nothing directly to do with human experience, beginning with music and coming up through Kasimir Malevich's *White on White*. And what is learned through mimesis that couldn't be learned by other means? Aristotle tells us that imitation teaches "what kind a given thing belongs to: 'This individual is a So-and-so'" (sec. 6) and that it is pleasurable to know this. I am not in the least denying that imitation is pleasurable and instructive, or pleasurable because instructive, but only suggesting that there is something of a gap in the relationship of one to the others. Is it possible that imitation is an elementary activity in some other sense, even underlying cases in which learning takes place by going through the motions in a mock way? For example, the play of young animals is apparently pleasurable even as it perfects, through imitation, the skill needed in the real stalking and killing to come.[2]

---

[2] As I write, the Center for the Neurobiology of Learning and Memory at the University of California–Irvine has announced "that 10 minutes of listening to a Mozart piano sonata raised the measurable IQ of college students by up to 9 points." Alas, the boost

Obviously, there are no clear answers to these questions. Nevertheless, in and around the whole idea of pleasure and instruction (*dulce et utile*), there is an air of the pragmatic and the referential, or an assumption that we should be getting something out of art, as opposed to *having* something during it. What the anglerfish helps us see is that, although the motive and the degree of awareness of imitating may be different in humans and lower animals, there is reason to believe that imitating is very much like eating, breathing, hunting, flight, sexual performance, and so on. An even more curious fact is that the pleasure of art quite often involves us in the display of intense pain: what can be pleasurable about this? One might say, metaphorically, that as the anglerfish has inherited (by natural selection) a useful appendage for luring prey, so *Homo sapiens* has inherited a disposition for making things stand in—or rather away from—the world in a special way, things made of the world and yet made in such a manner as to transcend the world. These stand-ins are called imitations—often mistakenly thought to be copies of things in the world. So the anglerfish and the human artist fall along the same biological continuum, the operative difference being that human mimesis, in its artistic phase, seems to be carried out for itself, for its own good, or at least to produce the immediate good we call pleasure, such as we see on the pleasure-glazed faces of Daumier's pleased audience. Imitation may serve still other ends, but creates its primary pleasure through something inherent in its nature and way of existing before us.

Perhaps we can sum up this purposefulness of theater by positing an imaginary moment of evolution on the seafloor. I would not want to press any analogy between an artist and a fish very far, but imagine our anglerfish one day discovering its filament for the first time, like a child discovering its toes, and becoming simply enthralled by the beauty of all the variable configurations and symmetries that are possible with this supple device. Here, so to speak, we have the first artist, a deep-sea actor. Now imagine other fish coming along and watching this display with

---

dissipated within ten minutes. The theory is that classical music probably enhances abstract reasoning by reinforcing certain complex patterns of neural activity (*Los Angeles Times*, Thursday, October 14, 1993, p. 1). In any case, this is certainly good news for Mozart lovers, and one can envision a revolution in which classrooms might be equipped with infrasound systems whereby rational skills in math and logic would be accelerated 10 percent.

equal pleasure and applauding the performance with a furious agitation of the pectoral fins. All the ingredients of theater are now present. Now imagine a smart friend of the anglerfish—call it the Machiavel fish—swimming out of the wings and whispering, Iago-like, "You know, you could probably use that thing to catch your dinner," and you have theater being adapted to a useful, though altogether secondary, purpose.

I am not suggesting that theater is a predatory institution. I am interested here in the question of how it is that mimesis can be an end in itself and adapt itself to other ends as well. Let us move up the biological scale: midway between the anglerfish and, say, a sumptuous performance of Verdi's *Aida*, let us place the cave drawings at Lascaux. Here is a clear case of primitive human imitation dating from 15,000 B.C., and we can no longer explain it as the consequence of an elementary motor program imprinted in behavior. Something has changed, but what? Several possibilities suggest themselves. For one thing, the imitation now survives its making, unlike the performance of the actor or anglerfish. We have now an objective artifact left by an absent maker—a *work* of art. And a new problem emerges in that the art object reflects back to the viewer a peculiar quality of expressiveness: it not only *is* something, it is also *about* something. And in this sense it has already detached itself from the cave wall. No one has been more eloquent on this aspect of the Lascaux paintings than Maurice Merleau-Ponty, who sees them as illustrating the "enigma" that occurs between the self and the things of the world:

> Quality, light, color, depth, which are there before us, are there only because they awaken an echo in our body and because the body welcomes them. . . .
>
> Things have their internal equivalent in me; they arouse in me a carnal formula of their presence. Why shouldn't these [correspondences] in their turn give rise to some [external] visible shape in which anyone else would recognize those motifs which support his own inspection of the world? Thus there appears a "visible" of the second power, a carnal essence or icon of the first. It is not a faded copy, a *trompe-l'oeil*, or another *thing*. The animals painted on the walls of Lascaux are not there in the same way as the fissures and limestone formations. But they are not *elsewhere*. . . . I would be at great pains to say *where* is the painting I am looking at. For I do not look at it as I do at a thing; I do not fix it in its

place. My gaze wanders in it as in the halos of Being. It is more accurate
to say that I see according to it, or with it, than that I *see* it. (1964, 164)

But what could have been the purpose, then, of the paintings? Was it
"pleasurable" *because* "instructive" to paint them or to look at them? Were
they intended as a historical record, or as a religious symbol of the animal
spirit? Were they sympathetic magic, as Wilson himself suggests, "derived
from the notion that what is done with an image will come to pass with
the real thing" (1978, 179)?[3] There is no need to discard these and other
possible answers, but, again, it seems to me they avoid the question of
imitation as a phenomenon by dwelling on a use to which it is being put.
For again, in another time and place, we will find the art of imitation
being used to different ends, such as making graphic and written records
of explorations, historical events, wars, and kingships (as in the Aztec
codices), depicting the identifying plumage of birds, preserving the faces
of leaders, revealing social and political abuses, and always we will find
children drawing animals and houses and shafted sunbeams without the
least prompting or instruction. There is no end to the uses to which
imitation might be put. But this is as much as to say that language is an
instrument of communication as opposed to something in its own right,
or that music can be used to create the proper ambience for sexual seduction. What is it about music that creates this ambience if not, to come
back to Dufrenne, its "ability to seduce the body" (in still another sense)
through its audible being?[4] So one is led to believe that if all the things

---

[3] Clayton Eshleman sees the cave paintings as originating what he calls "the history of
image" (1981, 10). "I felt that I was witnessing the result of the crisis of paleolithic people
separating the animal out of their thus-to-be human heads, and that what we call 'the
underworld' has, as its impulse, such a catastrophe behind it" (11). And, in a slightly later
book: "I have attempted to get beyond the traditional archeological approach that
Paleolithic art reflects only survival concerns. My vision is that behind these cave wall
'signings' is a crisis that was going on for thousands of years: the separation of the
hominid/animal constitution. Ice age severity, plus tools and fire, had brought people
into dialogue to the point that at around 30,000 B.C. this crisis began to be 'imagined,'
that is, a metamorphic act took place: the animal was taken out of the Cro-Magnon and
wrestled onto rock. . . . (thus positioned and signed the cave wall became his first 'lab,'
and like a microscope deepened and narrowed him—released of animal, dependent
upon animal, he became obsessed with animal. The timeless caul was torn)" (1983, 86–
87). I owe this interesting reference to my colleague Donald Pearce.
[4] For instance, in music there are no conceptual rewards or cause-effect expectations,
no descriptions of real things, and no events brought on by people. Yet music palpably

that imitation might do for us or teach us (and in teaching give pleasure) were otherwise accomplished by other means, we would go on imitating all the same. And this gives rise to the possibility of a form of elementary purposefulness beneath all these secondarily purposeful ends.

Coincidentally, it so happens that Theodor Adorno also identifies an enigma at the heart of the artwork. For Merleau-Ponty the enigma occurs between the self and the thing-other, the outside and its internal equivalent in me. It is effectively the enigma of the spectator of art (or of the world). For Adorno the enigma—a possible variation of the same enigma—occurs in the work itself: it is the work's way of being, as a consequence of "having been broken off" from the world (1984, 184) and put in this special neither-here-nor-there relationship with the world. The enigma is that the artwork is a riddle, in that it "hides something while at the same time showing it" (178). Any answer that art offers is mimetic, rather than judgmental, conceptual, or discursive, and this throws us back on the enigma that art is itself a "thing negating the thing-world" (175)—a fancy way of saying that the animal paintings are neither part *of* the wall on which they are inscribed nor are they "elsewhere."[5] One may say that the imitation cancels (negates) the world by putting another world, not of this world (sometimes called a fiction), in its place. Consequently, we are "at great pains" to say where we are in the presence of a work of art. It evades us, even in its most realistic forms. And it is possible that a work of art fills us with emotion because of this evasion, or this way of being *enigmatically* there between the world and the self of the maker or on-looker. The work becomes what Georges Poulet calls a "subjectivized

---

reorganizes our sensory faculties and produces what we might call *pure plot*—that is, an uncontaminated experience of balance, contrast, variation, repetition, elaboration, disclosure, reversal, and crescendo. It is, in a word, *thrilling*. And yet music is nothing but organized sound, with zero verisimilitude, no likeness to anything "real" (except perhaps our experience with space), no semantic relevance to life. Can we not suppose that the pleasure of music is simply a different, nonrepresentational species of the pleasure we have in plays and that, indeed, the more conceptual and ideational pleasures we derive from plays (moral lessons, awareness of universals, etc.) are forthcoming precisely because they ride on the rhythmic current of the pure pleasure of the audible?

5 The classical document on this idea, of course, is Heidegger's "The Origin of the Work of Art," principally in the notion of the rift-design or the struggle between World and Earth in the created work of art, so that its createdness "stands out from it, from the being thus brought forth, in an expressly particular way" (1975, 65).

object," or a mental object "in close *rapport* with my own consciousness" (1981, 43). For example, Nelson Goodman, by way of pointing out that the proper question is not "What is art?" but "When is art?", writes that "a Rembrandt painting may cease to function as a work of art when it is used to replace a broken window or as a blanket" (1978, 67). When I think of the *Self-Portrait*, for example, stopping a hole (as Hamlet says) to keep the wind away, something deeply disturbing occurs inside me. I think my reaction is only remotely connected to the painting's reputation as an Old Master or to the waste of a priceless work of art, though these may be factors. Primarily, I think what has occurred is a violation of the work's Being, which is to say the erasure of its equidistance from empirical reality, on one hand, and the world the painting arouses in me as a carnal formula, on the other. How sad to see that the painting has lost its proper footing in the world and has become one of the things. As countless examples will indicate, damage done to works of art carries the same implications of outrage and pain as damage done to human beings, certainly more (or of a different kind) than to inanimate things like buildings and parking meters. And the reason is that works of art are, in part, human—the unique signs of the human soul projected into a space between world and self.

We can see this principle working in reverse form on an even simpler level. As a virtually automatic act, we very often see faces in the foliage of shrubs or in the billows of clouds. Sometimes the faces are filled with character and nuance, and we are even moved to imagine they have a history or are involved in some immediate drama ("This face has experienced something painful."). We know they are only there in the mind's eye, but the objectivity of the effect produces a strange sense of their being detached from the shrub or cloud, yet at the same time "out there," outside the mind, unlike a thought-image. They exist, in short, as imitations; and what makes them imitations is not that nature is doing the imitating or that they are copies of faces we already know, projected onto a natural mass, but that they are collusions between objective nature and the subjective holdings of the private brain: they are both fictitious and real, rather like the actor or the puppet. The pleasure such images produce is not joy or some immediate thrill of the senses: it is not exactly fun to look at them. The pleasure, rather, arises from a dimension of actuality in which the self and the other are joined and exchange natures, thus offering a momentary solution to the enigma of our ontological isolation from the things of the world.

Beside Aristotle's defense of mimesis—"the habit of imitating is congenital to human beings from childhood . . . , and so is the pleasure that all men take in works of imitation"—let us place a modern biological version of the same idea by Jean-Pierre Changeux:

> The fundamental capacity of the brain of the higher vertebrates, particularly humans, involves the construction of "representations," either as a result of interaction with the environment or spontaneously by an internal focusing of attention. If one adopts the theory put forward here, these representations are built up by the activation of neurons, whose dispersion throughout multiple cortical areas determines the figurative or abstract character of the representation. A mental object is by definition a transient event. It is dynamic and fleeting, lasting only fractions of a second. (1985, 277)

Changeux is not referring here to the representations of art, but to the neuronal wiring that makes all representation possible. The possibility arises, however, that the images of art may indeed spring from still another enigma, born of this fact that mental pictures are transient events lasting only a fraction of a second. It would seem, then, since they constitute the fair share of our subjective life, that they require fixing or what Adorno calls objectivization. That is, we are driven to produce equivalences, as internal pain or pleasure requires bodily equivalences in the form of crying or laughter, which are, in a certain sense, imitations of neuronal feelings. Mental images must be brought outside to this unspecifiable *nonplace* between the self and the empirical world, where they are given duration and audience—where they serve, as it were, as arbitrators of the enigma. For without external representation our subjective understanding of the world remains fleeting and ephemeral, bottled up in the ether of thought, without extension or concrete being—and this is apparently an intolerable loss.

Finally, to our biological ledger we may add the phenomenon of the dream which, on still another neuronal level, is midway between the anglerfish and *Aida*. Jean-Paul Richter rightly calls the dream "involuntary poetry"—more to the point, involuntary imitation. So it would seem that we have no choice but to dream; it is simply not a volitional matter. The question then arises, Is it pleasurable and instructive to dream? We have debated this question at least since Freud, and we are still offering different kinds of answers. Certainly in the dream what pleasure we experience belongs to the plane of the dream's content (sexual arousal, the exhilaration of flight, the magnificent vista, etc.), not to our presence before the workmanship of an expressive object we ourselves are making. For in a dream we simply exchange one reality for another, both equally real; without knowing it, we ourselves become images or representations in which we fall to our death, drown, make love, or fly, although we are doing none of these things. In short, there is no artwork in the dream, even though the dream itself is the consequence of the same creative process that produces art. It is possible, of course, to have the feeling of viewing an art object *as* an art object in a dream, and to be aware that it is different from other things in the dream—a mimesis as opposed to a part of the dream reality. But such is the nature of dream images that thought, image, speech, and event often blend into a composite sensory confusion (without the dreamer's awareness), wherein any image has unnatural properties (animals talk, landscapes think, speech occurs without words, etc.). So although you may view a painting objectively *as* a painting in a dream, there is no guarantee that you will not disappear into it, like Akira Kurosawa into the Van Gogh landscape in *Akira Kurosawa's Dreams*, just because a painting in a dream has the same ontological status as another dream person or thing. In a dream, the enigmas described by Merleau-Ponty and Adorno simply disappear.

It is virtually certain that the Lascaux draftsperson was a dreamer (even animals dream) and that dreaming preceded the making of external mimesis both in the life of the individual and the life of the species. There is also a good possibility that he or she learned how to make images as an extension of the habit of dreaming. For the baffling thing about dreaming is that it occurs spontaneously, without art or experience in making images. Thus one already knows, at a deep level, what representations are before it occurs to one to make one. In the dream, one has already seen a world whose origin is within one's self. One is tempted to think, then, that the occurrence of dreams may have supplied the biological precedent for the painting of the animals, indeed the making of all art, and that when we find out why biology leads us to dream we will also find out why it leads us to make art. One of the things we do know about dreaming is that it is no more possible to keep back than sleep itself; perhaps the same is true for the imitations of waking life.

I certainly don't mean that everyone involuntarily writes poetry or paints pictures, but rather that a share of life is given over to the making of representations in the form of private fictions, daydreams, hypnogogic predreams, or imaginative (what-if?) reconstructions of reality, visual projections (the face in the cloud), memory, or fantasy. Perhaps, as Shelley suggested, those in whom these tendencies are excessive are apt to become artists. We may at least speculate that imitations may have occurred first as the waking exercise of the neuronal need to represent the world of concern in objective images, something as indispensable to survival as the anglerfish's filament, and that these imitations were a natural extension of the mental representations most fully realized in the nocturnal dream.

In any event, in divining purposes for the phenomena of experience, we sometimes get the cart before the horse. There is some reason to think that making metaphors is a pleasurable activity in itself, irrespective of what descriptive or instructional purposes the metaphors may be intended to serve. That is, the purpose of metaphors may be to make metaphors, which is to say, to make little perceptual symmetries out of a dispersed content of the world, to bring things together in a way they aren't together, or pinned down to a specificity, in rational discourse. Consider the biologist who named the anglerfish: on one hand, there was the pragmatic scientific need to give the fish a name so that it can be distinguished from other fish; on the other hand, what drove the biologist-poet to choose "anglerfish" rather than "filament fish" (which is, alas, also a metaphor of sorts) or "appendage fish" (which is less so)? Where do the interests of science and poetry begin and end? In any case, I will bet that our biologist—unless it was a fisherman—experienced a degree of pleasure in finding an appropriate name for this heretofore nameless creature. Indeed, the act of making a metaphor, or reacting to one made by someone else, instantaneously produces a *good* feeling—a small burst of *ekstasis*—and it would seem to have something to do, as I suggest in Chapter 5, with the parts of drama Aristotle calls "peripety" and "recognition," the means by which plays connect unlikely likelihoods into a meaningful unity. Like metaphorical naming, peripety too implies a purpose, but it has the virtue of being something that is immediately purposeful, good in itself, as opposed to being attached to a further or long-range good, like making you more aware of the world or better able to cope with life (artists, for what it is worth, are notorious noncopers). If there is an unaddressable riddle in imitation rising from its equivocal status as a world-negating thing, as Adorno suggests, one might explain its "purpose" as being to imitate the enigma. The enigma of art as riddle is a perfect imitation of the enigma of the riddle of life—there is on one hand the subjectivity of the personal self and, on the other, the objective world that surrounds us, something invariably different from—and indifferent to—one's subjective plan for it. I probably entertain a notion of the function of mimesis very different from that of Michael Taussig, but in his book *Mimesis and Alterity* he puts very well the issue I have been examining from a quasi-biological standpoint. In a sentence reminiscent of Sir Philip Sidney, he says that mimesis is "the nature culture uses to create [a] second nature" (1993, 252). The beauty of this definition lies in the seemingly tautologous way in which it keeps the act of mimesis within the nature that mimesis is often thought to copy. There is no question of copying nature but of blending consciousness in with it. One might imagine the imitator asking the question, "Why is the world *other than me?*" and then satisfying it artistically by "grow[ing] in effect another nature," as Sidney says, that includes the poet-maker in it. If the world weren't other than me, of course, there would be no problem. But there would be no art either. So perhaps the art is a compensation of sorts in that it splits the difference between world and self and allows me to be in two places at once.

As a boy, I used to think that science was coming closer and closer to the Truth and that one day it would run out of problems to solve. Later on, when I had given up the idea of being a scientist and had taken up art, I thought there was a great danger that we were running out of good plots, and in a few years there would be none left. It did not occur to me that every plot is, in a sense, the same plot, just as every scientific problem is the same problem and that scientists probably don't become scientists, or artists artists, to discover new things, but to perform the activity of discovery, which is one of the great pleasures of life. Discovery, or what I refer to as unconcealment, is probably the central principle of dramatic action and a main source of our pleasure in reading or witnessing plays. It is not pleasurable to the likes of poor Oedipus, of course, but then he is only an imitation of the real thing.

CHAPTER 2

The Actor as Musical Instrument

Aristotle barely acknowledges the actor beyond reference to "the persons who are performing the imitation." But since one of our primary perspectives is that theater is an exercise for realizing the possibilities of the actor, the proper place to begin is with our personal experience with the actor and with acting—that is, the physical (and psychic) act of pretending you are someone you *aren't* before a group of people who have paid to see you do just that. For one definition of an actor is, as John Harrop has phrased it, someone who "does artificially what everyone else does naturally" (1992, 7). Or perhaps I should say *think* we do naturally, for it turns out that a great deal of our behavior, from riding a bus to sitting in a restaurant, is dictated by sets of expectations endlessly rehearsed on the stage of the empirical world. Social psychologists these days are calling such sets *scripts*, and this would seem to make all of us actors, to one degree or another. Moreover, the anthropologist Victor Turner, among others, has identified a phenomenon called the "social drama" in which cultural tensions move through a series of phases (breach, crisis, redress, and reintegration and/or recognition of schism [1982, 69]), an overall plot or narrative complete with actors and performances (e.g., ritual and juridical procedures).

It is possible to overstress the likeness of theater to life, but at bottom there is a relevant similarity between a person sitting in a theater on, say, "good behavior" and an actor up on the stage on "bad behavior" playing Richard III: both involve a certain degree of restraint in the deportment of the body and mental concentration on the imaginary. Indeed, commentary in present theory seems to stress the creative and participatory role of the audience in theatrical performance (see Blau 1990; Rayner 1993). In any case, the professional actor is a strange sort of being and until recently has been treated as a stranger, if not an outcast, in our society. Plato thought the actor possessed, if not mad; Rousseau deplored the idea of someone who "annihilates himself," sacrificing identity to that of a chimerical being. Through most of our history, the actor has been persistently identified with loose morals, prostitution, disease, atheism, and unrestrained behavior. The myth continues today in the popular conception of Hollywood as Sin City, a reputation that is probably based as much on the content of its films as on the behavior of actors. The myth is also the consequence of certain inevitable factors attendant on the communal and spectacular nature of theater itself and finally on the fame the actor accrues as a portrayer of fictional people. For the actor is inevitably thought of (unless you come to know one personally) as a composite of his or her roles, as somehow leading an ideal life different in kind from our own. And even though, on one hand, a lucrative industry is devoted to proving that actors are just like us (they buy homes, love their children, and get divorces) by making public their most private behavior, we are invited, on the other hand, to think of actors as living a storybook life uncluttered by trivia (eating, bathing, driving to work)—unless we imagine these events in vivid color and accompanied by a studio orchestra. Indeed, this double interest in the actor as a real and a mythical being is a direct extension of the actor's ontological double status on the stage.

It is important to see what underlies this paradoxical suspicion/fascination with the actor. Suppose I am in my backyard pulling weeds and singing "Somewhere Over the Rainbow." My neighbor beyond the fence overhears me and makes a smart remark to the effect that I am frightening the birds. But it is all very natural: my singing is taken as a sign of good cheer, an occasion for levity, and nobody objects to that. Now suppose, instead of singing "Somewhere Over the Rainbow," I am saying (in a low voice), "If it were done, when 'tis done, then 'twere well it were done quickly. . . ." Even if my neighbor recognizes the lines from *Macbeth* or knows that I am given to such indulgences or that I am rehearsing a role in a play, his or her response is apt to be rather different. Song is one thing, talking to yourself (in iambic pentameter) is another, and the difference takes us to the whole mystery and essence of impersonation. What has happened is that I have somehow "left myself" and, as Sartre puts it in his essay on the actor, have become "totally and publicly devoured by the imaginary" (1976, 162). In short, as Plato would say, I am mad, at the very least troubled by something that has eclipsed my normal self-presentation to the world.

What has happened here, in effect, is that without all the trappings of theater (beginning with a stage and an invited audience) that make such behavior virtually normal, what is left is the unframed, seemingly serious, and outrageous text of a man contemplating a murder—at the very minimum speaking *in a strange way*. Without the proper frame, such behavior is drained of its fictionality and becomes monstrous in the old-fashioned sense of something unnatural. It is true, as Aristotle argues, that the habit of imitating is congenital to human beings from childhood forward; still, every unframed instance of imitation in real life arouses either amusement or suspicion in the spectator, a good sign that it occurs on the behavioral fringe. Yet my imitation of Macbeth contemplating murder is really no stranger, in itself, than the words of the song, in which I audibly yearn for a land where troubles melt like lemon drops, and it is no stranger, really, than a social occasion (attending a party, for instance) in which my behavior is informed by a certain polite style and I follow a script, however routine, established by my society. Why is it natural to sing aloud in public and unnatural to "become" Macbeth in public without the frame and authorization of the stage? Certainly, the difference must have something to do with cultural habit, with a principle of normalcy whereby usage (manners, do's, don't's) is dictated by role expectations in the social drama. (For example, in a country addicted to theater or inhabited only by actors, my imitation of Macbeth would probably go as unnoticed as, I presume, yodeling does in Switzerland.) But it also has to do with seeing and with the sense in which the actor offstage in real life always strikes us (unless we are also actors) as a slightly transcendent creature, that is, real in an unreal way.

Theater is poised at this mimetic boundary between two worlds: the world of the real outside and the world of the felt interior of the self, of "is" and "isn't," that unfolds in the same indeterminate space as the Lascaux cave paintings. But theater is unique among the arts (if we include in it the dance and opera) because it is made of real human beings who have "annihilated" themselves in order to become unreal human beings for our pleasure and instruction. This boundary is the subject of endless speculation by theorists; for even though mimesis is, after all, a simple matter of an actor undergoing an easily performed change into a fictional character, and even though this act entails little more self-annihilation than that of an athlete entering the scripted world of a basketball court (where movement, concentration, and behavior are even more focused), the resultant confusion presents immensely interesting perceptual problems. What precisely are we now seeing? How is it that these players, but in a fiction, a dream of passion, can force their souls so to their own conceit, that they weep for Hecuba—a still more unreal being than themselves—and make us weep for her in the bargain? For the human habit of accepting the real world as given by nature is extended onto the world of the theater stage, which assumes its own reality. And although Samuel Coleridge spoke of this transaction as a "willing suspension of disbelief," the consciousness of our *willing* it is lost in the suspension. It would appear that the suspension is willed, or that we are willing to undergo the suspension, only in the sense that we weren't forced to come to the theater in the first place: once there, we are helpless expectant victims, and two of the few things that can rescue us from its grip are poor acting and a boring play. And of course poor acting is nothing more than a painful reminder that actors are human after all—in the one place we don't want them to be. But in this state of suspension, when the theater is on its very best behavior, we experience feelings that are often more powerful than those we experience in the normal world.

Let us briefly draw some comparisons between theater and some adjacent experiences that are probably more familiar. On the affective scale, theater would be situated somewhere between cinema, on one side, and the nocturnal dream, on the other. Of course the dream is not an art form, but I invoke it for reasons I hope will make sense. Like the dream, cinema is a projection of visual images onto a screen (to speak metaphorically about the brain) which lends it the quality of a direct unmediated experience. Moreover, the dreamlike quality of the cinema (or the cinematic quality of the dream) is such that the auditor, thanks to the infinite versatility of perspective, also becomes a participant in the illusion, or at least is enabled to see precisely what a participant would see (as when a character's viewpoint is replaced by the eye of the camera). Both in a dream and in the cinema one is, so to speak, "on location," or in the same scene as the actors. Obviously there is the sense that the cinematic screen and the light patterns striking it do not constitute a scene at all, but are simply the site of a physical "event" less than a quarter-inch thick in the world of matter. As Christian Metz puts it, "What unfolds [on the cinema screen] may . . . be more or less fiction, but the unfolding itself is fictive: the actors, the 'decor', the words one hears are all absent, everything is *recorded* (as a memory trace which is immediately so, having been something else before)" (1975, 21). The unusual thing about this fictive "unfolding," however, is that the very absence (of actors, decor, etc.) removes the fictive aspect of the cinematic experience and establishes it as a reality—not iconic but fully present, not significational but actual. Again, it is like the dream in that *nothing* is there in any physical sense (except light and screen), but this nothing produces a world of unparalleled realness, a world of "memory traces" that have lost all trace of memory *recalled* and have gained the character of a first and only time.

In the theater, on the other hand, the very real presence of the actor and the setting, however natural or stylized, creates a drag on the illusionary real quality of the experience and converts it into a spectacle of virtuosity. No matter how realistic the stage picture, it cannot escape the fact that real people and real things do not present themselves to the view of others in this manner—or when they do, as in a beauty contest or a presidential procession, or a wedding, they are, to that extent, not themselves but actors in a scene. The expression "She makes a lovely bride" tells the entire story of the theater's affective power to convert the real into an iconic status of a "role." For about the bride, and the groom as well, is an aura of Brechtian self-division into person and performer: Mary Lou Simmons and Mark Wilson as Bride and Groom. Together, they enact a wedding ceremony; they are real people cast into roles, and it thus comes about that the bride having trouble with her veil before the kiss or the groom misplacing the ring are evidences of an erstwhile humanity, vaguely reminiscent of actors missing a cue, but wonderful examples of the "real" persisting into the performance. These actors are such stuff as people are made of.

Thus it is that the theater offers a double paradox: the paradox of the character being at once fictive and real, and the paradox (within this paradox) of the realness contributing to an artificiality whose intentional basis is the project of "showing off" the skills of a woman or man behaving in the performing mode. One might easily argue that this second paradox operates in reverse—that is, that the realness, before our eyes, of the actor and the setting in real space enhances the illusion and takes the audience affectively into a willing suspension of disbelief similar in kind to that of the realness of cinema and the dream. But such a view overlooks the affective truth that the real "anchor" provided by actor and setting constitutes the site of an unnatural refinement of real human behavior and real environment.[1] In a word, theater would place between illusion and reality the parenthesis of aesthetic display, or a zone of "making" in which intensive "work" is being done.

Couldn't one say this of cinema as well? It must be understood that I speak of these two media strictly in their relation to each other. Certainly there is a visible virtuosity in the film's aesthetic project, and we can, and do, speak of the power of the film actor's performance. But Anthony Hopkins and Glenn Close are, as Metz says, absent from the performance. We do not see and hear the performance but rather its "memory trace," which has canceled out the toil and fabrication, as memory itself cancels out its source in the original empirical occurrence of which it is only a trace. I have elsewhere called this the endangerment of the actor, someone who can *be* someone else before our eyes and also *fail* in trying to be someone else (1985, 119–28). This possibility of failure is quite different from that of the film actor, who may fail to be convincing or to carry the part off well (witness our fascination with "bloopers" or outtakes in which the failures of the actors become hilarious, in part *because* the final take is always so error-free). The stage actor performs in tension with the world of the audience, and each moment floats between victory and potential disaster. This is something of an exaggeration: the actor is not *that* endan-

---

[1] In *Frames of Reference*, Erving Goffman lists these "unnatural" conditions as follows: (1) the spatial boundaries of the stage itself which "cut off the depicted world from what lies beyond the stage line"; (2) the open room with no ceiling and one wall removed, "an incredible arrangement if examined naively"; (3) the artificial position of speaking characters in relation to the audience's point of view; (4) the focus on one person at a time and the placement of nonspeakers "out of focus"; (5) the sharing of "talking" time and the pause between speeches for audience response, when expected; (6) the systematic and covert disclosure of information necessary to the audience's comprehension; (7) the elevation and projection of the actor's voice above normal range; (8) the elimination of all nonsignificant information or action (1986, 139–44).

gered, and every actor has a thousand tricks of the trade to get out of trouble. At the very last resort, the actor can simply shrug his or her shoulders, wink at the audience, and get a nice round of applause. But, even so, performance is a *process* of liberation from the world which is signified by the glowing EXIT signs that flank the stage. Thus theater is a dare ("Can this cockpit hold the vasty fields of France?") in which the actor's power is waged against the always potential incredulity of the audience.

Let us look briefly at the famous speech from Shakespeare's *Henry V*:

CHORUS: O for a Muse of fire, that would ascend
    The brightest heaven of invention,
    A kingdom for a stage, princes to act,
    And monarchs to behold the swelling scene!
    Then should the warlike Harry, like himself,
    Assume the port of Mars; and at his heels,
    Leash'd in like hounds, should famine, sword, and fire
    Crouch for employment. But pardon, gentles all,
    The flat unraised spirits that hath dar'd
    On this unworthy scaffold to bring forth
    So great an object. Can this cockpit hold
    The vasty fields of France? Or may we cram
    Within this wooden O the very casques
    That did affright the air at Agincourt?

                 (Prologue)

Here, under the guise of making an apology, Shakespeare is bragging about the temporal and spatial versatility of his theater. What is such a speech doing in the play if not proclaiming in every syllable the limitation that defines the peculiar power and virtue of theater? It is rather like the magician who claims to have doubts that the woman can actually be sawn in half and levitated ("Let's hope it works this evening"). Imagine a motion picture—say, a James Bond film—opening with such a chorus: "Can our camera cram within its eye the fearful battle of Fort Knox, take the warlike Bond beneath the coral sea and into starry space?" Of course it can; that's why we're here—to see the camera do what it does best, "jump o'er times" and "digest the abuse of distance." Despite whatever jumping the theater may occasionally do, however, what we want to see in it, finally, is a play that, once having decided where to jump, maximizes the faculties of the actors and the stage space. In short, it isn't the jumping that impresses as much as the settling into a scene where theater can work its peculiar magic with its relatively modest toolbox. It is true that in battle scenes we are asked, as the Chorus says, to "piece out [theater's] imperfections" in our mind's eye, and "into a thousand parts divide one man," but this is not what theater does best. And when it is done well we are amazed, not because *we* have pieced out the imperfections, but because the theater has used its slim art to produce the effect, knowing full well that the best art always leaves a creative role to its audience. It is not always the case that theater achieves this, of course; some of the most painful theater occurs when a dozen actors with bucklers and wooden swords recirculate their number, as on a conveyer belt, trying to create the illusion of two armies clashing.

As for stage space itself, I think of two examples of scene design which use the theater "cockpit" to perfection: the baroque operatic theater of the eighteenth century (and after), which created in a relatively cramped space highly realistic and "vasty" prisons, fierce island temples, and architectural interiors that were, in point of *opsis*, the *Jurassic Park*s of the day. This effect was achieved by the so-called keyhole principle, which uses the aperture of the proscenium arch (perhaps 25 feet high, 40 feet across) as a frame (often reduced still further) through which the audience could see only the first order of architecture, the rest of the structure, presumably, soaring out of sight beyond the stage opening. To the trapped eye, in short, it is as if space's attribute (infinity) had been released by being bound in: the presentation of a vista would be tautological. What you see in the theater is not all you get, as we see in the living rooms of natural- ism, which are but samples of the house beyond the doors and the house itself but a sample of a thousand such houses you might see in the society beyond.

On the other end of the scale is the stage of Thornton Wilder's *Our Town*, which deliberately strips away everything and leaves it up to the actors to summon a world out of thin air through the pure skill of gesture and mime.[2] Again, this isn't piecing out imperfections: the theater is no

[2] I deal with this aspect of *Our Town* in *Great Reckonings in Little Rooms* (Berkeley: University of California Press, 1985), pp. 97–98.

more imperfect in its physical limitations than the violin is impoverished by having only four strings. In either case, the attraction for the audience lies in what can be done with the potentialities that are built in to the instrument's design, either by historical evolution or as a means of achieving a certain purity and expressiveness. When theater manages to perform one of its optical miracles, our reaction is always to some extent founded on our knowledge that the effect was produced by thoroughly probable means (flats, lights, wires, etc.). For the effect of the achievement depends on seeing how much it owes to its physical origins, rather as a painting is impressive not because the subject is lifelike, realistic, arousing, and so forth, but because it is created through a manipulation of pigment on a flat surface. "It is Van Gogh's brush-strokes and colors," Mikel Dufrenne tells us, "which express despair and love, not the bedroom or the wheatfield he depicts" (1973, 137). To which I add a small refinement: it is Van Gogh's brushstrokes and colors arranged *as* a bedroom or wheatfield that produces the effect; it is in the fusion that the effect resides.

Let us say a theater audience was confronted—unaccountably and without precedent—by a sudden display of the virtuosity that is easily achieved in another medium—say, the cinema—but impossible in theater itself. To take an extravagant example, suppose Peter Pan not only flies across stage and over the orchestra pit, in the usual manner, but out into the auditorium, into the balcony, round the chandelier, and back to the stage, all the while performing loops and figure eights that couldn't conceivably be achieved with wires or the duplicity of photo-projection. Any possible audience appreciation of this event, this jumping through space at will, would be canceled by disbelief, consternation, and distraction, and it is possible that the play would have to stop. This example is deliberately founded on an impossibility in order to show what happens when the rules of probability—the specific gravity—of one medium get confused (if such a thing were possible) with those of another.

I intend the example to illustrate how a medium's affective power depends on its manipulation of its own material potentials and how at the bottom of a medium's *possible* art there is a tension between formal limitations and the performance arising from them. Even within the theater medium itself the same principle obtains. The potentials of speaking theater are very different from those of the mime, where performance is bound by the limits of a body which, to quote Patrice Pavis, "says nothing other than what it does" (1982, 53). Speech in the mime would strike one as a contamination, like a soliloquy in an opera that was spoken rather than sung. So too a photograph offers a more accurate representation of a subject than a painting—or, to be more cautious, if the painter could achieve the realism of photography to the point of obliterating all optic signs of the medium, bewilderment would set in, because the foundation on which artistic expressiveness is assessed would be in doubt. On what basis is one to judge the achievement? Are we in the presence of the limitations of brushstroke and color or those, as in my *Peter Pan* example, of the camera? Why send a painter to do the work of a photographer? At the very least, the painting would be viewed as a tour de force.

I am aware that the school of realism, which has produced remarkable trompe l'oeil effects, might invalidate this claim. But hyperrealism, in my experience at any rate, does not obliterate the signs of painterliness. It is precisely the hyperclarity that sets the painting apart from a possible photograph of the same scene. I should add also that I have seen mime performances that incorporate speech and dialogue. I am not claiming this can't or shouldn't be done, simply that it seems to me a confusion of media and is, to say the least, something that you would notice as peculiar after the eloquence of pure body speech. Finally, one might make an interesting kind of theater by having a film simultaneously projected on the scrim as the actors enact a play before it (I have in mind something more sustained than the projections often used in Brecht productions).

My main idea in this discussion is not to prescribe limitations or to keep artistic media pure but to illustrate how dependent they are on limitations for their effects. To put it simply, we go to the film with different expectations than we go to the theater; we don't expect paintings to be three-dimensional or sculpture to be flat. It is possible to produce such mergers of media, but the effect would itself be a merger of effects—not necessarily a confusion but a confrontation of different frames of organization of the experience, as Goffman would say. This is hardly a denial that technical progress can increase a medium's versatility, or that there can be successful mixtures of media (e.g., in performance theater), but these advances and intermixtures rarely create fundamental modifications in the medium. Advances in stagecraft have hardly displaced the actor as the defining expressive tool of theater for the same reason that robots have not replaced the athlete in the theater of sports. Like athletics, theater belongs to life and the resources of the human body, and it is on these resources that theater founds its special expressiveness. The cinema and sculpture and painting and music may use human life and its resources as their subjects, but they can also produce interesting art that has nothing to do with these things.

I should say a word or two about speech in the theater, or what Aristotle called verbal expression (*lexis*). Is it possible, according to internal formal characteristics, to define certain kinds of speech as more suitable to the theater, and other kinds as less suitable? For example, the following words do not seem to have the characteristics of dramatic speech:

1 cup coarsely chopped green bell pepper
1 cup coarsely chopped celery
2 teaspoons minced garlic
1 cup tomato juice
12 ripe plum tomatoes . . .

Whereas these words from *Death of a Salesman* do:

BIFF: I am not a leader of men, Willy, and neither are you. You were never anything but a hard-working drummer who landed in the ash can like all the rest of them! I'm one dollar an hour, Willy! I tried seven states and couldn't raise it. A buck an hour! Do you gather my meaning? I'm not bringing home any prizes any more, and you're going to stop waiting for me to bring them home!
WILLY: . . . You vengeful, spiteful mut!

But the distinction is spurious. It may be that one can legitimately claim, on the evidence at hand, that there is more drama and tension in the second example, and virtually none in the first, unless you are a gourmet who is excited by the plot of a good recipe. But of course one can read a recipe under all sorts of conditions, and if this one were spoken in a play, say, by a man named Atreus while preparing dinner for his brother Thyestes, you might be on the edge of your seat, or (depending on the vérité of the production) on your way to the rest room. Or, in another vein, imagine Carol Channing or Gilda Radner speaking the words to the accompaniment of a lugubrious cello. The basic recipe for dramatic (or stageworthy) speech, then, would be an arrangement of words (or events) in such a way as to feed an opposition or a tension, either serious or comic, that serves other ends than communicating information (which recipes are usually intended to do). So it is impossible to determine whether speech is dramatic or stageworthy from the content of the speech alone. On the stage, speech is always indentured to "a greater semiological system" (Barthes 1972b, 116), that of mimesis itself. And one of the characteristics of mimesis is that it is an "as if" sign system in which speech is used to create tension between the literal meaning of the words and their occurrence in an illusionary situation. The speech from *Death of a Salesman* happens to be more dramatic only because it contains in the sample itself the tension *and* the evidence of mimetic reduction. Indeed, it is a classic Aristotelian case because the opposing forces are "persons who are near and dear (close blood kin) to one another" (sec. 14), people one would normally expect to hold no such enmity toward each other, therefore productive of the highest possible emotional potential.

To come to the matter of length, as opposed to content, one of the characteristics of speech designed for the theater is that it is tailored to the "two hour traffic of the stage" and, even more important, to the actors who speak it. Dramatic speech is not simply any language used by the actor but language that "uses" the actor in speaking it. That is, dramatic speech is not there for its own purpose or end but to actualize the potentialities of the performer. The actor may be compared, in this regard, to the filament of a light bulb: when the current passes through it, the filament glows, its very resistence being the source of the light. And so it is with stage speech: it illuminates the actor—or, rather, it illuminates the work of the actor, who survives less as a performer than as a performance. My recipe doesn't achieve this end because it is simply a recipe for chicken creole, but, as we've said, an actor might make the words interesting in the theater by resisting their informational value—speaking them in a certain style and motivational context—that would make the recipe incidental to the achievement of its conversion into something else. Indeed, one notices that cooking shows on television ("Julia Child," "The Frugal Gourmet") have learned to theatricalize their presentations by allowing the personality of the chef to become, as it were, a main ingredient in the stew. Thus (presumably) people might tune in not simply to get new recipes but to watch the performance of the cook who converts them *stylishly* into attractive food before your eyes. This may seem trivial or obvious, but kitchen shows, in the end, are faced with certain theatrical requirements, being a species of framed reality and therefore subject to certain expectations that include using the medium to best advantage.

If I wanted an example of speech that makes full use of the actor, I couldn't imagine a better place to look than Shakespeare, if only because Shakespeare's speech, unlike naturalistic speech, is designed, like music, to appeal to the ear. There are of course the great arias of the soliloquies, the "glist'ring Phaeton" speech of Richard II's deposition, the stunning opening of *Richard III*, and so on. One of my favorites happens to be a prose speech from *Much Ado about Nothing*. Beatrice and Benedick are carrying on a merry war of words; one is absolutely anathema to the other, or so their public behavior would suggest. But their friends, seeing the situation differently and observing that "Cupid kills [some] with arrows, some with traps," set up the famous garden scenes in which Benedick and Beatrice successively hear how one is secretly pining away for the other, but is simply afraid to confess his or her love for fear of the other making "sport" of it. All the while, of course Benedick and Beatrice are listening and visible to the audience during the two scenes. Let us take the first of the two soliloquies, Benedick's:

BENEDICK [*Coming forward*]: This can be no trick. The conference was
    sadly borne. They have the truth of this from Hero. They seem to
    pity the lady; it seems her affections have their full bent. Love me!
    why, it must be requited. I hear how I am censur'd. They say I will
    bear myself proudly, if I perceive the love come from her; they say
    too that she will rather die than give any sign of affection. I did never
    think to marry. I must not seem proud. Happy are they that hear
    their detractions and can put them to mending. They say the lady is
    fair; 'tis a truth, I can bear them witness; and virtuous; 'tis so, I
    cannot reprove it; and wise, but for loving me; by my troth, it is no
    addition to her wit, nor no great argument for her folly, for I will be
    horribly in love with her. I may change have some odd quirks and
    remnants of wit broken on me, because I have rail'd so long against
    marriage; but doth not the appetite alter? A man loves the meat in
    his youth that he cannot endure in his age. Shall quips and sentences

and these paper bullets of the brain awe a man from the career of his humour? No, the world must be peopled. When I said I would die a bachelor, I did not think I should live till I were married. Here comes Beatrice. By this day! she's a fair lady. I do spy some marks of love in her. (3.1.228–55)

A good deal of the conversion has taken place visually, by this time, in Benedick's changing reaction to the scene from his position in hiding. We must think of speech here as a vehicle for demonstrating a mind being led down the path of desire. It is precisely sufficient to express the change taking place in Benedick's affections. And there isn't an instant in which the actor is either idle or redundant as a physical presence in the grip of an evolving emotion—the actor is, in a word, glowing. Every sentence, every phrase contributes to the progress, and an actor can move through the speech without a single repetition of affect or addition of "business" beyond that implicit in the words themselves. From start to finish, it is a thing of beauty that would show off the genius of any actor who is up to its demands.

Unfortunately, it is often difficult to appreciate what we have in a verbal performance of this kind because, having the performance, it is hard to imagine it otherwise. I can think of two different ways this speech might have been written. Shakespeare might have shown Benedick gradually falling in love before our eyes through a slow evolution from skepticism and doubt to a tug-of-war between love and the old "war" game; and we would watch him gradually falling into a weakness, thence to a lightness, as Polonius would have it, and into the love wherein he now raves and that we saw coming all along. And this might have produced an interesting scene. Shakespeare didn't write this scene, however. The speech grows from momentary consternation to almost immediate acceptance, at "Love me! why, it must be requited." The balance of the speech, then, is devoted to the spectacle of rationalization of the condition. So we get two treats in one: not only the falling in love (which was virtually accomplished in the overhearing scene anyway) but falling so *deeply* in love, and so fast, that casuistries are necessary—any moral cliché will do—in order to convince the remnant of the rational man left in Benedick that the love has adequate grounds, that his sacrifice of requitement is well worth the quips and paper bullets he will dodge hereafter, all of this ending splendidly in the ardent altruism of "No, the world must be peopled." This speech is exactly what Samuel Johnson meant in saying that Shakespeare's people "act and speak by the influence of those general passions and principles by which all minds are agitated, and the whole system of life is contained in motion" (1986, 11). To fall in love is human, as we say, but to love is also to fall into one of the deepest stupors of helplessness the human creature is capable of, or so runs the argument of comedy. Here we see, comically, how the entire psyche of a man is "agitated" into a reversal of affections before our eyes, how indeed the mind works overtime to satisfy the imbalance between desire and reason, and how all of this is contained in the motion of the actor's body—all in all a perfect instance of what Hamlet referred to as suiting the action to the word and the word to the action. The scene is as hilarious as any in Shakespeare, but it is also a delicate rendering of the modesty of human nature, all the more perfect because it so thoroughly realizes the physical possibilities of the actor. Thanks to the efficiency of Shakespeare's speech the actor's "whole system of life is contained in motion."

To sum up: dramatic speech is thin and muscular; it is, one might say, a musical score for body and voice, and as in music there can be no such things as superfluous notes. Dramatic speech—I should say, rather, speech for the drama—can afford no fat, no excess of itself, or the actor's body begins repeating itself and becomes behaviorally obese. Even Falstaff's speech is thin, though Falstaff himself is fat. Falstaff is given no more words than the quantity necessary to realize the humorous possibilities of his corpulence. Anything more would diminish him as a character by making him excessively excessive, like a person who tells too many jokes. For instance, take any of Falstaff's speeches, or Hal's anatomizations of Falstaff's appetite and size, fatten it by one-third, and it begins to resemble a catalogue out of Robert Burton's *Anatomy of Melancholy* which, knowing no limits of discretion, is not speech intended for the motions and commotions of an actor's body but strictly for the mind's eye.

This principle must clearly be adapted very elastically. It is possible that Shakespeare might have extended Falstaff's part and made the character even richer, but we can assume that he wouldn't achieve such a success by simply fattening Falstaff's lines. In dramatic speech the quantity of lines stands in direct ratio to the tension produced, and of course there are many different kinds of tension. Then too, sustaining a tension obviously depends on the power of the individual actor and on the tolerance of the audience, which varies widely from one period to another and from one kind of audience to another. Moreover, something might *become* dramatic, hence actable, by virtue of its fashionability in the immediate culture. Some epochs, for example, have a high tolerance for rhetorical embellishment that becomes embarrassing and unactable in the next. Finally, sometimes the principle of economy I have outlined might be upstaged by the opposing principle that if something is good, more of it is better. One of the most brilliant improvements on Shakespeare's rhetorical art occurs in Laurence Olivier's rendering of the opening monologue of *Richard III* ("Now is the winter of our discontent . . ."). Realizing the charisma of Richard's personality and the spectacular occasion for a performance afforded by this speech, Olivier grafted parts of still another of Richard's monologues from *3 Henry VI* (3.2) and made it twice its original length. This worked principally because Richard's charisma (not to mention Olivier's) is essentially founded on his rhetorical skill and his intimacy with the audience. Richard is that rare dramatic character who is as interesting when he is talking to himself or to the audience as when he is interacting with other characters. Indeed, in Richard and others of his tribe we have the spectacular beginning of a monologic tradition most lately exampled by Spalding Gray. If *Richard III* has a shortcoming, it is that Richard's charisma declines as he runs out of victims and hence occasions for sharing his electrifying imagination with the audience, and the action becomes more and more centered in mere battles, murders, and court scenes.

Obviously, Hamlet's fascination is of this ilk as well. Hamlet has no such intimacy with the audience (only villains seem aware of the audience), but he is probably the hero with whom the audience is on most intimate terms, owing to the peculiar quality of his mind. "I *am* Hamlet," Steven Berkoff writes, "since when you *play* Hamlet he becomes *you*. When you play Hamlet, you play yourself and play the instrument which is you. If you can make a good tune as an actor your best tunes will come out of Hamlet and if not then that does not matter but you will be a better actor for having played it, and been there" (1989, vii–viii).

This is the opinion of a single actor, but it could be duplicated many times over. Why should it be that "when you play Hamlet you play yourself and play the instrument which is you"? I have never played Hamlet (or any other Shakespearean character), but I do have the impression that when I read Hamlet I am, so to speak, reading myself, a sentiment that goes back at least to Coleridge and probably has something to do with Berkoff's point. Why should this be so? I think it is because Hamlet is the rare case of a hero who has nothing to do but be himself, which—it turns out—is to be many things to many people. By virtue of his famous delay, or refusal to play the role assigned to him, he becomes something of a wild card or free agent who is left, as it were, with all nature as his plaything. On the other hand, when we play, or watch, or read *Macbeth* or *Othello* or *Lear*, we are, to a great extent, observers of characters caught in the grip of a single passion and dilemma, a feature which to a degree *objectifies* them in our eyes and emotions.

Not so Hamlet: Hamlet is like us, a versatile and highly variable instrument that plays many different tunes. As a result, the actor cannot simply act vengeance—or murder or rejection or anger (as in the cases of Macbeth, Lear, and Othello); he (or, on occasion, she) must act a spectrum of emotions and attitudes—now friendship, now love, now wit, now wonder, now philosophical curiosity, bitter disappointment, irony, anger, self-recrimination, suspicion, and so on, until he has run through the alphabet of human behavior. There may be other reasons for our intimacy with Hamlet, which I leave to actors to determine. But the commentary in general suggests that of all the heroes Hamlet is the most difficult, or at least the most demanding character to perform—partly because he displays this capacious behavioral range (often turning his mood on a dime), partly because he has fewer stage breaks and more lines than any other character in a single Shakespeare play, and partly because so many people in any audience *know* these lines and are authorities on how they should be played. For they are all, themselves, Hamlets as well.

CHAPTER 3

The *Poetics* as Ur-Text

To the casual reader, Aristotle's *Poetics* is hardly a stimulating book, and much of it deals with archaic topics (the various forms of recognition) that no longer have much relevance to drama or theater. It never ceases to fascinate me that the immense influence of the *Poetics* can be traced to a few pages in which Aristotle sets forth principles of Greek tragedy which have become, by common consent of the ages, virtually permanent. This is not so astonishing in itself. One would expect, for example, that if a skillful observer in ancient China had set out to enumerate the characteristics of athletic games in his or her native city, at least some of them would be valid for athletic games everywhere and for all time. The reason is that the activity of play, like that of playmaking, is itself universal. Games in one era aren't apt to differ terribly from games in another era simply because play is based on a principle of structured give-and-take limited only by the possibilities of the human body. A more psychological way to say the same thing is that the human brain, as a matter of survival, follows certain conceptual and organizational patterns, both innate and acquired, that are used in the conceptualization of problems arising from experience. In recent years, cognitive psychology has discovered that the brain is richly endowed with conceptual systems that are in certain ways fixed and at the same time adaptable to widely different uses. The French psychologist Jean Piaget calls these thought structures "schemes." Albert Bregman, more recently, refers to them as *ideals*, and in a way they are similar to Platonic Ideas—the very structures, ironically (it turns out), that Plato felt were lost in artistic imitation. Ideals (or schemes, or conceptual frames, gestalt structures, paradigms, whatever one wishes to call them) have the additional property of entering into composition with one another in order to generate variant structures capable of dealing with still different problems and materials. "In the process of composition," Bregman says, "the standard form of the ideal is transformed so that the ideal may appear in a different form in each different composition." Ideals "have the potential of unifying our accounts of a wide variety of psychological phenomena" (1977, 250). So if we have new thoughts and make new discoveries about the world, we do so with the same old mental equipment that operates in the same old way.

One such phenomenon would be the drama, an art form designed to offer a certain conceptualization of human experience. As I suggested in my Introduction, the aim of drama is to portray human experience in its aspect of change; or, as Susanne Langer nicely puts it, drama is the art in which the "future . . . is made before our eyes" (1953, 307). This is not the place to discuss the purposes art might serve, but it would seem that human beings, who are obsessed by time and change, by beginnings and endings, need the drama (including its close neighbors, fiction and cinema) as a way of showing, in Aristotle's words, the kind of thing that *can* happen to people (as opposed to history, which shows what *has happened* in the past). And these kinds of *possible* things, when contemplated by the artist, bring into play certain ideal structures that can be used in a variety of combinations yet still retain certain generic features. Just as human beings play many different games within the conceptual limitations of structured give-and-take, so they create many different kinds of plays within the limits of a principle we might call "maximization of magnitude." I borrow this term from Ignacio Matte Blanco's study of the unconscious. It relates to one of the fundamental characteristics of what he calls emotional thinking (as distinguished from logical or analytical thinking), and it means simply that we tend to "carry to their extreme and utmost potentialities the characteristics of a given situation or person." We always "idealize" a situation (his term), whether it is frightening (like being alone in the dark) or joyful (like falling in love). Thus the loved one or the person one hates (to use Blanco's examples) is always maximized, or idealized, and contains all attributes of "the type." In short, "there are no half measures" in emotional thinking; "everything which is good or bad is so in an extreme degree" (1975, 243–45). In contemplating possibilities that might be thrown up by the world, we create a worst case or best case scenario, depending on our mood; rarely does one hear of a middle case (or break-even) scenario, except perhaps in the business world where people plan investments and expectations on the basis of a spectrum of possibilities. My claim of course is that Aristotle's *Poetics* is an analytical description of one generic application of this principle—the drama—and how drama goes about embodying in mimetic representations the emotional maximization of human experience.

In one respect, then, Aristotle achieved something he hadn't intended: like a biologist observing a particular species in his own backyard, he inadvertently fell upon the main characteristics of a much larger genus. The genus in this case is not simply Greek tragedy but drama as a mode of poetic expression distinct from such primary modes of expression as the lyric and the epic, which follow *their* own ideal principles of development. Indeed, as a way of illustrating comparative distinctions, we might begin by separating out the strategic principles of these three timeless poetic voices in a simplified chart (Figure 1). Many things can be said about the three modes—lyric, epic, and dramatic—that would complicate the over-neat arrangement of the chart. For example, one might argue that there is typically more conflict in the epic (e.g., Homer's *Iliad*) than in most dramas. Moreover, Aristotle himself noted that epics have both simple and complex plots and "need peripeties and recognitions as well as tragic acts" (sec. 24). Then too, most of the plots and actions of Greek tragedy

FIGURE I

Lyric	Epic	Dramatic
Subjective, personal (1–thou)	Social, communal (We)	Objective, detached (He, she, they)
State of private soul at rest (joy, grief, resignation, etc.)	Human *activity* in world (war, peace, work, etc.)	*Action* as process of change Interpersonal conflict
Private values (but may be shared by others in love, grieving, etc.)	Shared values (tribal codes of honor, patriotism, etc.)	Values, beliefs, desires in conflict
Descriptive (intensive)	Descriptive (extensive)	Dialectic (intensive)
Short form	Long form	Three-hour length

were borrowed from epic poets such as Homer, particularly from the *Iliad*. But if we are looking at the functions served by both forms, we see that conflict, peripety, and recognition in the epic tends to be subordinated to the larger rhythms of the episodic plot in which individual actions are dwarfed by the movement of armies and peoples. This is the sort of scope that tragedies, being intensive in form, can't indulge. Another difference between the epic and the tragedy is that in the epic each group (person, army) in conflict tends to have equal chances of winning, skill in combat or superior numbers usually being the deciding factor; in the tragic conflict, however, "the dice are loaded," as Thomas Pavel puts it (1986, 133), and skill in arms is scarcely a factor (Hamlet seems to be a better swordsman than Laertes, and look what it gets him.). Finally, though Aristotle did not comment on it, the epic seems to be motivated by a principle of shared communal values and deeds. Epic is what we may call the patriotic form par excellence, as one sees in the American war movies of the 1940s. Hence, the epic is a "we" form, its overriding purpose being to "sing" the great events of tribal life, usually beginning with an invocation to the gods by the poet-narrator. So an epic might minimize conflict (war) and emphasize communal life (*Growth of the Soil*, *Giant*), or it might shift back and forth between the two (Tolstoy's *War and Peace*).

The lyric, on the other hand, is distinct from both the epic and the dramatic in being the poetry of the private soul in a state of rest or unrest. Its purpose is to describe this state in what Northrop Frye calls "an internal mimesis of sound and imagery" that ends when the feeling has been fully described and submitted to a pattern (1957, 250). The lyric is thoroughly subjective and typically uses the "I" voice. The dramatic mode, on the other hand, presents its poetry directly to an audience without the mediation of a narrator or speaking-soul: hence the third-personal basis. The characters are perceived as others (he, she, them), however much their drama may move us.

But we must immediately note that as poetry's three principal modes (or expressive ideals) lyric, epic, and dramatic are quite compatible in each other's company and have, like all ideals, the capability of interbreeding with each other and creating hybrid forms that would have surprised even Polonius. Thus Bertolt Brecht called his dramatic plays epics, chiefly in view of their episodic form of plot development. They also represent "shared values and tribal codes" and differ from the normal epic in that the values and codes displayed by Brecht's characters are drawn largely from the negative column of human traits (greed, personal ambition, opportunism, etc.), producing, ironically, the effect of an anti-epic, or an epic put to purposes almost the reverse of communal integration and patriotism. Shakespeare's history chronicles, like Brecht's, are epic in form and dramatic in terms of objective presentation. Moreover, though it may seem odd to make such a claim, Thornton Wilder's plays—chiefly *Our Town* and *Skin of Our Teeth*—fall into the epic tradition by virtue of their episodic development and orientation toward communally held values as against conflict between competing values. Finally, the lyric is commonly found as an element in both epic and drama, chiefly in short bursts (prayer, lament, elegy) or choral odes (as in Greek tragedy), but often in a pervasive mood such as we find in the plays of Anton Chekhov, which commonly attract the adjective "lyric" as a consequence of their impressionistic atmosphere, or *nastroenie*, as it is called in Russian. (Francis Fergusson once used the term "ensemble pathos" in connection with Chekhov, an excellent description of the choral quality through which each character seems to be a voice in a single harmonic, or disharmonic, action.) Indeed, the endings of plays tend toward lyric rest in the sense that the characters have become what they are, having reached through their drama a *state* of acceptance, resignation, or peace. The later plays of Samuel Beckett (*Footfalls, Rockaby, That Time, Nacht und Träume*) come about as close to pure lyric stillness as the drama is likely to get without becoming recited poetry.

What then is the value of making such distinctions, if they are so continually breaking down in practice? The point, after all, is that they aren't breaking down in practice; in combining with each other they are behaving as naturally as paint on a canvas. My objective is not to find a set of rules or principles and expect it to apply purely or in all cases. Even the physical universe doesn't work that way in practice, inasmuch as elements combine to form compounds and compounds coexist side by side in still larger confusions of pure forms. But, as with the physical universe, it helps to know which things are elementary and which things aren't and how and why combinations of elementary things come about to produce new forms. In order to do that we need first principles, and in the universe of art first principles are based inevitably on emotional needs shared by members of the species. In short, art is an interplay of feeling and form, in

Langer's useful term. One can actually feel the presence of form in a poetic composition and, by common consent of theorists since Aristotle, the most elementary formal principles are those of the lyric, the epic, and the dramatic. These, one may say, constitute a three-stringed musical instrument on which the poet may play all the tunes of the world and all of those yet to be conceived.

The anthropologist Laura Bohannan (1966) once described her frustration in trying to tell the story of *Hamlet* to a circle of elders in the West African bush country. The elders incessantly interrupted her to correct her faulty interpretation of the events of this story they had never before heard. As one might expect, the "right" version of *Hamlet*, for them, was one that coincided precisely with their rules for storytelling, which are directly based on their rules of social and personal conduct. At every point, they change Bohannan's reading of *Hamlet* to make it coincide with the one possible "true meaning" it possesses: their interpretation. In this, obviously, they are no different from literary critics the world over. The interesting thing, however, is that no one complained about the story itself, which they felt was very good. In short, as a dramatic action plotted "accordingly to probability and necessity," *Hamlet* transported quite well from one culture to another about as far removed from it as you can get— only its meaning and certain plot details needed repair. Though Bohannan does not mention it, I am tempted to think that the whole frustrating occasion was made possible because, despite all the cultural differences in play between Bohannan's world and that of the African elders, *Hamlet* is, for all parties, faithful to an ideal that rises from such elementary facts as that we all live on a nitrogen-dependent planet, we reproduce through sexual means, our societies are organized into family and tribal units of government, and our life span is roughly seventy-five years in length, infinitely longer than that of the fruit fly but considerably less than the elephant's or the sea turtle's. With only these facts, it should be no surprise that every culture would arrive at something like the drama: an art form that specializes in imitating the most radical consequences of human action, centering usually on people of close blood relationship, brought about contrary to expectation, and giving rise to such emotions as pity and fear. "Plots of that sort," Aristotle says, "cannot fail to be artistically superior," no matter where you live, and if one were to discover a life-supporting planet similar to ours in another galaxy, there is a strong chance that its peoples would have created stories and plays identical in structure to those we tell here on Earth.

If we look at the *Poetics* in this light, we are free to think of it as describing one ideal, or conceptual framework, that is infinitely capable of self-variation, of entering into combination with the ideals of the lyric or the epic or as many other poetic ideals as there may be. Like the species of the plant and animal kingdoms, the species of ideal described in the *Poetics* is capable of interbreeding. It may, in other words, become diluted, or less purely observable in a particular instance, but that has nothing to do with its potency as an ideal in its own right.

Unfortunately, we still think of the *Poetics* as applying primarily to tragedy (even, in some opinions, to Greek tragedy alone), though the term (*tragoedia*) covered a far greater range of plays for Aristotle than the genre we define as tragedy today (for example, Euripides' *Helen* is almost closer in spirit to the American musical than to the *Oresteia*). Moreover, we still refer to plays as being Aristotelian in form if they manifest a certain orderliness of parts to which we can directly apply the key terms set forth in the *Poetics*. The closer a play is, say, to *Oedipus Rex*, the more Aristotelian; the closer to Ionesco's *The Bald Soprano* or Peter Handke's *Offending the Audience*, the less likely that Aristotle's name or ideas will come up in the discussion—unless by way of indicating what such "anti-plays" were trying to avoid. And that is another value of the *Poetics*: if nothing else, it offers an ideal yardstick; for if we want to know what something is, and how it behaves, we need a standard against which to judge it, and the *Poetics*, apart from its other uses, is our most durable and straightforward description of what drama is and how it does what it does.

For me, the most remarkable thing about the *Poetics* is the almost un-canny sense of "nestedness" or interdependency among all the parts. If you start with any single term and wonder how it got there, you will arrive eventually at all the others by a kind of sympathetic logic wherein one part is explained and made necessary by another. For example, if the end of a tragic play is, as Aristotle believes, to produce both pity and fear, it must have a certain kind of tragic hero (neither saintly nor evil) who commits a deed that is neither repulsive nor admirable, one that is closer to an error of judgment (hamartia) than a crime (of which there are few in Greek drama). Moreover, if the error is to play its role in the drama, it must eventually be brought to light and to produce some consequence. But how is this discovery (recognition) to occur? Obviously it would be boring (and gratuitous) if the hero were simply to remember committing the error at some convenient point in the play. Hence the need for a divulging event (a peripety) that is completely unexpected when it comes—"the opposite of the intended action," as Aristotle says—and yet occurs according to probability from the causal train of events already set in motion.

This principle of reversal is easy to accept once Aristotle has pointed it out, but what this crucial element implies is no less than the symmetry in human experience that drama specializes in arranging. For the peripety— often only the entrance of a character, as in *Oedipus Rex*—is really a means of giving shape to the seemingly unconnected and endless events of a human history. Finally, a tragic play cannot simply end in a recognition, like a joke; the recognition must, to have its full consequence, lead to the brink of a pathetic event that is either averted or carried out, according to whether the poet wants either good or bad fortune for the hero. These three "parts," then, may be considered as the drama's principal means of rounding out a human history; they are to the imitation of tragic actions what Kohler's law of dynamic direction is to gestalt theory, "a genuine cosmic principle, directed toward the maximum of orderliness obtainable under the given system" (Arnheim 1974, 27).

On still another level, there is Aristotle's claim that a dramatic action must have "a beginning, a middle, and an end," thus forming a "whole" with a "certain magnitude" (sec. 11). As a student, this idea always struck me as belonging in the same book of tautologies as Calvin Coolidge's remark that the more people are out of work the higher the unemployment. How could it be otherwise? But if one takes Aristotle's statement as a necessary first step—in effect, as a beginning, in his own sense of a beginning as something that has nothing before it and from which something else follows—one has the advantage, in one clean shot, of separating the action of plays from human action and experience in the open world where things, more often than not, go on and on in all directions and get hopelessly mixed in with other things. In other words, the idea of the whole may be obvious, but it is a *first* principle in which virtually all the constructional subprinciples of the *Poetics* are nested.

Once you start thinking about what a whole *is* and how a play achieves wholeness, you have to invoke the principles of metabasis (a change of fortune), peripety, and recognition (in complex cases at least) ending in the pathos, which, as I have suggested, are the whole-making instruments of the plot. The whole amounts to a whole, becomes perceivable as a whole, precisely because of the manner in which these internal principles operate through each other to create a whole with its own unique integrity. All of which brings us back to the key Aristotelian term "mimesis," or imitation of an action. For a mimesis, as recent literary theory is urging, is achieved precisely through wholeness in the object—if one thinks of wholeness as the object's separation from the continuity of the world as a thing *made of and about* the world which is observable as a representation rather than as a reality—that is, something framed in and by its art, something peculiarly distanced from the real world (by virtue of this reduction) yet endowed with meaning and intention respecting our concerns in the world. In a word, it is through its wholeness that the play becomes a fiction that obeys its own laws.

In a certain sense of Aristotle's meaning, one might even say that a play that had lost some of its text—say, its opening lines, an incident from its middle, or even its ending—would exhibit, in what remains, the characteristics of wholeness and magnitude. For wholeness is not so much a matter of everything being *there* as of what is there displaying a certain genetic integrity. There is more wholeness in the *Nike of Samothrace*, though the statue has lost its head, than in countless inferior sculptures where everything is intact and yet the "whole" seems a mélange of parts conceived by a committee of artists. Moreover, there is a certain sense in which a perfectly conceived but incomplete work of art (like the *Nike* or Kafka's *The Castle*) even leads us to imagine or to "replace" its missing parts in the style of those already there. This should not be considered a literal replacement of parts but rather an impressionistic projection to which aestheticians have given the term "consistent continuation"—the sympathetic extension of a work "beyond its frame" (Sparshott 1983, 142). Consistent continuation is rather like the sensation of a phantom limb or the trick by which the eye compensates for its own blind spot. Actually, this principle has something in common with our perception of a stage setting, which (though we never see it) continues on and on in all directions beyond the "sample" living room, throne room, or country road with a single tree, which soon becomes cluttered with invisible elsewheres. (More about this in Chapter 10). At the very least, we feel no less aesthetic regard for the work because it is incomplete, though we may be disappointed because it is. The incompleteness is simply an accident endured by the work *from an outside agency* (usually) and has no effect on the quality of the rest of it.

Thus we might claim that wholeness can be found anywhere in a work that has been wholly designed; wholeness is a symptom, like blood type, of the work's self-sufficiency and "just measure," as Samuel Johnson would call it. For example, take this fragment from *Macbeth*:

> —Whose horrid image doth unfix my hair,
> And make my seated heart knock at my ribs,
> Against the use of nature? Present fears
> Are less than horrible imaginings.
> My thought, whose murther yet is but fantastical,
> Shakes so my single state of man,
> That function—
>
> (1.3.135–41)

What is self-sufficient about these lines (which I leave deliberately incomplete) is their power of fully rendering the spectacle of a mind undergoing excruciating thought. One couldn't predict the rest of the passage, in specific verbal terms, but what we have exhibits a thoroughness in demonstrating the mind at work, very much as a Rembrandt sketch of a hand or a thigh is perceived as sufficiently rendered without the help of the body from which it has been "severed." Subtly, we begin scaling our perception to a certain character and measure of expression that we expect to be present, in kind, in whatever might precede or follow, if we were lucky enough to have it. Indeed, with only this much of the play, one can make certain claims about Shakespearean style, density of character, and magnitude which separate it from, say, the style of a contemporary, Thomas Kyd, who wrote the following fragment, equally whole in its own Senecan terms:

> O eyes! no eyes, but fountains fraught with tears:
> O life! no life, but lively form of death:
> O world! no world, but mass of public wrongs,
> Confus'd and fill'd with murder and misdeeds.
>
> (3.2.1–5)

Wholeness, then, is manifested in the invisible principles of selection and arrangement of the parts, as mimesis is manifested, not in the work's likeness to the real world, but in its wholeness. In the end, it is as impossible to separate the two principles as it is to separate plot from action. One might say that wholeness is a characteristic of the work, something the work possesses (or doesn't possess) and that mimesis is the act that brings the principle of wholeness into finite form. Wholeness, then, is an impression formed by the skillful conduct of the mimesis. On the other hand, can we not say that mimesis is a characteristic, or a consequence, of wholeness and that what constitutes mimesis—or at least a successful mimesis—is the understanding, on the artist's part, of wholeness and what the work demands in order to become whole? Wholeness and mimesis, then, behave very much like M. C. Escher's self-drawing hands: one hand is drawing the other, but the other is also drawing the hand that draws it. It all depends on where you start. In any case, if theorists like Wolfgang Iser (1993) are correct, when you speak the first word or draw the first line of a mimesis of an object in the real world or in your mind's eye, you have taken the first step toward wholeness. Rather than turning to Iser's highly complex proof of this claim, however, I offer an entry from the diary of a painter—or rather, the diary of a woman, Joanna Field, who is struggling to *become* a painter. The struggle consists in overcoming the powerful impulse in the amateur to paint the object as it exists before the eye. This enslavement to the "copycat" principle is exactly what prevents wholeness, which can only come when the "me" of the painter is fused, or con-fused, with the "not-me" of the object in nature. Here is Field, writing, one might say, at the moment of her recognition of what the solution to this problem entails:

> I now remembered Goethe's idea of colour as something which happens when white light and darkness meet; although not true of the physicist's world, it looked as though it might be true metaphorically of

the world of psychic experience. For here was the fact to be faced that there was a startling change in the quality of experience itself when imagination was brought down to earth and made incarnate in the body, a sudden richness that was like the sun coming out over a world that had been all greyness. And not only did the weather change in one's soul when imagination was made incarnate and took its flesh upon it, but the very way one moved was affected. Without such an incarnation one seemed to move as if by the commands of an internal drill master, with it one could achieve the state of wholeness in which

> "It doth not by another engine work,
> But by itself; which in the act doth lurk."
>
> (1983, 112)

The second remarkable thing about the *Poetics* is Aristotle's discovery of the principles of reversal and recognition, which will occupy me on many different levels in the chapters that follow. It is almost certain that someone would eventually have discovered them if Aristotle hadn't, but one's respect for the achievement rises when one considers the task of trying to determine the common characteristics of hundreds of plays by dozens of artists and arriving, out of all possibilities, at this particular formulation: the course of tragedy describes a change of fortune (metabasis), and complex tragedies achieve this through a peripety, or reversal, and a recognition. These principles are so familiar to students of drama that we take them as self-evident, rather like the roundness of the earth (which was once a fresh discovery). But the very linking of these two elements was a profound formulation, for as Gerald Else has put it, it is through this means that tragedy is able "to concentrate an intense emotional charge [for both protagonist and audience] upon a single event, a change of awareness [in which] the whole depth of a human tragedy can be 'contained'" (1967, 353).

Moreover, reversal and recognition run so deeply in human experience in the world that instances of their coupling are virtually inexhaustible. For me, this is the heart—or in Aristotle's own word, "soul"—of the Aristotelian Ideal. For example, consider the structure of a joke: the inevitable emergence of the punch line from the junction of two heretofore incompatible or unrelated chains of reference (Q: What can go up the chimney down, but not down the chimney up? A: An umbrella.). Or, consider the moment long, long ago when one of our Paleolithic ancestors, walking one afternoon along a hillside, dislodged a round log and conceived through the action of its descent the principle of the wheel. These are simple instances of the unexpected leading to a sudden realization. While we cannot call them peripeties and recognitions in the formal sense in which Aristotle defined these terms, we can at least see the metaphorical respect in which they are all variations of the same pattern and that peripety and recognition themselves are therefore simply instances of a species within a much larger genus. Actually, I've taken a page out of Arthur Koestler's *The Act of Creation*, which eloquently makes the same point: that humor, scientific discovery, and art all share a common creative process that consists in the uncovering of hidden similarities. His term for this process is "bisociation": "When two independent matrices of perception or reasoning interact with each other the result . . . is either a *collision* ending in laughter, or their *fusion* in a new intellectual synthesis, or their *confrontation* in an aesthetic experience. The bisociative patterns found in any domain of creative activity are tri-valent: that is to say, the same pair of matrices can produce comic, tragic, or intellectually challenging effects" (1969, 45). Let us begin with an example in which this process of bisociation produces a tragic effect. These are the key lines from Aristotle's favorite instance of the coming about (together) of peripety and recognition, the arrival of the Messenger from Corinth in *Oedipus Rex*:

MESSENGER: Son, it's very plain you don't know what you're doing.
OEDIPUS: What do you mean, old man? For God's sake, tell me.
MESSENGER: If your homecoming is checked by fears like these.
OEDIPUS: Yes, I'm afraid that Phoebus may prove right.
MESSENGER: The murder and the incest?
OEDIPUS: Yes, old man, that is my constant terror.
MESSENGER: Do you know that all your fears are empty?
OEDIPUS: How is that, if they are father and mother and I their son?
MESSENGER: Because Polybus was no kin to you in blood.
OEDIPUS: What, was not Polybus my father?
MESSENGER: No more than I but just as much.

(David Grene trans., 1008–17)

Many people consider this the most tragic peripety in drama. As Else would say, it concentrates an intense emotional charge on a single event, a change of awareness in which all of the assumptions on which Oedipus had lived his life are suddenly reversed by a simple fact. And if these assumptions, which constitute one matrix or chain of reasoning are false, it follows that the truth leads inescapably to a diametrically opposite matrix of assumptions. This is immediately confirmed by the arrival of the herdsman (for this is a two-part peripety) and the convergence of two chains of evidence:

HERDSMAN: If you are the man he says you are, you're bred to misery.
OEDIPUS: O, O, O, they will all come,
    all come out clearly! Light of the sun, let me
    look upon you no more after today!
    I who first saw the light bred of a match
    accursed, and accursed in my living
    with them I lived with, cursed in my killing.

(Grene trans., 1180–85)

It is interesting to note that Nietzsche found this "horrible triad" of fates the paradigm of discovery itself: "'the same man who solved the riddle of nature (the ambiguous Sphinx) must also, as murderer of his father and husband of his mother, break the consecrated tables of the natural order . . . ; wisdom is a crime committed on nature': such are the terrible words addressed to us by myth" (1956, 61). Friedrich von Schiller called the play a "tragic analysis. Everything is already in existence, and has only to be unravelled" (Letter of 2 October 1797 [1877, 1:411]). Freud saw in it the paradigm of the psychoanalytic method of uncovering the truth hidden in the unconscious (1965, 294–95), and others have called the play the world's first great detective story. In still another vein, I have an impish friend who insists that the play is the world's first great comedy. This is certainly a perverse reading, but it does make a point that brings us back to Koestler's triptych. If you think of *Oedipus Rex* shorn of seriousness and cathartic value, the play is distantly funny in the Bergsonian sense of something mechanical encrusting itself on the human. Radical irony carried to this degree reaches a point where human value is eclipsed in a spectacle of impossible symmetry that recalls the structure of the joke.

Here we arrive at Charles Baudelaire's idea of the absolute comic as indifferent to moral value which becomes the plaything of an extreme idea. Indeed, there is a very clever joke based on Oedipus's meeting with the messenger from Corinth. Here is the version I know:

> MESSENGER: I have good news and bad news.
>
> OEDIPUS: Well, speak.
>
> MESSENGER: Do you want the good news first or the bad news?
>
> OEDIPUS: Give me the bad news.
>
> MESSENGER: Very well. Your father is dead.
>
> OEDIPUS (*Brightening*): My father is dead? DO YOU SAY MY FATHER IS DEAD?
>
> MESSENGER: Yes. However, the good news is that . . .
>
> OEDIPUS (*Euphoric*): O speak no more!
>
> MESSENGER: . . . he wasn't your father.

In short, the difference between discovery ("I've found it!"), a joke ("I get it!"), and a tragic recognition ("I am Fortune's fool!") lies not in the structure but in the perspective one takes on the content. And one is led to suspect that if Aristotle's lost treatise on comedy were found, it would be a reverse image of the *Poetics* in all its particulars, with special emphasis placed on the triadic pattern of peripety, recognition, and felicitous (as opposed to pathetic) event. One of the reasons that a peripety/recognition can concentrate such an intense emotional charge on a single event is that it is activating a conceptual pattern that the brain has used or confronted on thousands of previous occasions.

CHAPTER 4

Plot and Action

A ristotle maintains that tragedy is the imitation of an action (praxis) and that "the basic principle, the heart and soul" of this imitation—hence, we can assume, of the action as well—is the plot (mythos). Plot is also defined as "the arrangement of the incidents," as distinguished from the incidents so arranged (which would be more appropriately called a synopsis). The parts of the plot, then, include the tying (or complication) and the untying (or denouement), the latter composed of the three main structural elements of the play—the peripety, the recognition, and the pathetic event.

The important thing is that plot and action are not two different *things* but two different perspectives on the same thing—the order of words and events that constitute the play, either in the text or in performance. Plot, then, is the unfolding, or arrangement, of the events that compose the action "according to probability or necessity." That is, the events seem to grow believably out of each other: it is probable that Oedipus would leave Corinth on hearing the oracle's warning; it is probable that he would flee over the mountain, meet a party of travelers at the place where three roads meet, and so forth. But this alone amounts to what we might call motion, or momentum, the sort of cause/effect pattern one can observe most simply on a billiard table: ball A strikes ball B, ball B strikes ball C, and so forth, until the energy in the system is exhausted. So in life too all our motions are probable, ending in a systemic exhaustion called death: It is probable that I would go to the grocery store for a carton of milk. It is also probable that I would meet a friend, or be struck by a car en route, and so on. Probability has nothing to do with statistical likelihood or expectation; probability is what is possible, hence believable, either in the empirical world or in the play-world where, of course, different kinds of probability obtain. Probability in Poe's or Stanislas Lem's worlds isn't the same as probability in Henrik Ibsen's or Sophocles'. Probability extends to "the way of the world" in the play, down to the smallest tics of behavior: it is probable that Harold Pinter's characters will not tell the truth; it is probable that Arthur Miller's will tell the *whole* truth (eventually); it is probable that David Mamet's characters will use the F-word a great deal; and so on. Of the reality of the fictional text, Wolfgang Iser says, "The reality represented in the text is not meant to represent reality; it is a pointer to something that it is not, although its function is to make that something conceivable" (1993, 13). And, we may add, to make it probable and necessary—that is, to obey a law of probability unique to its own world.

Unfortunately, Aristotle did not deal very extensively with the concept of action; his main point about it is that it should represent a single change to good or bad fortune. A bad play would be one that dealt with several unconnected episodes in the protagonist's life, one that attempted to cover an entire lifetime (as an epic might), or one that dealt alternately with two protagonists. But the concept of action is far more versatile than all this suggests, and here we reach one of those points on which Aristotle might be extended, without changing his basic idea, to include plays as diverse as Shakespeare's *Winter's Tale* (which covers the events of sixteen years), Caryl Churchill's *Cloud 9* (which covers 125 years and has multiple protagonists), and even a play as seemingly barren of everything dramatic as Peter Handke's *Offending an Audience*, which is, in effect, a lecture to the audience explaining that it has no action, plot, character, and spectacle. I will return to two of these examples in a later connection.

Perhaps the central point is that Aristotle's notion of the change of fortune involves the kind of action that centers on a crucial tragic deed (the murder of Agamemnon, the revenge of Orestes or Medea, the burial of Polyneices). In this regard, Greek tragedies are like Greek statuary: they are executed in the Severe Style in which every shape is dominated by the solemnity of the whole, above and beyond any possible crosscurrents of agitation in the parts. Greek tragedy, one may say, is stubbornly about *one thing* alone, and the master function of the chorus is to extend this unity of effect to all parts of the dramatic world, much as metaphor in Shakespeare's world serves to bind all the parts through analogical correspondence. However, if one reduces Aristotle's conception of action (and its relation to plot) to its bare essence, ignoring the fact that it is based on his observation of plays with very strong local requirements (e.g., three actors, a chorus, the trilogy form), we might define an action as any sequence of events which is complete and whole (with a beginning, a middle, and an end) and possesses a certain magnitude. In short, apart from the relation of the *Poetics* to Greek tragic art, there is good reason to think of action as adaptable to any play that exhibits wholeness.

Still, we need a clearer sense of action and its relation to plot. Unfortunately, it is difficult to illustrate the difference between plot and action through the examination of a play. This is one of the great frustrations of dramatic analysis: every time you talk about action as a series of parts, the phenomenon has a way of disappearing, much as if you were to show me a single still photograph from Eadweard Muybridge's series on the running horse and say, "This is a running horse." And indeed it is a running horse, as anyone can plainly see—or it *was* one, for whatever we mean by *running* is now a half-mile down the road. Action is like music: there is no way to stop it and have it. The other problem is that if you *do* stop it (for example, by quoting the text) and think of the play as a spatial construction with its parts in a hypothetical repose, you discover that each part is made of littler parts that are made of still littler parts, right down to the syllables that compose the words. As in Zeno's paradox of the flying arrow, there is no end of "places" the play has been, or will go, and since it is always in a place equal to itself, as Zeno claims of the flying arrow, you end back at the absurdity that you are treating something you know to be in motion as if it were at rest.

One way around the problem may be to take a unit of text small enough to allow us the luxury of seeing a complete action unfold before our eyes. Unfortunately, short of Beckett's thirty-five-second *Breath* (which isn't a good example), there isn't a play that will serve the purpose. But we can achieve the same effect by observing the drama that sometimes occurs in prose. Indeed, a nonfictional prose passage might be the best place to begin, because the concept of action is not necessarily confined to plays, and it may well be that an action in a play owes its power to our familiarity with action as it occurs in unrelated forms of motion, action being definable as motion that makes sense. To this end I choose a passage from Kenneth Burke's *Attitudes toward History* which attempts to characterize Socratic irony. The specific subject and context are not important, though it would be useful to have some sense of the personality of Socrates as revealed in the Platonic dialogues. But even without that, the passage will make the point:

> Socratic irony is perhaps the most ingenious possible development of phatic communication. The asking of questions is obviously a masterly shortcut for the establishment of "phatic communion." The young girl, with little to talk about, soon discovers how easy it is to establish communion by asking the young man about his plans. So Socrates, by asking questions, was apparently doing the most *social* of acts. But Socrates was an ironist. He did not merely ask questions. He *kept on* asking questions. He persisted. He *insisted*. And by driving on and on, piling one question atop another, he subtly converted the business of phatic communion into an extremely annoying occupation. In fact, people felt like killing him. In fact, they did kill him. (1984, 235)

Students usually find this very funny. Among other things, it illustrates the natural impulse of language to "wave its hands" while it talks—that is, to enact its subject while describing it. Here is the perfect instance of what Yeats called "the thinking of the body," or at least the body thinking along with the mind. The "plot" of this text could, for convenience, be thought of as the arrangement of the individual phonemes, clauses, and sentences that lead in a certain intelligible direction according to probability: one sentence leads to the next, and you can follow the sequence without any trouble. These are the "events" in Burke's characterization of Socratic irony, a tepid synopsis of which might reduce to some such statement as, "Socrates asked so many embarrassing questions and was such a devastating ironist in doing so that the Athenian fathers sentenced him to death." But at mid-paragraph (roughly at "But Socrates was an ironist") something "peripetous" happens to the prose. The sentences get shorter and more staccato, and we soon become aware that the true intelligibility of the passage, the thing that gives each part new life, is the metamorphosis of a description into a *representation* of Socrates actually "doing his thing." It is as if Burke, the historian, is suddenly seized by the spirit of his topic and, to invoke his own phrase, begins dancing the attitude of Socratic persistence. Plot is "subtly converted" into an action that culminates in the death of Socrates. Moreover, behind the spectacle of Socrates' agon, we sense the presence of a pattern we recognize from other forms and places: for here we encounter the ghosts of such figures as Oedipus, Antigone, Christ, Medea, Macbeth, and all those unrelenting tragic heroes who persist, who insist, driven on and on by a hubristic energy that brings them finally to disaster. Thus the passage enacts not only a specific drama but a master plot—or, as Aristotle would say, a *universal*. In Socrates' drama we are in the very presence of the dramatic principle.

On a much larger scale, all plays achieve their actions through such rhythmic arrangement of events. Thus Hamlet's famous delay is established not simply through Hamlet's soliloquies ("Why is this thing yet to do?") but in the play's habit of interrupting a possible direct course (like those of *Macbeth* or *Othello*) and continually interposing delays in the form of subplots, comic relief, and long descriptions between promise and fulfillment. It is not simply Hamlet who delays: it is *Hamlet* itself. Hamlet's psychology and the action of *Hamlet* stand in a synecdochic relation to each other. So too after ten minutes of watching Chekhov's *Three Sisters*, we arrive almost unconsciously at the realization that the Prozorovs will never reach Moscow and that the play is really *about* a certain psychical characteristic that prevents them from doing so. The structural source of this understanding is far too subtle to describe in detail here, but it consists, among other things, in the characters' continual resort to what we might call the ostrich syndrome whereby all urgencies are either ignored completely or bathed in philosophy. In either of these cases, action (on one of its perceptual levels) is, as John Jones has put it, an "indwelling form" (1968, 23), something invisible, like gravity in nature, going on in the motion of the visible. So we can see the sense in which action is simply another perspective on wholeness and magnitude, just as action itself is another perspective on plot.

How does an action take its shape? Let us take an unpromising case of pure motion such as we find in empirical reality. Suppose you see a dreadful head-on collision on the highway, the sort of thing the newspaper might later describe as TRAGEDY ON 101. However tragic such an event might be for the people involved, it would not be a very good subject for a play or a film; it is not an action but an instance of raw causality rearing itself into visibility. We call such events accidents, and in them we see the indifference of the causal order to human desires. (Hence the expression "meaningless accident.") The strange thing is that accidents, even in Aristotle's theory, play a strong role in dramatic structure as well, and I will examine this role in due course. But how might one make this "simple" highway event into an action in the Aristotelian sense?

One way might be to develop the sort of plot that we find in Harold Pinter's *Betrayal*, which traces an adultery from its conclusion to its beginning, moving backward in time (more or less) from the denouement to the origin. Or, our case might best take the form of a double plot in which the lives of the occupants of the two cars, who otherwise have nothing to do with each other, are traced through the fateful day (or prior weeks) as they undergo their individual problems and frustrations, and we would arrive finally at the moment when their lives are "bonded" by the collision. And one would probably contrive the plot in such a way as to suggest that these two individuals, though complete strangers, somehow deserve each other (like Oedipus and Laius at the crossroad) or are in some key respect the perfect complementary ingredients of an action (otherwise, we would have only two instances of pure motion). For everything that occurs in a dramatic action must, on the principle of wholeness, contribute to a pattern. From the standpoint of a casual onlooker, or a highway patrol officer, this event is still an accident; but we, who have seen it evolve through the window of mimetic art, would perceive in it a unity, the sign of a fateful order inhering in human events. This is the sort of action that Thornton Wilder chronicled in his novel *The Bridge at San Luis Rey*, which traces the lives of a group of travelers back in time from the moment they fell to their deaths in the accidental collapse of a bridge over a deep chasm. Indeed, this is the same retrospective method Thomas Hardy used in his poem "The Convergence of the Twain: Lines on the Loss of the Titanic" in the year (1912) of the great maritime disaster, which so shocked the world in its unexpectedness. First, Hardy describes the great ship resting in "the solitude of the sea" following its collision with the iceberg. Then he asks, "What does this vaingloriousness down here?" And the answer, in retrospect, is:

> Well: while was fashioning
> This creature of cleaving wing,
> The Immanent Will that stirs and urges everything

Prepared a sinister mate
For her—so gaily great—
A shape of ice, for the time far and dissociate.

And as the smart ship grew
In stature, grace, and hue,
In shadowy silent distance grew the iceberg too.

Alien they seemed to be:
No mortal eye could see
The intimate welding of their later history,

Or sign that they were bent
By paths coincident
On being anon twin halves of one august event,

Till the Spinner of the Years
Said "Now!" And each one hears,
And consummation comes, and jars two hemispheres.

Of course Hardy has designed the event as a tragedy, complete with hubris, hamartia, pride, peripety, and the pathetic event. It may strike us today as somewhat romanticized, but beneath the poem we sense an old pattern accomplishing itself irrespective of human will and desire. Moreover, the idea of such convergence is familiar to everyone, if only in the "small world" principle. Take any relationship or turning point in your life, any instance in which something crossed your path and somehow changed things. Now imagine the incident from a perspective outside of your self-interests, some superior viewpoint from which you see the thing coming about. From origin to conclusion, you see the convergence of two independent lines of motion. Would you not be tempted to think that some force, some "Spinner of the Years," was guiding the process? What if you had done x instead of y on April 14 of that year? What if you had taken the job in Illinois instead of the job in Philadelphia? In short, the deep appeal of drama, as the art of catastrophe, is that behind anything you *do* or *are* at a particular moment stands the causal pyramid of your life—all its choices, givens, accidents, and mistakes—and, it turns out, the causal pyramids of everyone with whom you have crossed paths. Your *now* is the product of a unique lifetime of *thens* and *others*. Indeed, what makes *Oedipus Rex* one of the world's foremost examples of tragic art is the steady impression of convergence, as Oedipus the child and Laius the father meet at the narrow mountain crossing and become "twin halves of one august event."

To put it another way, action is motion with an attitude, or motion manipulated toward some end by something. It may be probable that Oedipus would meet a party of travelers while crossing the mountain, but you probably wouldn't buy a used car from someone who told you that one of the travelers was his long lost father. Still, this is probable, or *barely* probable (it *could* happen, given the conditions of Oedipus's birth, etc.), but more important it is what Aristotle would call "marvelous": what such an event lacks in hard probability (in the sense of likelihood) it makes up in wonder, for "such things don't happen by chance," as Aristotle puts it (sec. 12). And if it isn't chance that causes them, then the operative probability—the one that really counts—is occurring at a higher level. And it is the interplay of these two levels of causality which creates all the interest of drama.

Before we return to the nature of action, however, let us look more closely at this interplay of causalities. We may begin by saying that drama is the imitation of causality. This is not a revision of Aristotle but an attempt to get beneath the level of plot and the content of the imitation to the conditions underlying the principles of wholeness and action. For we cannot understand the nature of wholeness without seeing wherein it is the frame that separates dramatic action from movement in open life. Causality, one might say, is the subject of drama's subject, the theme of its themes. This is something the dramatist does not consciously write about, any more than he or she is conscious of breathing while writing. Why should the dramatist worry about something as remote and abstract as causality as long as the play is believable? And why should an audience distract itself from its immediate interest in poor destiny-dogged Oedipus as long as the play moves along smoothly to an exciting climax? But then, what are these interests but reflections of the operation of causality? Beneath our interest in Oedipus, then, is the larger base of the current of change on which Oedipus is carried along. By himself, Oedipus would be nothing: for drama is not the imitation of men but of the actions wherein they are happy or the reverse. And action, so to speak, is simply causality on a leash.

Here we are back at the bedrock of playmaking and playviewing: drama is made of causes and effects—change made perceivable, in Susanne Langer's phrase. Under all its local and cultural mimetic preoccupations, drama is the art of making causality intelligible, and the concept of the whole rests securely on the foundation of the laws of causation—which include, incidentally, those of fantasy. The simplest bedtime story observes the principles of causality in its unfolding ("And then . . . And so . . , Next . . . At last . . . "). Its plot, like the stages of an arrow's flight, is a harvest of causality in the sense that it brings in the unexpected fruits of the probable. Its whole is a process that secretly pays homage to the fundamental predicament of life: the fact that the causal future is always concealed from us. I go to the store to buy milk: I may meet an old friend, or I may be struck dead. Neither was planned; all I wanted was a carton of milk. As poor, distracted Ophelia puts it, "Lord, we know what we are, but know not what we may be." Drama, then, is a poetic strategy for *unconcealing* the concealed future, and it is at once a lament and a consolation for this fact. Which is another way of saying that drama offers its audience a kind of pity and a kind of terror. Both bad news and good news, at the same time: the bad news is that these sufferers are people, like ourselves, undergoing a radical change of fortune; the good news is that they don't really exist.

By a simple extension, we can understand the role of accident in drama. Accident, the coming about of the unexpected, is a form of reversal, and reversal of fortune is the armature of dramatic development. It is surely an accident that Oedipus meets his father, of all people, at the crossroads. As we have said, it is also probable, but it is such a spooky form of probability that we even have a word for it: coincidence. This is a two-edged word that carries in conflicting definitions the ironic spirit of dramatic reversal. In its secondary meaning, a coincidence is "a notable concurrence of events having no apparent causal connection" (*OED*). Roland Barthes has given us the best treatment of this phenomenon in his analysis of the structure of the newspaper feature story (the *fait-divers*), based on an event with an unusual symmetry. To take two examples from my own collection: COMPUTER MATING SERVICE RE-UNITES DIVORCED COUPLE; ROBBERY

VICTIM BECOMES BANDIT'S BRIDE. And we might as well add: FATHER
AND SON RE-UNITED AT FATEFUL CROSSROADS. Such events, Barthes
says, are based on chance (nevertheless probable), and chance implies "a
certain idea of Fate. Every coincidence is a sign at once indecipherable and
intelligent . . . ; antithesis or paradox, all contrariety belongs to a deliberately constructed world: a god prowls behind the *fait-divers* (1972a, 193–
94). This idea is also expressed by the modern playwright, Friedrich
Dürrenmatt, in his "21 points" on playwriting:

- A story has been thought to its conclusion when it has taken its worst
  possible turn.
- The worst possible turn is not foreseeable. It occurs by accident.
- The art of the playwright consists in employing, to the most effective
  degree possible, accident within the action.
- The carriers of a dramatic action are human beings.
- Accident in a dramatic action consists in when and where who happens
  to meet whom. (1984)

Accident in drama, then, is not simply an isolated occurrence or something extraneous dragged in by the playwright to get our interest. It is
always paradoxical, as Dürrenmatt goes on to say: accident is always what
produces the "worst possible turn." To put it another way, accident is
always the agency that unconceals the future (or the ending, as in beginning, middle, and end).[1] Unconcealment is a continuous process in the
play, for even when things seem to be more in doubt, more questionable,
the play is moving, however obliquely, toward its master unconcealment,

[1] I am using this term, *unconcealment*, in Heidegger's sense of disclosure in "The Origin
of the Work of Art." For example, Heidegger examines Van Gogh's painting of the
peasant shoes as an unconcealment of the "equipmentality" or "reliability" of the shoes,
in which their "truth" is vested (1975, 33–36). I am suggesting that if one were to seek the
fundamental truth disclosed by drama, as an art form, it would be located in the
disclosure of causality, or how things come about in the world of experience. Above
this, of course, drama might disclose, or unconceal, many more specific aspects of
experience, all of which would take us into the province of theme or idea, what the play
is "about." See also Kierkegaard's discussion of "concealment [as] the faction of tension" in drama (1954, 93–94).

and this unconcealment is what gives force and depth to all dramatic speech. For example:

> What parents? Stop! Who are they of all the world?
> (*Oedipus Rex*)

> Nothing, my lord.
> Nothing!
> Nothing.
> (*King Lear*)

> Nothing, my lord; or if—I know not what.
> (*Othello*)

> Yesterday I heard in passing that they might transfer our brigade somewhere far away.
>
> (*Three Sisters*)

Each of these lines opens, by a thin crack, the hidden abyss of the future. It does not matter that the character, as in Iago's case, may be intentionally concealing something from another character (Othello) or that a character, such as Cordelia ("Nothing, my lord."), may be intentionally unconcealing an attitude she suspects will lead to trouble. Concealments or unconcealments of this sort are simply the surface upon which paradoxical fate writes its own cryptic order, be it tragic, comic, historical, or fantastic. Thus we may say that the great dramatic plots are fait-divers writ large:

GENERAL SACRIFICES DAUGHTER IN WEDDING CEREMONY (*Iphigenia at Aulis*)

GENERAL STRANGLES WIFE IN HANDKERCHIEF ERROR (*Othello*)

SAINT BURNED AT STAKE FOR NOT RENOUNCING RELIGIOUS VISIONS (*St. Joan*)

WIFE FORCED INTO ADULTERY BY HUSBAND, MOTHER, PRIEST (*Mandragola*)

FAMED ESTATE BOUGHT BY FORMER SERF AS OWNERS DANCE (*Cherry Orchard*)

MAN'S STATUE AVENGES HIS MURDER

This last one, of course, comes directly from Aristotle, who clearly saw this relation between drama and the fait-divers principle: "even among chance occurrences the ones people consider most marvelous are those that seem to have come about as if on purpose: for example the way the statue of Mity's at Argos killed the man who had been the cause of Mity's death by falling on him while he was attending the festival; it stands to reason, people think, that such things don't happen by chance—so plots of that sort cannot fail to be artistically superior" (sec. 12). Let us put this ancient passage beside a recent modern treatment of the phenomenon of paradox by A. David Napier:

> A paradox is something that appears self-contradictory, a thing that at some time, or from a particular point of view, appears to be what it is not. Logically, paradoxes appear to infringe upon the law of contradiction, upon the logical prohibition against a thing being and not being at the same time. . . . Vexing as this problem may be, we can say with certainty that a paradox must by definition lead us at some time to perceive a contradiction, and in so doing necessitate an acceptance that things may look like what they are not. Our ability to accept this ambiguity is also fundamental to our recognition and signification of change. We know what things look like and recognize specific change because we are aware that something no longer is what it was. Our awareness of change is, thus, essential for resolving the ambiguity that is basic to paradox. (1986, 1)

Here we have a constant gestalt of terms belonging to the same phenomenon: paradox, contradiction, change, ambiguity, recognition. Indeed, as Napier goes on to point out, the phenomenon rests on the problem of identity and how we are to come to terms with the potential for paradox that inheres in the illusion of security. Napier himself is concerned particularly with the mask which exhibits the paradox in identity in one stunning presentation of the self that isn't itself. Oedipus too, we know, wore a mask—that is, the actor who played Oedipus wore a mask, as was conventional in Greek theater. But one might, in a more philosophical or thematic respect, say that this mask was an unnecessary repetition, since the plot of Oedipus's life enacted the same paradox, a disguise of true identity, unearthed finally by the ambiguity of the causal series itself.

We can round out the idea by invoking Walter Benjamin's definition of Fate as "the entelechy of events in the field of guilt." Benjamin is specifically addressing tragic events (hence the emphasis on guilt), whereas we are interested here in the behavior of drama at large. But we can also speak of Fate as the entelechy (or design, purpose) of events in the field of happiness (comedy), of danger (melodrama), social and psychological conflict (naturalism), fantasy, and so on. In each of these forms, Fate—in order to *be* Fate—admits nothing by halves. Fate is thus the incarnation of Matte Blanco's principle of maximization of magnitude. It admits no such halfway plot as KING DISCOVERS HE KILLED UNCLE AND MARRIED AUNT. Fate strives for the ideal form, for the causal law of drama rests on the endowment of events with a perfect design—KING DISCOVERS HE KILLED FATHER AND MARRIED MOTHER. In such cases, as Benjamin says, "everything intentional or accidental is so intensified that the complexities . . . betray, by their paradoxical vehemence, that the action of this play has been inspired by fate" (1977, 130). A god prowls behind the event.

Yet such events, as Aristotle says, "must grow out of the very structure of the plot itself, in such a way that on the basis of what has happened previously this particular outcome follows either by necessity or in accordance with probability" (sec. 12). To come down to cases, we are reacting to two different orders of causal determination during a play. Let us refer to them as *empirical* and *entelechial* causality. These are pretentious terms, but they are the most descriptive that occur to me. Empirical causality is what we observe taking place as an illusionary sequence of events and speeches, one giving place, or rise, to another: the Watch awaits the appearance of the Ghost in *Hamlet*; it appears and is confirmed by Horatio; they tell Hamlet, and so on, together with each nuance of interaction that complicates the plot and leads finally to *Exeunt marching*. This is roughly Aristotle's probability and necessity (the two terms covering both likelihood in social interaction and what necessarily happens under specific physical conditions).

It is likely that Aristotle would find many of our plays highly improbable in this regard, but with some study of our modern freedoms he might decide to update his idea of probability rather than abandon it as a permanent principle of plotting. Among other things, he would see that so-called absurd, irrational, or postmodern deconstructive experience, so characteristic of our drama, would have its own form of probability and

The Pleasure of the Play

that a play such as *The Bald Soprano* might do almost anything it liked, within unreason, as long as it didn't begin making sense like an Ibsen play, or, if it did, that possibility would somehow have to be built into its causal assumptions early on. Moreover, a play such as Pinter's *Betrayal* might quite plausibly move backward in time, putting, as it were, the effect before the cause, but having begun doing so, it would only confuse us if it would suddenly restrict itself to moving forward in time, like the rest of reality. Empirical causality, then, is simply what we see happening according to a probability based in part on a logic of normal expectations and in part on a logic of convention, or what the play announces as its own rules of development (e.g., in Poe's world people rise from the dead, but in Zola's when you're dead you're dead).

Entelechial causality leads us beyond mechanical cause-effect (A causes B, etc.) to the realm of design or purpose in nature, or of things reaching the potential inherent in their form. It is the tendency of things to unfold according to some "whole-making" process, or vitality. As such, entelechial causality takes us to the sphere of the divinity that shapes the work's end—that is, the author's superimposition of form on the seemingly "probable" events of the play. But bearing in mind Aristotle's idea that the plot is the soul of the drama, we might think of entelechial causality as that sense of form being imposed on the events not only by some absent author (who, we realize at some perceptual level, has already created the play) but by an internal principle of form imposed by the medium itself, much as DNA predictably produces similar creatures in any given species. A more colorful term might be Kenneth Burke's notion of "internal fatality, a principle operating from within, though its logic may also be grounded in the nature of the extrinsic scene, whose properties contribute to the same development" (1962, 517). So we sit at a play with one part of our attention fixed on the mechanical order of events, the "accidental judgments, casual slaughters, and purposes mistook," as Horatio puts it, and the other part focused on the ambiguous coherence in all this disorder taking place before us.

To sum up: the unified process through which these two forms of causality cooperate in a play is illustrated by the diagram in Figure 2. Here our wheel of fortune is dramatically refined to illustrate not only how kings rise and fall but how plays get from A to Z.[2] Through dialogue

[2] This diagram by O. R. Kline appeared on the dust jacket of my *Irony and Drama: A Poetics* (Ithaca: Cornell University Press, 1971).

FIGURE 2

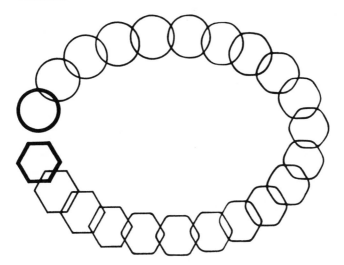

(which, for present purposes, I will enlarge here to include gesture, movement, silence, etc.) the play moves gradually to its ending. Each unit of
dialogue is represented by a circle, and the area of overlap may be construed as the cause-effect linkage of any two units—as, for example, when
Bernardo in *Hamlet* says, "Who's there?" and Francisco responds, "Nay,
answer me. Stand and unfold yourself." Thus through the spontaneity of
dialogue and physical interchange the play appears to move by happen-
stance one step, or link, at a time in a probable direction, much like
conversations or motions of real life. In this respect, the play unfolds as
life unfolds, taking its energy and momentum from what is being said or
done at, and to, that point.

But we notice that as the chained circles advance they begin getting
"edgy" and the arcs gradually sharpen into angles. Moreover, the direction
of movement becomes elliptical, so that while the circles "return" as hexa-
gons, the path by which they do so is a perfect orbit that could in no
purely mechanistic or realistic sense have been determined by the drive of
dialogue alone. This is the entelechial process, that invisible homing instinct by which the full potential of the drama is realized in "the worst
possible turn"—or, in the case of comedy or sentimental drama, the best
possible turn. As Kenneth Burke has suggested, the dramatist is like the
dialectician in the sense that he or she is driven on to antithesis, to a

The Pleasure of the Play

continual sharpening of distinctions into ironic oppositions: "We could lay it down that 'what goes forth as A returns as non-A.' This is the basic pattern that places the essence of drama and dialectic in the irony of the 'peripety,' the strategic moment of reversal" (1962, 517).

We are now in a position to enlarge our use of the word "coincidence." In its primary meaning (*OED*, defs. 1–3), coincidence refers to the sense of things coinciding, agreeing, or corresponding exactly in substance, character, time, or place. In all meanings, the denominator is a coming together or joining (*incidere*: to fall upon or into, to happen to), or the formation of a unity out of diverse elements, as when we speak of an "incident" as something special that happened in the causal flow of normal experience. So there is an overlap in the meanings, and a co*IN*cidence in the fait-divers sense could be thought of as a coin*CID*ence in the primary sense of bringing two causal chains together in a single event, like the "independent" journeys of Oedipus and his father. Obviously, we are speaking in a metaphorical way here, since no two elements in a play can coincide (occupy the same space or time) in the sense that geometricians speak of angles or circles coinciding or that Zeno thought the arrow coincided with the space it occupied at each moment of its flight. Still, as a play is performed, we do feel something akin to such a coincidence; we have a complex impression of something "building up" in the play's space, of all its elsewheres and thens somehow nesting in the here and now of each instant, and in the end of all its "parts" having been stored in the whole that, in the process of passing, manifests itself as a kind of emotional Big Bang. Indeed, catharsis may be explained as the advent of coincidence in this primary meaning of the term, and we might even think of a play as a space-time event that gradually falls *into* us and becomes reembodied (having given up its own "body" in the performance), creating something like a temporary soul.

So we now see that the true coincidence of a play does not simply lie in such bizarre occurrences as Oedipus meeting his father at the crossroads, then marrying his mother. These, and all of their kind (e.g., the "moment" in which Pozzo is struck blind in *Waiting for Godot*) are only sympathetic of the more pervasive form of coincidence in a chain of events that seem to grow out of each other casually: in short, the process crudely represented by the overlapping circles in our diagram. The play is a continuous overlap, since at no point is anything happening that is absolutely *new*. All of its events are continuations (Polonius hides behind the arras; Hamlet stabs him; Hamlet is sent to England; Laertes returns from Paris) held together by the cement of probability. Hence the entelechial wonder of the ending: the sense of convergence of all the parts, of everything leading precisely *here* to this *now*. We suddenly see the import of Polonius's avid detective work, of Ophelia's frailty, of Claudius's poisoned cup (not meant for Hamlet after all), of Gertrude's ambiguous innocence, of Fortinbras's willingness to invade Poland rather than Denmark. But even these gross coherences are inadequate as approximations of the experience aroused by the play. Coincidence is the microevolution of the play's unity-in-time, and in order to appreciate this fact we must now consider the theatrical event as a temporal structure that is merely seen in space. In short, the paradox of the play's flight can only be resolved by thinking of it as occurring, somewhat literally, in three places at once.

CHAPTER **5**

The Unity in Time

The simplest text to illustrate this point is Saint Augustine's famous division of human time into three zones of consciousness: *memory* ("the present of things past"), *sight* ("the present of things present"), and *expectation* ("the present of things future") (1973, 193). It should be said that Augustine is describing our consciousness of time, not time itself in some abstract or measurable sense. The distinction, of course, is that consciousness can only occur in a present, and from this perspective the most impure (I am tempted to say the *weakest*) of the three presents is the one Augustine refers to as *sight* or "the present of things present." This is the zone of time philosophers refer to as the "specious" (or seeming) present, and its singular quality is that it cannot be contemplated *as such* because it is continually being bumped into the past (memory) by once-future events. I am not suggesting that dramatic power is *not* concentrated in this present, however fugitive, but rather that in the theater, of all places in the world, sight is an intensified composition of memory and expectation. This is one of the truths behind Gaston Bachelard's statement, "Sight says too many things at one time. Being does not see itself" (1969, 215). Or, more matter-of-factly, being does not recognize what it sees *as* being because sight is a (con)fusion of stimuli coming from different temporal sectors. In the theater, you would have more luck apprehending being, or the present of things present, if you ignored the play and concentrated your gaze on the back of the head in front of you or on the EXIT light over the door—on anything that wasn't *doing* something or *spending* time—which is to say, retreating from expectation into memory.

So we should think of the theatrical *now* not as a point or an interval that is succeeded by another point or interval (as in Zeno's paradox of the arrow) but as the window of our consciousness on the temporal flux taking place in the space before us. The present—sight—is my contribution to the flow of time; without me, or another like me, the present is an unnecessary category. The present, Merleau-Ponty says, is the passing of time itself, or "that which does not pass in time" (1978, 423). That is, the present does not come and go, and what comes and goes *in* it is of a different order from the present itself. The theater, with all its metaphors of "on" and "off" and "enter" and "exit omnes," is the place par excellence that preserves the *passage* of time in its purest form. And the inadequacy of our circular diagram, of any diagram, is that it cannot show how the present is *made of* the past and the future. Merleau-Ponty continues:

> Since in time being and passing are synonymous, by becoming past, the event does not cease to be. . . . Instant C and instant D, however near they are together, are not indistinguishable, for if they were there would be no time; what happens is that they run into each other and C becomes D because C has never been anything but the anticipation of D as present, and of its own lapse into the past. This amounts to saying that each present reasserts the presence of the whole past which it supplants, and anticipates that of all that is to come, and by that definition the present is not shut up within itself, but transcends itself towards a future and a past. (420–21)

What we see *in* the present, then, is a fraction of succession in the process of the whole. But the particular demand of theater—and the dramatic texts on which it depends—is that it be time-efficient and, like the March Hare, always worried about being on time with the next event, the next "now." Of all forms of fictional plotting, dramatic action demands a rapid transmutation of tenses. The novel can quite easily relax the flow of tenses into extended time warps of description or reflection in which the translation of causes into effects and effects into new causes will be secondary to the accumulation of homogeneous detail or background—for example, the historical essays that interrupt the narrative flow of *War and Peace*, the textbook on cetology in *Moby-Dick*, the catalogue of ships in the *Iliad*. Susanne Langer's notion of "change made perceivable" is absolutely critical to theater, and it is explained phenomenologically by the "paradoxical vehemence" (in Benjamin's phrase) with which theater processes time as a perceptual convergence of past and future.

To put this another way, one might say that theater (hence dramatic texts) must process time at the speed of the actor's body, which means simply that everything that passes in theater must be *actable*, as opposed to merely speakable. There are charismatic actors who could recite a phone directory and maintain our interest, but on stage during a play the actor becomes a passive, uninteresting vessel the moment the text ceases to supply him or her with the cues that arouse passion and change in both body and voice.

The dramatic illusion, then, is not simply, as Langer says, "a present filled with its own future," but a present filled with its future and its past. Moreover, this is as much a phenomenon of sight as of expectation and memory. Since sight consists of peripheral as well as direct vision, we may say that in the immediate *now* of stage action the eye sees the entire triptych of "Augustinian" time as it flows from future into past, like a row of chorus girls dancing through a spotlight on an otherwise dark stage.[1] The *now*, in short, is not a knife edge but the spotlight of vision that bathes the passing act and allows us, like Thomas Mann's Hans Castorp, to "see time spacious," or, what amounts to the same thing, to see space drenched in time. Thus every act has a trinocular—or, if you wish, a

---

[1] This point is of course a central issue in deconstruction's critique of *presence*. For example, Jonathan Culler: "Consider . . . the flight of an arrow. If reality is what is present at any given instant, the arrow produces a paradox. At any given moment it is in a particular spot; it is always in a particular spot and never in motion. We want to insist, quite justifiably, that the arrow *is* in motion at every instant from the beginning to the end of its flight, yet its motion is never present at any moment of presence. The presence of motion is conceivable, it turns out, only insofar as every instant is already marked with the traces of the past and future. Motion can be present, that is to say, only if the present instant is not something given but a product of the relations between past and future. Something can be happening at a given instant only if the instant is already divided within itself, inhabited by the nonpresent" (1985, 94). This presence/absence may present a valid problem for some kinds of linguistic or textual inquiry, but it seems to me the underlying condition behind anything we do or think in life, and theater is perhaps the primary art—being *lively* in its very composition—that depends on and makes capital of this *différance*, or endless elusiveness in the motion of things.

tritemporal—structure. If, as Merleau-Ponty says, being and passing are synonymous, what is enacted in time is virtually consubstantial with it. The force of Hamlet's sword thrust through the arras rests entirely in what I already know to be behind it and what I expect will surely follow as a result. Even if I halt the act in mid-progress on the knife edge of a photograph, it will retain at least memory-traces of its "temporal ubiquity," like Muybridge's running horse. I will see Hamlet's body, in other words, in an unnatural posture (lunging, futurely, sword in hand) that can only be explained if it is distributed over time.[2] Moreover, because my consciousness is, as Augustine puts it, "divided amid times" (1973, 201) between memory and expectation, I am bound to miss a great deal of the act itself. I *see* the act but I am too busy seeing *through* it, in the same sense that I see through the words on a page to the flow of significance behind them. Instant C is at once the denouement of instant B and the exposition of instant D, and each is nothing more than the specious visibility of the *now* in which my attention is trapped between "something is happening that was going to happen" and "something is going to happen to what is happening." What I see clearly, then, is the collusion of past and future in which the present is swallowed in a praxis.

To sum up: the composite *now* is the perceptual ground of dramatic action and the source of its emotional affect. Without the past, the present is simply motion, not action, and the future is random openness, not anticipation. As a simple instance, if I happen to arrive late at the theater, I must allow the play to accumulate more "past" (in me) before I can fully convert what I see on stage from unintelligible motion into intelligible action. As we have seen, what distinguishes action from motion is the sense of implicit wholeness, or wholeness in the making. Motion is continuous and belongs strictly to the sphere of physical behavior; action—at least dramatic action—is a discrete manifestation of motion that belongs as well to the sphere of value; or, as Aristotle would say, something done for the sake of something, and we will get to this part of the problem

---

[2] Along this line, I am reminded of the photographs of baseball pitchers in the act of pitching. Viewed "in time," this is a graceful and efficient bodily act, but I have yet to see a photograph of a pitching pitcher that does not render the act as an awkward, if not grotesque, distortion of the body. The same thing is true of many comparatively still photographs, in which otherwise attractive individuals are caught in unattractive postures.

when we discuss character. Motion would broadly correspond to empirical causality. If I may paraphrase something I've said in another connection (1992, 146), action would correspond to entelechial causality, the realization of a thing's potential. In the *Physics* Aristotle gives the example of the falling stone that strikes a man. It did not fall for the purpose of striking him but rather it fell spontaneously or incidentally; that is, it fell as an effect of an empirical cause, some sort of nearby motion that dislodged it. But in the case of Mitys' statue, which fell on the man who had been the cause of Mitys' death, the sheer symmetry of the values involved forces us to seek some extrinsic or intentional cause, some form of poetic justice. Thus the event becomes an action, scarcely one worth dramatizing, unless perhaps as a fait-divers story in the Argos *Times*. But it does demonstrate the idea that what we experience in the presence of an action is a virtual personification of the world, as if events could think.

Drama imitates time, then, not simply as a construct of human will or as something whose passing can be measured ("T'is now struck twelve. Get thee to bed, Francisco.") but as a fusion of presents which has, as the Gravedigger would say, "three branches." These meet in the agony of the hero, the sacrificial vessel in which we see reflected "the fullness of time." This is the source of that joy I. A. Richards places at the heart of the tragic experience, the sense in which "everything is right here and now in the nervous system" (1961, 246). There are at least two ways to read the key word "right" here. You can think of it as meaning "correct" or "just," or you can think of it, as I prefer to do in this context, as a combination of "exactly" and "totally." For the idea is that the cathartic experience, our response to tragedy, is a loading of our perceptual circuits to capacity through a process from which everything "irrelevant and extraneous is excluded" (244). This loading has nothing to do with assuring us that Fate is either kind or unkind, only that Fate is a full harmony of the causal and temporal orders, as we see at the end of *King Lear*. The deaths of Lear and Cordelia are joyful, as Richards would say, not as a moral solution to the play's tensions but as the inevitable resolution of the *Lear* music; and the infamous eighteenth-century deletion of the "accident" that produces this joy (the hanging of Cordelia) amounted to little more than a preference for immediate socio-temporal harmonies over full orchestral ones.

One might say of tragedy, then, that the real purging begins at the beginning of the play rather than arriving at the end, inasmuch as the ending is already implicit in the beginning, as Mary Stuart said of her own situation. Indeed, it is debatable whether catharsis or ecstasis is the better word for what tragedy does to us. Are we full or empty at the end of tragedy? Are its "lendings" of pity and fear drained off, as Aristotle seemed to believe, or are they retained as psychic possessions that lead to bad habits, as Plato feared? Or might we take a middle course that sees catharsis as purification, in the sense that if you purify something you don't necessarily get rid of it, you have simply thrown the worser part away. Behind the concept of catharsis, of course, is theater's paranoic self-defense against its critics, since there has always been (and remains) the question of what happens to moral poisons that are, as Hamlet (the play-producer) put it, ingested "in jest." But when the mood of paranoia declines and theater becomes less defensive, we note that discussions of catharsis tend to become ecstatic. For Nietzsche, to take a well-known example, what is purged is not pity and fear but human individuation; in its place tragedy puts "a metaphysical solace" through which "for a brief moment we become, ourselves, the primal Being." Like Richards after him, Nietzsche would have it that the spectator "seems to see all the possible events of life and the world take place in himself" (1956, 99). Indeed, the nervous system runneth over.

   We are led to the seeming paradox that theater is timeless in as much as it contains all time. Timelessness must be understood as a metaphorical concept and not as an interval in which one has no awareness of time passing (as in the timelessness of being under anaesthesia). Georg Lukács's idea that tragedy's "moments exist in parallel rather than in series" (1974, 158) is aimed at this distinction, and it has partly to do with the way the elements of a play keep repeating themselves as the play evolves. For instance, the reduplication of the "passion's slave" theme in *Hamlet* occurs on all levels, from physical movement and gesture to rhetorical imagery. When we encounter several verbal events "in parallel," for example—

> Is it not monstrous that this player here,
> But in a fiction, in a dream of passion.
>
> (2.2.545–46)

and

> What to ourselves in passion we propose,
> The passion ending, doth the purpose lose.
>
> (3.2.189–90)

and

> . . . Give me that man
> that is not passion's slave.
>
> (3.2.71–72)

—we are experiencing at once a unit of timelessness and a synecdochic reduction of the whole of *Hamlet* into three of its parts, which now become one. For these three passages, together with countless others tending on the same theme, form a kind of running metaphor whose tenor (in this case) is passion bound on one side by the notion of playacting (as in a fiction or a theater) and on the other by proposing or promising ("Ay, thou poor ghost. . . . thy commandment all alone shall live within the book and volume of my brain." (1.5.96, 102–3); in the space between them we perceive an infinitesimal "imitation" in small of the actions of Hamlet (and *Hamlet*) at large. Thus repetition in dramatic poetry—of word, phrase, motif, scene, plot, etc.—is a device for "obliterating" time. I take this word from Samuel Beckett's discussion of the recurrence of the past in the present (involuntary memory) in Marcel Proust: "Thanks to this reduplication [of parts]," Beckett says, "the experience is at once imaginative and empirical, at once an evocation and a direct perception, real without being merely actual, ideal without being merely abstract, the ideal real, the essential, the extratemporal" (1931, 55–56). Of course, you couldn't say that the more repetitions the greater the sense of timelessness. Indeed, excessive repetition produces too much time-awareness, another word for which is boredom. Timelessness must be discovered, come upon by rhythmic surprise; it must be experienced as a sudden glimpse into the tritemporality of the now, for the "now," like ecstasy, will not tolerate much extension. Timelessness is, in short, not being literally *outside* of time, or dead to time's passing, so much as being "amid" times, as Augustine says, where one experiences the woven texture of expectation and memory in the timeless moment of the now.

Behind the famous unities of time, place, and action, in other words, is a single generic unity, a striving (even in nontragic drama) to make the play a simulacrum of life's transtemporal brevity. In the theater, we witness a stylization of time. First, time has been framed off from world time and space by the proscenium arch, the platform, or the circle, and by the actor whose art is founded less on mimicry than on the elimination of the random. Time has been given rigor, cleansed of excess, and framed again by a beginning and an ending within which are countless beginnings, middles, and endings called moments, or events, all merging so rapidly that they appear, out of one eye, to be stationary, like the spokes of a spinning wheel. In the theater, we are standing still at great speed, a metaphysical condition that has its humble origin in the actuality of a stage and a theater seat, or a seat in one world that looks into a (w)hole in another world. Thus the phenomenon of stationary movement, of the moment that belongs to all moments, is the result of empirical change within entelechial causality. To put it less abstractly, one might see this fusion, in pure stylistic terms, as an elaborate display of déjà vu, or of the *plus ça change* principle whereby, as Vladimir puts it, in *Waiting for Godot*, "the essential doesn't change."

In what respects we should limit the term "catharsis" to certain kinds of dramatic experience, I am not prepared to say. Catharsis still has the status of an *idée reçu*, as if tragedy's homeopathic purpose were, always and everywhere, to produce a special emotion that is five parts pity and five parts fear—moreover, an emotion one can presumably identify when it occurs and also differentiate from other emotional combinations. Thus, it would seem, we have a true (or full) catharsis in certain works of Aeschylus, Sophocles, and Shakespeare (otherwise, where else?), less so in certain of Euripides' plays, something slightly less (perhaps seven parts pity) in Chekhov, and none at all in Brecht (who preferred five parts reason and five parts social indignation). To my knowledge, no one has bothered to differentiate these other reactions, but then no one seems to worry about what catharsis is either. All that seems to be important is that we have a word to indicate any powerful feeling we experience at the end of a (usually tragic) play. What is supposed to happen during the rest of the play isn't clear, but in most casual uses of the term, "catharsis" indicates a kind of payload, like delivery in the birth process. Catharsis is, I suspect, more a term of dignification than of definition, and, like expensive wine, we seem to reserve it for special theatrical occasions.

In some respects, I am inclined to agree with Theodor Adorno that, as we view catharsis today, the whole notion "is an outmoded piece of mythology, hopelessly inadequate for understanding the impact that art does have" (1984, 338), including tragic art. On the other hand, the idea as expressed in Aristotle has a certain value in accounting for the balance one finds in tragedy (at its best) and in other forms of drama, if only because pity and fear preserve, better than some other pairings (joy/outrage, desire/revulsion) a certain oppositional suspension that mirrors the state of practical suspense in which we view the artwork (as we say: pity—the impulse to approach; fear—the impulse to withdraw). More specifically, as we will see, Aristotle couples catharsis (as a balance of pity and fear) with the character of the tragic hero by way of showing how tragedy seeks to avoid certain other emotional responses that would throw us out of the work—chiefly, moral repugnance. To claim, however, that catharsis is what we go to plays to have or that it explains art's purpose does seem an incomplete idea of the pleasure afforded by drama. And the point deserves to be made by Adorno himself, who draws a distinction between "aesthetic feeling" and the various emotions raised by art:

> Aesthetic feeling is not what is being aroused in us. It is more like a sense of wonderment in the presence of what we behold; a sense of being overwhelmed in the presence of a phenomenon that is non-conceptual while at the same time being determinate. The arousal of subjective effect by art is the last thing we should want to dignify with the name of aesthetic feeling. True aesthetic feeling is oriented to the object; it is the feeling of the object, not some reflex in the viewer. Furthermore, one has to differentiate this viewing subjectivity, properly understood, from the subjective moment in the object itself, which is located in expression and form. (1984, 236)

Like Adorno, I consider as pleasurable, then, our entire orientation to the aesthetic object which contains its own "subjective moment" located at the level of expression and form. "Subjectivity [in the process of creation]," Adorno says, "comes into its own not as communication or message [or presumably as emotion], but as labour" (238). The labor in question here is that of the artist who "functions as the executor of [the work's] balance." This labor is what makes it possible *to feel* the particular presence of Sophocles or Shakespeare or Ibsen or Brecht and to feel, beyond that, the presence of aesthetic composition, shared by all artist-laborers, which separates the work from the world of experience it is adapting to mimetic representation. And here I am concerned primarily with this labor rather than with the particular emotion it produces. All plays, it seems to me, produce something *like* a catharsis (a particular emotion), and I see no real way in which the cathartic charge, however narrow or generalized it may become, can be separated from the aesthetic feeling itself. Plays are not emotion-producing machines, they are objects of "wonderment" which overwhelm us, in the best cases, by their way of being present before us as "expression and form." One might claim, then, that aesthetic feeling invites its own cathartic reaction, not simply as pity and fear felt for the hero, but as pity and fear—or joy, indignation, sadness, grief, woe, wonder, etc.—purged of their normal visceral force by the economy of expression and form.

Thus all plays behave in an Aristotelian way insofar as they are set off from empirical reality by wholeness, which itself implies certain strategies of containment. Indeed, one could write an interesting study of beginning-ness, middle-ness, and end-ness and the sense in which these three formal time zones control our emotions differently and successively as the *clues* of the beginning pass into the *symptoms* of the middle and the *consequences* of the ending. To outline briefly: in the beginning a play behaves like a mystery, giving us something behind which a great deal is withheld. What is perfectly intelligible to the characters in the play-world is news to us and must be treated as we treat clues—for example, the line "Nay, but this dotage of our general's / O'erflows the measure," which introduces the on-again off-again imbroglio of *Antony and Cleopatra*. We pass into middle-ness without awareness, but the middle is roughly the point where clues have become symptoms, or repetitions. The characters have become reliable but the situation, having now emerged, is not, and it is exactly the reliability of the characters which increases the instability of the situation. That is, it is because Antony remains Antony (reliably undependable), Cleopatra Cleopatra, Caesar Caesar, and so on, that the play reaches its "worst possible turn." The function of the reversal, of course, is to resolve middle-ness and put us at the threshold of end-ness, where the "turn" enters its final spiral. Symptoms have begun to produce consequences, which arrive like messengers (and usually through them), and there is an aura of inevitability about the proceedings which actors are often tempted to overstress. It is also at this point that plays have a habit of looking back over their shoulders to their own beginnings ("And all our yesterdays have lighted fools the way to dusty death . . . ") or into the future ("Give me my robe, put on my crown; I have immortal longings in me"), and such moments can usually be assigned to the recognition. The ending, finally, freezes the causal series in a Grecian-urn effect, often through a theatrical tableau (as in O'Neill's *Long Day's Journey into Night*) or, in the cinema, by the frozen still, as in the ending of *Butch Cassidy and the Sundance Kid*.

It might be argued that some modern plays do not have true endings and that some plays even repeat their opening lines as the closing lines, producing a "Here we go again!" effect. But this is a confusion of ends and means. Even such endings firmly seal off the future, putting causality to rest in a terminal holding pattern that says simply, "Here they go forever!" like the time-stopped Butch and Sundance who, as we see them through the rolling of the credits, are always *about* to die. One might also treat beginning-, middle-, and end-ness as extensions of Augustine's time categories: the beginning would be the present of things past (in the sense of the play carving its present out of the past in exposition); the middle would be the present of things present (in the sense of in-between-ness or indetermination in things); and the ending the present of things future (as they will be).

In any case, early on in a play we are drawn into the felt orders of wholeness in which the laws of time and causality parade before us in human masks. And, as the ending draws near, something happens to us which is not accounted for by our interest in the outcome of the plot. One suspects that this something is born of a built-in physiological recognition that endings per se are extraordinary experiences, like our highway accident. We see proof of this principle everywhere: in our rich vocabulary of "final" things; in the ritual of goodbyes; in our fascination with infinity and the circle; and in the mystical notion that our whole life passes before our eyes at the moment we enter the realm of timelessness for the last time. Coleridge once described poetry as a dim analogue of the Creation. The ending of a play is what we might call a dim analogue of the Last Day, which is associated of course with divine revelation and the raising of all the earth's dead: the past has run out of future and the *now* itself flickers and goes out. But for a brief moment—the death of the hero in tragedy, the mating of all the right people in comedy, the taking up of what's left of life in naturalism—time is full: all the returns are in; effects cease causing further effects; and everything seems to be right here and now in the nervous system.

> . . . the one life within us and abroad,
> Which meets all motion and becomes its soul,
> A light in sound, a sound-like power in light,
> Rhythm in all thought, and joyance everywhere.

Most plays do not live up to these lines from Coleridge's *Eolian Harp*. But even in weaker ending experiences, excepting outright boredom, there is usually some surge of feeling, if lower on the cathartic scale, at the passing of the play's world and the fullness of its inhabitants' lives. Endings of plays are like the codas of music, and play directors take great pains orchestrating their movement and rhythm, for the simple reason that all characters in plays, even those of comedy, die before us in the end in the sense of completing their three-hour lives. Such time-deaths simply remind us that music is art's greatest regulator of the body's response systems: with enough violins you can make the death of a pet snake unbearable.

CHAPTER 6

Peripety and Recognition

Some years ago, I suggested that peripety could be considered not only as a plot device but also as a principle of plot development, and that the former was really a symptom of the latter: "We could say that drama *is* peripety, and that the objective of drama is to make human experience as *peripet-ous* as possible" (1971, 27). This idea was inspired by Kenneth Burke's discussion of irony as internal fatality in "The Four Master Tropes," where drama is virtually equated with irony and dialectic ("Where the ideas are in action, we have drama; where the agents are in ideation, we have dialectic" [1962, 512]). In the light of recent theory in semiotics and phenomenology, however, I think there is more to be said on this point, particularly in connection with the relation of peripety to recognition and both of these to the interaction of audience and play. Here I want to advance the notion that the principle Aristotle calls peripety occurs in many modes and manifests itself in different forms, not only as a device or the principle of reversal in the plot, but as a strategy through which the drama might directly or indirectly throw curves of all sorts and sizes at the audience. All in all, peripety may be considered the *copulative* of dramatic spectacle, its means of enjoining the audience in its (always) peripetous acts of representation. For inherent in representation itself is what Burke calls "the paradox of the synecdochic" (509), a process of reversal whereby the world is transformed, or reduced, to a sign of itself, much as Oedipus the king is reduced to Oedipus the symbol through the Messenger's news from Corinth.

But let us begin with Aristotle's own meaning of peripety. It is perfectly clear that Aristotle was referring to a moment in the play—moreover, a single moment in the whole play—whereby the fortune of the hero is changed, literally, before our eyes. But Aristotle was really borrowing the term from a number of possible terms standing for related or overlapping concepts. All of these possible *other* terms for the phenomenon, however, stand in a relationship of contiguity and constitute what Douglas Hofstadter calls a "semantic network" (1980, 371). Crudely, a semantic network is a mental map in which the "towns" and "cities"—the terms composing the network—are all connected by neuronal "roads" and have names that are at least partially synonymical (as one might expect to find North Clearfield next to East or West Clearfield, and so on). Thus on a map encompassing the province of Peripety, the capital city would be Peripety itself, next to which we might find Coincidence, Reversal, Metabasis, Contrast, and so on. My own personal network—and networks of the same phenomenon are necessarily different for each individual— would include outlying towns and boroughs like Reciprocity, Tension, Bisociation, Polarity, Inversion, Dialectic, Irony, Antagonism, Strange Loop, Crisis and Catastrophe (connected by the Möbius Strip), Change, Internal Fatality, Feedback, Oxymoron, M. C. Escher and Magritte, Joke, Metaphor, and countless other terms that participate in the principle of retaliation or recursive action. Even this list does not begin to exhaust the holdings of a single mind respecting the potentiality of such a network. Moreover, any term in a semantic network might conceptually trigger any other one; for as signifiers and signifieds they stand "in a relationship of mutual substitution," as Umberto Eco puts it in his own version of this idea (1984, 73). Obviously some of the terms in my network are less substitutable than others, some are borderline terms, and some are virtually synonymous. Witness in the Aristotle commentary, for instance, the overlap between "change" of fortune (metabasis) and peripety itself: translations sometimes refer to the metabasis as the reversal of fortune and peripety as the finite moment in which the reversal takes place. In any case, the metabasis is always, in Aristotle's view, a reversal from good to bad fortune or from bad to good.

The most important feature of a semantic network, however, is that when you use one of its terms, you can never tell whether that is all you meant or whether the term isn't simply the best one you could find to stand in for something of much greater conceptual density. All in all, we are never really not using semantic networks, and Freud's entire psycho-analytic approach to dreams can be said to depend on tracing one dream-term or thought through the dreamer's entire network of associated terms. (For example, Freud's entire discussion of his botanical monograph dream is effectively an attempt to map a single dream-image through a lifetime of associations [1965, 202–9]). In short: if something is doing a certain kind of work, or having a certain kind of effect, at one level of perception, we shouldn't be surprised to find that a variation of it may be going on at other levels of perception. So when you invoke the term "peripety" you may be evoking a great deal more, of which the peripety was only symptomatic.

I should add that I am not trying to water down Aristotle's definition of peripety, but to see what sorts of variations of the principle one might identify by moving away from the specific thing it was intended to define. As Morris Weitz has suggested in an important essay on the role of theory in aesthetics, Greek tragedy is a closed concept in the sense that all its examples are already in. But tragedy and drama are open concepts, in as much as "unforeseeable [examples] are always forthcoming or envisage-able" (1962, 54–55). It seems reasonable to assume, then, that the proper-ties out of which the forms are created are also subject to change, as opposed to disappearance, or that we needn't throw away or limit the property because one form of it has been closed by history. In effect, then, I propose to treat the peripety/recognition complex much as history has treated metaphor: we once considered metaphor as a humble figure of speech in which two things were compared without a "like" or an "as"; then it was seen as a "tension" in language (simile itself became a form of metaphor); then as an indirect speech act; then a means of discovering nonconceptual meaning; and so on, until today metaphor has overflowed poetics and is widely regarded as a way of making conceptual models of reality and human experience (see Lakoff and Johnson 1980) or as any linguistic short circuit (Eco). Even scientists use things called "theory-constitutive metaphors" to express claims for which literal language is simply inadequate (Boyd 1979, 360). I suspect that somewhere along the line metaphor and peripety cross paths, inasmuch as peripety itself is a way of bringing two things together and producing a new meaning or a recognition. Metaphor, as Walker Percy once defined it, is a big thing happening in a small place, an excellent definition of the effect of peripety.

As Burke might say, speaking metaphorically, metaphor could be called a figural peripety, and peripety an actional metaphor. Hence Metaphor may be considered as yet another city, however far-flung from the capital, in the province of Peripety.

But let us begin by going back to the original description of peripety and recognition in the *Poetics*. Aristotle's scientific interests, of course, led him to view peripety from what we might call a middle distance from the play (roughly that of the scene) where discrete parts could be identified. In essence, peripety is a change to the opposite of the expected. We are still debating what Aristotle really meant by this: for instance, whether the change must occur in something the hero was undertaking at the time, in something that comes to the hero unexpectedly from the outside, or both (or something else). For example, Oedipus did not undertake to bring the Messenger from Corinth; he simply comes. On the other hand, Oedipus himself sent for the Herdsman and so brings something about through his own will. And although Aristotle does not include the Herdsman as part of his description of the peripety in *Oedipus Rex*, it seems untenable to omit the incident on the grounds that it simply confirms what the Messenger says. Gerald Else (1967, 348) feels, to the contrary, that the peripety occurs with the Messenger because it is at this point that the audience's expectations are reversed; the recognition, then, occurs in the Herdsman scene where Oedipus finally finds out the truth.

It is possible that this is what Aristotle meant. I certainly agree with Else that the shift to the opposite happens for *our* benefit, but unlike Else (apparently) I think our benefit is satisfied largely in seeing its effect on Oedipus. This is the so-called Sophoclean or dramatic irony: we know; he doesn't. Or, more likely, we know, and he only *suspects*. But it is the growth of the suspicion in Oedipus's mind (which surely begins way back in the Tiresias scene—"Stop! My parents? Who were they in all the world?") into full recognition that makes the whole scene, from Messenger to Herdsman, one of the most compelling units of action in all drama. Else also discusses the point that we know Oedipus's fate before seeing the play, as opposed to knowing it "in the course of the play—that is, before the climax." He feels that Sophocles takes this prior knowledge "subtly into account in writing the play . . . and plays with it as a cat plays with a mouse" (346). I agree but would add, on the contrary, that anyone who had never heard of Oedipus would know, virtually from the beginning—

or at least from the Tiresias scene—that Oedipus was the killer he seeks. How? First, the suspicion is built into the play on many levels. Mainly, though, it is built into dramatic expectation as part of the so-called Butler-did-it syndrome—in short, the same psychology of oppositional or peripetous thinking that operates in the murder mystery which invites us to seek the least likely suspect as the real murderer. We go to melodramas like *Oedipus* precisely to be played with like a mouse, and much of the thrill comes in trying to outguess the cat who wrote the play. Thus our generic expectation of a peripety leads us into peripetous thought patterns, wherein the actual peripety, when it comes, is a kind of lightning bolt that discharges pent-up energies that have formed throughout the play.

So the realization is Oedipus's, not ours: what we get is the satisfaction of seeing his recognition, and neither the reversal nor the recognition are complete without the Herdsman's verification. Altogether, it is like watching the face of a person who is hearing a joke you have already heard: you look at the eyes, "the windows to the soul," in which the punch line will register its effect, and you have the thrill of a vicarious second hearing. In "Oedipal" terms, your first hearing of the joke parallels the news brought by the Messenger from Corinth; your second hearing parallels the confirmation of the Herdsman.

So we have, in this only extant example of Aristotelian peripety, a kind of double action: an external event that reverses the facts of the hero's situation and a simultaneous internal mental event—realization—that reverses his understanding of it. The two are fused inextricably as a process, rather than occurring as a one-two punch to the soul. And this would be true in most cases: for example, if a teacher should say to a student, "I'm afraid you flunked the final exam," the recognition would begin roughly with "I'm afraid" (if not with the gravity of the teacher's tone or the look in his or her eye) and reach a quick fulfillment at "final exam"—about as long as it takes a guillotine blade to fall.

Theater, obviously, wants to spin out such fast mental transactions because they are, after all, what we go to the theater to see. And indeed, it's hard to imagine a more satisfying instance of peripety and recognition occurring together than the one in *Oedipus Rex*. Moreover, if one reflects the instance against the play at large, it can be seen as a replica in small of the overall action of the play, with which it is structurally isomorphic. It fits "inside" the play like the Russian doll within the doll, or as a perfect example of the holographic principle of *mise en abîme* in which the whole is contained in miniature in one of its parts. It is this relentless internal symmetry that makes *Oedipus* one of the most perfectly constructed plays in the world (and incidentally the easiest to study from a structural point of view). The play is an extended exercise in peripety; or, as someone else has put it, it is one long recognition scene.

But let us look more closely at the Aristotelian view of recognition. Perhaps this is the most curious example of how Aristotle's principles carry unforeseen applications. Aristotle's discussion of recognition limits it to a recognition of inanimate objects, events, and persons. The chief recognition, the one at least that carries the heaviest charge, is that of persons. It is understandable that Aristotle should have confined the concept to such narrow terms, which turn out to be not so narrow after all. Greek tragedy deals primarily with family conflicts, and it is quite common in the plots that members of a family should be separated and, in the vagaries of the small world of myth, find themselves unknowingly confronting a kinsman, usually under terminal stakes (Thyestes, Oedipus, Electra and Orestes, Iphigenia, and Clytemnestra). However, there are many examples of this form of recognition in Shakespeare as well, from Hamlet's recognition of Polonius after stabbing him fatally ("I took thee for thy better") to Emilia's recognition of who has driven Othello to murder Desdemona ("My husband? . . . My husband?"). Moreover, the recognition of persons is almost indispensable to comedy (where it is called the *cognitio*), because disguise and misapprehension of identity tend to be the most durable motifs of the "double take" in the comic plot; then too, comedy is much more tolerant of such unlikely confusions (as we see in the Abbott-Costello routine "Who's on first?"). And finally, recognitions of this kind supply the denouements of whodunits and detective fiction.

Understandably, however, critics have insisted on enlarging the range of recognition, even when it involves personal identities, to include any form of knowledge or understanding gained by the protagonist. Thus Oedipus not only recognizes his own identity and that of his mother and father, he also recognizes, as Francis Fergusson puts it, "the piteous and terrible sense of the mystery of the human situation" (1949, 31). O. B. Hardison, who quotes this passage, maintains, on the contrary, that "the concept should be understood in its narrow sense. It means just what it says. In

Oedipus, which is atypical, the hero recognizes himself. He does not gain insight as a result of the information supplied by the messenger; he simply learns who he is" (Aristotle 1981, 171).

I am moved to respond, like the Greek chorus, by saying that both sides have spoken well, they simply misunderstand each other. Hardison is trying to determine exactly what Aristotle said, and there is no textual evidence that Aristotle had anything like a metaphysical or spiritual discovery in mind. But then, as the remaining scenes of *Oedipus* make clear, the larger meaning of Oedipus's fate is not lost on anyone in the play (and surely wasn't lost on a reader like Aristotle), and it amounts, as the Chorus puts it in the concluding line, to proof that we should

> Count no mortal happy till
> he has passed the final limit of his life secure from pain.
>
> (1529–30)

which is quite a conclusion to draw from one mistaken identity. But again, it all depends on whether you are interested in what Aristotle said or in what the drama does to you. It is certainly more than accident that the recognition of persons, as it became vestigial in drama (in Aristotle's sense), gave way to other forms of discovery resulting from reversal and that the recognition of persons was simply a local variation of a universal realization as steady in its occurrence as the rule that a joke must have a punch line. For every peripety, in other words, there is some sort of recognition, for the simple reason that the peripety would have no function if it did not have a human consequence. It is hard to conceive of a change of fortune that wouldn't be accompanied by a change in awareness, or a recognition that what has happened has somehow affected the participants or—and this is critical—the audience.

To draw a more general conclusion: over against the sphere of causality (discussed in Chapter 4), we may place the sphere of comprehension. The sphere of causality consists of all divine, natural, and human agencies that bring about the change of fortune, and its effect is most visible in those moments we call peripeties, which may be likened to cairns defining the course of a path that might otherwise be obscure. There is every reason to assume that a play may have several discrete peripeties (there are at least three good candidates in *Oedipus* alone) but that audience psychology demands a master peripety somewhere near the end which will bring the wheel full circle, as the Elizabethans were fond of saying. Despite Aristotle's seeming belief that there is one peripety per play, then, we may say that, in principle, peripety is at the heart of a play's *aiming* system. We might describe the peripety as the "strange attractor" of drama. I borrow this concept from chaos theory, where it is related particularly to the behavior of orbits. "An attractor is any point of a system's cycle that seems to attract the system to it"—for example, the midpoint of a pendulum's swing, a hole in the bottom of a pan of water, and so on (Hayles 1991, 8). A strange attractor is one that "combines pattern with unpredictability, confinement with orbits that never repeat themselves" (9); moreover, the strange attractor displays the system's "recursive symmetry" or "the predictability that lies hidden within [its] unpredictable evolutions" (10).[1] And that is precisely what plays, as examples of organized chaos or unforeseeable chains of events, are always demonstrating: the predictability that lies at the heart of unpredictability. Again, Napier conceives of paradox as a thing that "appears to be what it is not" (1986, 1). Thus it is in the discrete moment of peripety where the play betrays the hidden systematicity that operates everywhere in it.

The sphere of comprehension, on the other hand, consists of all that may be learned from a dramatic (or any other) work, not only by the people in the play, but by the audience watching the play. It is the audience that primarily interests me here, since my concern bears centrally on the question of pleasure. Obviously recognition belongs to the sphere of

---

[1] I am using these terms metaphorically, rather than scientifically, and I take my liberty from the chaos scientist's tendency to think of strange attractors in aesthetic terms. For example, David Ruelle: "I have not spoken of the esthetic appeal of strange attractors. These systems of curves, these clouds of points suggest sometimes fireworks or galaxies, sometimes large and disquieting vegetal proliferations. A realm lies there of forms to explore, and harmonies to discover" (Gleick 1988, 153). The discrete Aristotelian moment of peripety, then, could be described as a point at which pattern and unpredictability meet, and the aesthetic appeal of such moments is obviously considerable, as we can see even in simpler figural transactions like metaphor, which relies, so to speak, on a mixture of surprise and pattern; but the moment itself is a manifestation of a continuous orderliness that is, once again, best described in Burke's term, "internal fatality." And this is the respect in which the almost invisible and pedestrian events in Chekhov (such as Astrov saying he won't return until summer at the end of *Vanya*) are doing precisely the work that their more emphatic counterparts are doing in *Oedipus Rex*.

comprehension. It is to the sphere of comprehension what the peripety is to the sphere of causality—a moment in which something thrown up by the causal chain is crystallized either in the minds of a character or the people in the audience. Moreover, recognition is related to what Aristotle calls thought, or *dianoia*, and it may be useful to recall Frye's remark that the plot (mythos) is the dianoia in movement, and the dianoia is the plot in stasis (1957, 83). This leads to still another dimension of recognition. Following Else, Hardison makes the astute observation that "the theoretical reason for the special excellence of recognition of persons is that it is 'part of the plot and the action' and is especially evocative of 'pity and fear'" (Aristotle 1981, 170). Or, as Else puts it, "catharsis is not a change or end-product in the spectator's soul, or in the fear and pity (i.e., the dispositions to them) in his soul, but a process carried forward in the emotional material of the play by its structural elements, above all by the recognition. For the recognition is the pay-off . . . , [or] the hinge on which the emotional structure of the play turns" (1967, 439). So catharsis, through still another of those terminological nestings, is linked to recognition, which is intimately linked to peripety, which is the extruded sign of the work's systematicity, or wholeness.

The reasoning here of course is that the sudden recognition of kin, either before or after a tragic deed, is probably the strongest source of emotion, not only in the character but in the spectator as well. The connection of recognition with catharsis is further strengthened by the two primary meanings of catharsis: it is, on one hand, a purgation or purification, a getting rid of something, and on the other a clarification, or simply "getting" something, in roughly the sense that one gets a joke. Even if the Greek term "catharsis" didn't have such different semantic connotations, the thing we feel when a play ends partakes of some such essentials that arise from the artistic economy of the presentation—a purging of the inessential and a stated or implied sense of its significance, together with the full pleasure of these two seemingly separate processes occurring together as a fusion of dianoia and praxis.

If this is a defensible idea, it gives rise to a further corollary: if the recognition is, as Else says, the payoff of the play, it follows that recognition occurs *even if no one on the stage recognizes anything*. As the main consequence of peripety, recognition is something like the sound a falling tree makes in the forest. If there is no one around to hear it, it is still a sound—or, more properly, the makings of a sound (an agitation of air)— and any ear in the vicinity can pick it up. And there are certain kinds of recognition that are heard only by the audience. I am thinking particularly of plays in the so-called ironic mode in which, as Frye points out, "pity and fear are not raised [in the characters, but are] reflected to the reader from the art" (1957, 40).

The most interesting examples of this kind are the plays of Chekhov, which typically bring the protagonists to a point of no return, with nothing in store but the bleakest of futures, and their response is to claim they will get a job or to speak of the happiness that others will glean from their suffering in future generations. This is an instance of what we may call the psychosis of deferral, or nonrecognition; yet it produces a cathartic effect for exactly the reason Frye suggests: the characters on stage have either missed the point of their lives or have succeeded in sublimating it, but the effect of this spiritual hamartia is passed directly to the audience as an acute form of pathos. In most strongly ironical plays (particularly in the Absurd vein), we probably don't care so much about the characters' future; but the thing about Chekhov is that he never destroyed a character for whom he didn't first arouse the deepest compassion, and when his plays are well done they can produce an overwhelming cathartic experience.[2]

I suggest that this affect belongs in the category of recognition: it is exacerbated by peripeties that, though probable in their occurrence, usually fall into the play out of thin air (the brigade "decides" to leave town; Solyony provokes Tusenbach to a duel; the professor and his wife simply leave the estate; Lopakhin buys the cherry orchard), just as the Messenger from Corinth arrives in Thebes without prior expectation. The characters certainly must feel the weight and import of what has happened to them, but in true Chekhovian fashion they reveal almost nothing; they take no

---

[2] Catharsis is another term that has been too narrowly confined to its Aristotelian meanings, as though there were something about tragedy that always produces the same effect, a combination of pity and fear. As a theater-goer, I find it impossible to separate my emotional experience with, say, Chekhov (when it is well acted) from my experience with, say, *Hamlet* or *Oedipus*. Catharsis seems to me a pell-mell effect, composed of different combinations of emotions, perhaps, but always what we may call a whelming experience.

action (like suicide or putting out their eyes); and the consequence is that the audience feels that peculiar disparity, common in irony (another word for what we're talking about), between what is said and what has been left unsaid. Irony, someone has claimed, requires three people: the ironist, someone who gets the irony, and someone (at least implicitly) who doesn't, or wouldn't, get it. In ironic drama there is, so to speak, something to recognize, and in Chekhov this something is exactly the characters' nonrecognition—or at least the gulf between the display of behavior and its possible inner consequence. A great deal of emotion is concentrated in these endings, and it flows directly into the audience, having no human vessel in the play-world in whom it is absorbed, as it usually is in Greek and Shakespearean plays where the dying hero is ringed by a circle of sympathetic mourners.

So we might describe Chekhov as a case—perhaps not the first (one thinks also of Büchner)—in which the principles of peripety and recognition are split between character and audience: the former gets the reversal, the latter the realization of its consequence—a virtual reverse of Else's theory. Imagine a version of the Oedipus story in which Oedipus strives to find the murderer of Laius, gradually uncovers clues that lead directly to himself, and finally, through some Chekhovian feat of hamartia, misses the point. And like John Marcher, in Henry James's story, he simply continues the search for "the beast in the jungle" long after the beast has come and gone. Even in this case the point would pass over to us, in the audience, who would see in the rift not only the chasm between truth and human understanding but a certain attitude in which the play is standing peculiarly aloof from its creatures, rather like a scientist observing the effects of induced deprivation in laboratory animals. This may seem a cruel thing to say about Chekhov, one of our most humane authors in other respects, but Chekhov's "gentleness" stands at one pole of a deadly paradox that Leon Shestov aptly referred to as "creation from the void" (1966, 3–60). Francis Fergusson once said that "the extraordinary feat of Chekhov is to predicate nothing" (1949, 175). This may be true, as far as propounding a thesis is concerned. But radical irony does predicate something, and it takes the form of an awareness of the audience, a "second person" whose presence is presumed in the conduct of the mimesis, and an invitation to put all language against a metalanguage, as one uses a codebook to translate a coded message. Thus in Chekhov we have a peculiar modern phenomenon growing out of nineteenth-century naturalistic assumptions, and we might call it the rise of the subtext.

In one sense it is incorrect to speak of the subtext as rising, for the subtext has always been with us. We see this even in *Oedipus Rex* when Oedipus refers persistently to "the murderer"—in the singular—though he has been told repeatedly that Laius was killed "by many hands." This would be a subtext belonging to the order of psychological behavior. The subtext I speak of here, however, is a distinctly modern form of ambiguation or outright avoidance whereby a play is built on "unspeakable" ground. What is unspeakable is not something to be disclosed, like an Ibsen secret or a Strindberg motive, or a social thesis. It is rather a steady state of being against which the dialogue is recursively played out. One might even say, in some cases at least (e.g., Pinter), that the subtext is the real subject of the work. Or perhaps even more relevant: in former textual interpretation, it was through the subtext that one discovered the meaning of the text. In the theater I refer to here, the text and the subtext stand in an adversarial or at least irreducible relationship, and the reciprocal operation of both creates our particular pleasure in the play. What comes forth is a two-part harmony, though it is more like a two-part dissonance. If you read a Chekhov play straight, listening only to one voice, as David Magarshack did, you arrive at the trivial theme that life is rough but if we work hard there is hope for all.

Here is an example of how all this works. If I were seeking an ideal sample of subtext "rising" in Chekhov—or anywhere else in modern ironic drama—my choice would probably be these oft-quoted lines in the opening scene of *The Three Sisters*:

OLGA: . . . This morning I woke up, I saw at once the sunlight everywhere, I saw at once that it was springtime, and I felt my heart would break with joy. I wanted desperately to go home again.
CHEBUTYKIN: The hell you say!
TUZENBAKH: Of course, it's all nonsense.

(Chekhov 1977, 104)

The subtext in this passage arises from the gratuitous coupling of the lines whereby possibilities in one conversation are set against an "echo" in another, and thereby flattened or at least framed by the indifference of a world running in counterrhythm to human longings. The author here is far from the scene; his work is seen primarily in the arrangement of the counterpoint, rather than in any statement made by either of the utterances. For instance, imagine, instead, Chebutykin telling Olga, "Dear Olga, forget the past. Forget Moscow! Live for today," and you have destroyed the Chekhov music. Of course, one might argue that Olga's longing is in itself a pure instance of Chekhov's theme (what one shouldn't be doing), but the larger question would be just how Chekhov's attitude about the longing figures in the theme. Try as you may, you can't find a line in the play which can be attributed to the author in the sense that it expresses his own belief or position (more about this problem in Chapter 10).

But let us distill the exchange even further and put it against its antecedent in the Messenger scene of *Oedipus*:

OEDIPUS: How is that, if they are father and mother and I their son?
MESSENGER: Because Polybus was no kin to you in blood. (1015–16)

OLGA: I wanted desperately to go home again.
CHEBUTYKIN AND TUSENBACH: The hell you say! Of course, it's all nonsense. (act 1)

Both of these exchanges, I suggest, are structurally and functionally isomorphic with each other in the sense that they perform the same service to the play by the same means, though to entirely different ends. To borrow a usage from music, they are what we might call *semi-demi-peripeties*, in that they contain in small the structure of a full reversal. In any case, both are single examples of what we find over and over in the plays at large, on various levels of organization, and if you traced them through the plays sooner or later they would lead to a full-throated peripety like this passage from Act 3:

VERSHININ: Yesterday I heard in passing that they want to move our brigade some place far away. Some say to Poland; others—to Chita, it seems.

TUSENBAKH: I heard that too. Well, hmm? The town will become deserted, completely so by then.

IRINA: We shall leave too!

CHEBUTYKIN (*Drops the clock, which is broken*): Smashed to pieces, to pieces!

(*Pause; everyone is upset and confused.*) (137)

I doubt we can say this scene actively represents a shift to the opposite of what is being undertaken, since nothing is being undertaken by the characters. But the rumor of the brigade's departure, thus punctuated by the smashing of the symbolic clock, has an immediate effect on the mood of the characters, and at the end of the act the prospect of being left alone brings on Irina's sudden decision to marry Baron Tusenbakh. This modest unfelt decision, in turn, is foiled in the last act by another peripety, the death of Tusenbakh in a senseless duel that reverses the plan for the marriage. But however different these scenes may be from Aristotle's idea of peripety, they are the direct means by which Chekhov reverses the fortune of the Prozorovs, and I see no alternative but to assign them to the peripety category. The fact that they aren't emphatic in their arrival and that they produce no immediate change in the situation as "expected" is simply a function of a radically different kind of entelechial causality operating in Chekhov's world. To borrow the term of Tzvetan Todorov, Chekhov's is a *mediated* (as opposed to an *immediate*) causality. That is, it is "a diffused, discontinuous causality, which is expressed not by a single action [and reaction] but by secondary aspects of a series of actions, often remote from one another" (1977, 68). There are no messengers in Chekhov because there is nothing to report (nothing has happened); or, to take that back, when there is something to report, such as the deaths of Tusenbakh or Treplev, it is muted to the point of releasing no emotion. Normally, however, peripety, when it arrives in Chekhov, comes on little cat feet, like Natasha's babies, and like them takes some time before it matures and fills the house with consequence.

Let us look at our two samples in a closer connection. With regard to dramatic technique, the chief difference between them lies in the plane of probability through which one voice cancels, or neutralizes, the other. In *Oedipus*, to put it simply, a question by one character produces a response from another character, according to the probability of normal human conversation. If there is anything improbable in *Oedipus*, it has to do with the world's capacity to throw up illogical coincidences, and these are usually kept, as Aristotle says, "outside the play like the one in Sophocles' *Oedipus*" (sec. 15), on the theory that what is out of sight is out of question. The "conversation" in Chekhov, on the other hand, is based on a different principle of mimetic probability. There is a kind of logic in the duet of voices—they *seem* to belong to the same conversation—but it cannot be explained on the level of characters communicating with or reacting to each other. The speeches of Olga, on one hand, and of Tusenbakh and Chebutykin, on the other, are independent chains connected by pure coincidence, like the stone that falls on Mitys' killer, and "such things don't happen by chance." So, again, there is the effect of a god prowling behind the play, though in this case the god is an ironic spinner who has arranged a convergence, or "twin-halved" event, that can only be perceived as such from a perspective outside the play—that is, from the omniscient position from which Hardy observes the meeting of the iceberg and the Titanic: in theater terms, the audience watching the play. For, as Frye tells us, in the ironic mode the audience has "the sense of looking down [or in] on a scene of bondage, frustration, or absurdity" (1957, 34). It is the looking *down* (or *in on*) that carries the effect of the audience's having a superior point of view to that of the characters. Of course, we also look down on the characters in Sophocles' play—for a while; the difference, as I have said, is that the recognition is finally contained in the mimesis, for the inevitable fruit of Oedipus's search for the truth is that he comes eventually to understand what we knew (more or less) from the outset. Chekhov, characteristic of the ironic mode, passes what recognition is available on to us. In this limited, yet pervasive sense, we may claim that in his own way Chekhov broke the fourth-wall convention and opened the way to self-reflexive theater, or theater based on its own conscious understanding that it was being watched by outsiders. Or, as Lionel Abel put it in 1963 (pursuing a very different point), "Thus Chekhov could produce a kind of metatheatre while remaining genuinely realistic" (109). It is to this phenomenon that I want to turn next.

CHAPTER 7

The Real Inspector Oedipus

I f peripeties in Chekhov are hidden in the paraphernalia of an eventless life and have only a delayed effect on the characters' fate, peripety can also become ostentatiously conscious of its own status as a peripety. That is, in semiotic terms, instead of belonging to the order of the signifier, or to the plane of expression ("These then are two elements of plot: peripety and recognition" [Aristotle 1967, sec. 12]), peripety might aspire in certain dramatists' hands to become a signified in its own right—that is, to belong to the plane of the work's content, the thing being imitated. We see this general principle in weaker forms in many cultural connections. In fashion, things (words, phrases, behavioral practices, clothing, cars) have a tendency to become ends in themselves rather than means to ends (of speaking, covering, getting someplace). In my playwriting days, I desperately wanted to write a play with a big third-act "scene" in which all the stops were pulled in a massive argument and a family collapsed in despair (preferably in the kitchen) following the revelation of a deep sexual secret. I hadn't a notion of what the secret was to be about and had no such secrets myself, but I had read and seen enough Anderson, Inge, Williams, and Miller to know that *that* was the whole point of writing plays and that all the business leading up to this *scène à faire* was an unavoidable trouble and a bore compared to the thrill of the discovery scene. So too poetry in the Gongoristic and Euphuistic traditions, the French Alexandrine, naturalistic argot, highly metaphoric theater (Edward Bulwer-Lytton, Christopher Fry), highly detailed or ornate realism, all to one degree or another, and at certain stages of usage, openly advertise their expressive wares and aspire to become imitations or ends in their own right. Language, in short, begins bragging about itself, just as certain actors, without intending it, seem to become their own objects of imitation when they repeat their tics with too much regularity.

The interesting thing about this inversion of ends and means is that it demonstrates the falsity of the idea, still assumed by some postmodern critics, that mimetic theorists have always been deluded into thinking art is imitating reality in the sense of copying something one can find in the empirical world. The truth is, mimesis has never had much to do with reality, except in the trivial sense of using it to prepare something that is of interest precisely because it isn't real—something that Sidney long ago called "a second nature." This is not a denial that art *always* has its field of reference in reality, but that question has to do with what we comprehend as the meaning of art. Mimesis has an infinite capacity to enlarge its confine, even to include itself in its subject matter, one of drama's favorite indulgences at least since Shakespeare, if not since Aristophanes. On this account alone, it is hard to understand Peter Szondi's claim that "the drama is absolute. . . . It can be conscious of nothing outside itself. . . . It is not a (secondary) representation of something else (primary). . . . The drama has no more room for quotation than it does for variation. Such quotation would imply that the Drama referred to whatever was quoted" (1987, 8–9). In a certain ontological sense, it may be true that the drama is *actual*, that it generates its own time and place, that each performance is original, and so on, but as much as any other art the drama is capable of quoting, of infinite variation, and of capitalizing on what has gone before in the way of convention. That is really my topic in this chapter.

However, this capacity to quote (sometimes called double coding), or to perpetuate a style into a content, is only the historical floor of a particularly modern phenomenon. When Euphuistic language, heavy realism, nudity, any newly discovered mode of expression, become ends in themselves—that is, interesting primarily for their stylistic appeal—we are not involved with a variation of the peripety principle, or, if so, only remotely. I am referring, rather, to a deliberate reversal of the audience's expectations along the axis from the plane of expression to the plane of illusion, as opposed to horizontal reversals that occur strictly within the illusion itself, like those in *Oedipus*. In other words, peripeties can occur within the play-world (the messenger/herdsman scene), and they can occur recursively, or vertically, between the illusion and its expressive source, between the signifier and the signified, producing a tangled hierarchy or a strange loop effect in which something *in* the system jumps out and acts *on* the sytstem, as if it were *outside* the system (Hofstadter 1980, 691). We might call these systemic reversals, inasmuch as they are systemwide occurrences, though in terms of the present discussion, I will call them Oedipal inversions, primarily because, as we will see, they are self-discovering, and often self-incriminating.

Some simple examples might be Escher's *Drawing Hands*, the paintings of Magritte, and the wonderful line Robert Alter quotes from Vladimir Nabokov's novel *Transparent Things*: "Hugh retraced his steps, which was once a trim metaphor" (1984, 15). In this latter example—a perfect reduction of the principle—one half of the sentence carries us into mimesis and illusion, the other half back to language as a vehicle of expression. This sudden split does not cancel the representation; it simply gives it away, like a panning camera picking up a mirror in a room in which it films itself filming. We suddenly see that representation is capable of bending back on itself, like time in the universe of quantum relativity. What happens in the Nabokov example is that we rediscover something that reading has taught us to overlook, that representations occur at a boundary between mental images and the material things that cause them (words, paint, ink, sound). Or, to move to a slightly different hierarchical level, on one side of the boundary is reality (words in a book held in your hand) and on the other involuntary illusionary life (dream, hallucination, delusion, etc.). The fictional, then, is a precarious balance between dream and/or imagination, on one hand, and reality, on the other. The fictional cannot be experienced by disappearing into it, as we do in dreams, because it then ceases to be illusory; nor can we experience the fictional by contemplating its material substance (a 14-ounce book): hence fiction occurs at a boundary which has the strange property, like the temporal present, of being specious, a nothing in itself but the knife edge where two contiguous states of awareness meet in a fusion.

At any rate, what the Nabokov peripety finally provokes is an old-fashioned recognition in which we discover, so to speak, the true identity of Hugh Person (for that is his name), who is not a person at all but an arrangement of trim metaphors got up to behave like a person. So there we are, back in Aristotle's country. Here is an example of the same form of inversion from Tom Stoppard's *The Real Inspector Hound*:

> MRS. DRUDGE (*Into phone*): Hello, the drawing-room of Lady Muldoon's country residence one morning in early spring.
>
> (Stoppard 1973, 15)

Here the signified is suddenly swallowed by the signifying system, which goes haywire and produces a surfeit of exposition through the channel of normal speech: that is to say, what is normally part of the "scene" (or written in the program, "one morning in early spring") is carried over into the "act." It qualifies as a peripety, or at least it *behaves* like a peripety, because it is one of those lurches that produces "the opposite of the expected"—at least until the audience gets used to it. But by that time the play is off and running with more complex permutations of the reversal principle through which it continually confuses the representational and the represented worlds. For as Moon, the theater critic reviewing the play, puts it, "What in fact is this play concerned with? It is my belief that here we are concerned with what I have referred to elsewhere as the nature of identity" (1973, 28). This is at once true (of *The Real Inspector Hound*) and a spoof on the clichéd idea of identity as a modern theme. However, the object of the imitation in Stoppard's play is not the identity of a murderer, as in Oedipus's search for the murderer of Laius, but the genre of detective fiction itself (*The Mousetrap, Night Must Fall, Deathtrap, Sleuth*, etc.), from which the play is continually "quoting" conventional motifs and re-marketing them (vaguely) as if they were its own. The laughter comes in our knowing where the motifs came from, not in anything intrinsically funny in the lines.

What such constructions, or confusions, introduce into the illusion is an element of self-doubt. Even though carefully planned and executed by the (absent) author, the fiction seems to be questioning its own empirical basis. One is reminded of Todorov's conception of the fantastic as a genre that introduces a moment of hesitation experienced by a person within the story (and by extension the reader) "who knows only the laws of nature, confronting an apparently supernatural event" (1980, 25). For example, this characteristic reaction from *The Saragossa Manuscript*: "I nearly reached the point of believing that fiends, in order to deceive me, had animated the bodies of the hanged men" (31). This is very much like Mrs. Drudge's line, even though she hasn't the least awareness of the oddity of her speech. The element of confusion is posited in the same way. The playgoer knows, so to speak, only the laws of playmaking (this is supposed to be an illusion, isn't it?), confronting an apparently nonillusionistic event (within the illusion). The effect is certainly not fantastic, but as the interest of fantasy is located precisely in the moment of hesitation between the natural and the supernatural, so the interest in the Oedipal inversion is located in the delightful uncertainty about where the "the real thing" is located. "By the hesitation it engenders," Todorov says, "the fantastic questions precisely the existence of an irreducible opposition between real and unreal" (167). This irreducible opposition continuously energizes the farce of Stoppard's play, and it is the same opposition on which much of modern metatheater is based.

Perhaps a better way to illustrate the idea is to borrow Roland Barthes's well-known conceptual diagram for mythical speech as a "second-order semiological system," a system in which one semiological chain (signifier + signified = sign) becomes the signifier of a second. Barthes intends the diagram to apply specifically to mythological speech, but it seems to me versatile enough to tolerate other uses. One of the things the diagram can illustrate, I hope, is this phenomenon of Oedipal inversion in which, as in myth, "a second language . . . speaks about [a] first" (Barthes 1972b, 115), and indeed uses the first as its own signifier. *The Real Inspector Hound* might look like the diagram in Figure 3. In the purely technical sense, of course, the signifier would be the actor (plus scenery, props, dialogue, lighting, etc.), and the signified would be a character (and an illusionary world made of props, lighting, etc.). For my own purposes, I am amending the diagram (offering, as it were, poor semiology) to illustrate in more or less gross terms what happens to the thriller in Stoppard's hands. By Signifier, then, I refer to such thriller conventions as murder/motive, false murder, corpse (false corpse), red herrings, contradictory clues, ingenious detection, discovery scene (false discovery scene), and so on, on the theory that, as Barthes puts it, the "discourse forms the signifier" (114) and the discourse of the thriller consists in such parts of speech as these; the Signified, then, is what Barthes refers to as "the crisis," in this case the display of "murder most foul," with its own implicit moral judgment, together with the "end" of suspense and clarification (whodunit?). Finally, the union of the two forms in a sign, which of course is nothing but "the

FIGURE 3

	1 Signifier (Thriller conventions*)	2 Signified "Murder most foul" (Suspense/ clarification)	
Thriller theater			
Stoppard's "Hound"	3 Sign I. SIGNIFIER (Conventions + S/C)		II. SIGNIFIED "The nature of identity" Tangled hierarchy
	III. SIGN		

associative total of the first two terms" (113). In any case, in Stoppard's "second order semiological system," the signifier is simply the stolen sign of the thriller suspense system, which is manipulated and exaggerated to the point of producing a Tangled Hierarchy—supposedly (on the mock-thematic level) devoted to illustrating the nature of identity, as Moon puts it, but *really* devoted to showing all the outrageous ways in which one can deidentify identity in the theater.

These inversions amount to "maximizing the magnitude" of all the givens of the thriller to the point of absurdity—including its suspense/ clarification mission as a genre. For the suspense of *The Real Inspector Hound* is not the audience's interest in the discovery of the murderer but the display of suspense for its own sake—the *lazzi* of suspense—in short, peripety for peripety's sake. So we are reacting not to the fortunes of the characters shifting in the unexpected surprise of experience but to the march of "stolen" reversals, the "trim metaphors" of drama. And indeed, the plot becomes precipitously peripetous until peripeties are going off like Roman candles in the foggy air around Muldoon Manor. And sure enough at the end there is a classical Aristotelian peripety cum recognition (of persons yet!)—right where it ought to be in good drama—when Moon realizes all too late that the murderer in the play-within-the-play world (in which he has got himself entrapped by answering the stage phone) is his rival drama critic from his own empirical world, if such an amphibious creature can be said to have one. Whatever the play may owe to the detective play, it owes at least as much to the great-great-great-grandfather of the genre, *Oedipus Rex*, which "prowls" behind every step and is nowhere more in evidence than in the denouement:

CYNTHIA: You mean—?

MAGNUS: Yes!—I am the real Inspector Hound!

MOON (*Pause*): *Puckeridge!*

MAGNUS (*With pistol*): Stand where you are, or I shoot!

MOON (*Backing*): Puckeridge! You killed Higgs—and Birdboot tried to tell me—

MAGNUS: Stop in the name of the law!

(MOON *turns to run.* MAGNUS *fires.* MOON *drops to his knees.*)

CYNTHIA: So you are the real Inspector Hound.

MAGNUS: Not only that!—I have been leading a double life—at *least*!

CYNTHIA: You mean—?

MAGNUS: Yes!—it is me, Albert!—who lost his memory and joined the force, rising by merit to the rank of Inspector, his past blotted out—until fate cast him back into the home he left behind, back to the beautiful woman he had brought here as his girlish bride—in short, my darling, my memory has returned and your long wait is over!

CYNTHIA: Oh, Albert!

(*They embrace.*)

MOON (*With a trace of admiration*): Puckeridge . . . you cunning bastard.

(MOON *dies.*)

(1973, 48)

The theater of Brecht offers a political variation of Oedipal inversion. Oddly enough, Brecht's method is closer to Chekhov's than one might think by looking only at the surface features of their work. Both are artists of what Umberto Eco refers to as "open work," or works in which "the author offers the interpreter, the performer, the addressee a work *to be completed*" (1984, 62). "The text sets out to stimulate the private world of the addressee in order that he can draw from inside himself some deeper response that mirrors the subtler resonances underlying the text" (53). And the common denominator is that both Brecht and Chekhov are consummate ironists. Brecht, Eco says, "does not seek to influence the audience, but rather to offer a series of facts to be observed, employing the device of 'defamiliarization'." Thus his plays "do not, in the strict sense, devise solutions at all. It is up to the audience to draw its own conclusions from what it has seen on stage. . . . A solution is seen as desirable and is actually anticipated, but it must come from the collective enterprise of the audience. In this case the 'openness' is converted into an instrument of revolutionary pedagogics" (55). Or, to put it another way, the spectator may be led to supply the solution to the problem posed by the work, but it will inevitably be drawn from a field of meanings informed by "a Marxist dialectic logic" (62).

Obviously, Chekhov and Brecht differ widely with respect to the problems for which solutions are not openly stated. But both are "open" artists to the extent that the recognitions their characters *fail* to have are passed over to the audience in such a way as to stimulate "some deeper response that mirrors the subtler resonances underlying the text." They are "open works" in a manifest sense, one might say, but they are more open to some meanings than to others. Even so, both artists activate in the audience an "attitude," to use Brecht's word, for which there is no direct semantic source on the stage. To come back to my earlier figure: the tree falls in Brecht's world, but the sound is heard only in the audience's. And this seems safe to say of Chekhov's world as well: the axes that fell the cherry orchard are heard only by the listeners in the auditorium.

Of course, Brecht's plays contain the usual kinds of peripeties (sometimes even with recognitions by the occasional "good person") in which fortunes are continually reversed on the actional level of the play, and in this his epic theater is hardly a deviation from normal dramatic practice. But Brechtian characters are walking versions of Nabokov's Hugh Person: that is, their believability as fictional creatures is always attached to the contrivance of their mimetic origin. This is not the place to examine something as well-known and complex as Brecht's *verfremdungseffekt*— quoting the character, historicizing the actor's behavior, acting in the past tense, transposing acting to the third person, and so on, all of which are designed, as Brecht puts it, to turn the characterization "from something ordinary, familiar, immediately accessible, into something peculiar, striking and unexpected" (1966, 143). It goes without saying that this technique is almost the direct opposite of Chekhov's way of drawing character (not to mention Constantin Stanislavski's way of enacting it on the stage). The idea of the "peculiar, striking and unexpected" finds its way into the Brecht playscript in many ways, but here is an example from *Mother Courage* of what I am referring to as Oedipal inversion as it occurs in the writing:

CHAPLAIN: There are people who think the war's about to end, but I say: you can't be sure it will *ever* end. Oh, it may have to pause occasionally, for breath, as it were. It can even meet with an accident—nothing on this earth is perfect—one can't think of everything—a little oversight and a war may be in the hole and someone's got to pull it out again. That someone is the King or the Emperor or the Pope. But they're such friends in need, this war hasn't got much to worry about: it can look forward to a prosperous future.

(Brecht 1961, 302)

This is what Brecht himself might call an instance of gestic playwriting, or a speech in which "people adopt attitudes of such a sort that the social laws under which they are acting spring into sight" (1966, 86). The whole attitude of the characters in *Mother Courage* toward war "springs into sight" in this single speech, much as the attitude of (at least most of) the characters of *The Three Sisters* might be symbolized in one of Vershinin's speeches or in Olga's "And I so longed to go home again!" To see the inversion, one has only to substitute the word "peace" for "war" and the speech becomes "classical," in the sense that there would be a direct correspondence between the prevailing ideology of the play-world and that of the audience (or the audience as we like to think of ourselves: i.e., antiwar). You might also defuse the gestus by adding a sentence or so in this vein: "I know what people say about war. I realize it destroys life, I know it is immoral, etc., etc. But it is economically indispensable." One wouldn't agree with the Chaplain, even so. But we have introduced a certain complexity, if not moral intelligence, into the sentiment: the Chaplain has made a *choice*, however wrongheaded, and such a choice reveals the presence—or conspicuous absence—of an alternative ideology and announces that the play, to this extent, is at least *openly* aware of the issue, in quite a different sense from Eco's meaning of the word. What would be *open*, in this case, is the *display* of the argument as the topic of the agon: in short, the theater that runs from Aristophanes through Ibsen to Shaw, Sartre, and Miller—the theater that argues a case before our eyes.

To some degree, one must include Brecht in this dialectical strain of socially committed theater, given his critical program respecting war as business by other means. I am referring strictly to dramaturgic procedure. The principle behind Brecht's theater, like Chekhov's—and here the resemblance ends—is deliberately to mute the contrary or alternative point of view, and in so doing to exaggerate the enacted deficiency that has no visible or audible opponent on the stage. The consequence (or at least

The Pleasure of the Play

Brecht's hope) of such a method is the creation of a vacuum that would be filled by the audience's shock of recognition. An extreme example of the same technique may be seen in Jonathan Swift's *Modest Proposal*.

To come back to Nabokov's Hugh Person, however, in Brecht we are dealing with another form of *metasemiosis*. Here again, Barthes's chart (Figure 4) is useful. The idea I intend the diagram to illustrate of course is that the Brechtian signifier—the actor in this instance—is equivalent to the total sign in so-called realistic theater—for example, Chekhov, or, for that matter, most traditional acting styles. Once again, in strict technical terms, the true Brechtian signifier (as in theater in general) is simply the actor alone, who represents a signified (character), which is the case in virtually every play. But the Brechtian actor is doing something else as well. What more or less disappears in realistic performances is the phenomenon of the actor-as-actor, though this does not imply that the actor isn't *there* at a certain (and indispensable) level of our perception. But as Brecht said of epic acting, "the actor appears on the stage in a double role" (1966, 194): "the acting Laughton [*den zeigenden Laughton*] does not disappear in the enacted Galileo [*den zegeitgten Galileo*]" (Hernadi 1976, 131). To accomplish this, the Brechtian actor "splits" the "associative total" of the first-order sign (the traditional actor/character) into two perceptible parts: he portrays not simply a character but an actor portraying a character as well—in short, an actor-actor/character—Charles Laughton acts Charles Laughton acting Galileo—or more accurately, Charles Laughton acts Galileo *and* Charles Laughton acting Galileo, since these are apt to appear as successive modes rather than as a simultaneous composite. And, presumably, this split creates a similar split in the attentiveness in the spectator as well, for the spectator, as Paul Hernadi tells us,

FIGURE 4

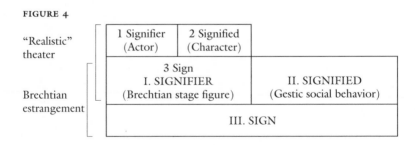

"Realistic" theater	1 Signifier (Actor)	2 Signified (Character)	
Brechtian estrangement	3 Sign I. SIGNIFIER (Brechtian stage figure)		II. SIGNIFIED (Gestic social behavior)
	III. SIGN		

"who realizes that the ACTOR [Laughton] and the 'actor' [Laughton acting Laughton and Galileo] are not identical, shares the ACTOR's apparently mixed attitude toward the character and probably evolves a similarly mixed attitude toward the one-sided 'actor' (132). Largely through this means, the recognition is passed on to the audience, in this case through what we may call an ambivalent sign, a sign that has it both ways. Brecht's preferred meaning is never in doubt (at least where war is concerned), but the play has communicated the right idea schizophrenically through a "false-self system," in R. D. Laing's term, which lays bare its own deceit.

An interesting recent variation of Brechtian schizophrenia is Caryl Churchill's *Cloud 9*. Here the first-order signification is sexuality (along with British colonialism), as the drama has depicted sexuality for over two thousand years: it is probable that people have sex, commit adultery, have sexual tensions, and of course this is the staple of drama. But as the song in the play goes, things are "upside down when you reach Cloud 9." What is striking and unexpected (for a while) in Churchill's play is the ubiquity of the sexual behavior that metastatizes into a massive display case for a crisis in gender identity. On one hand, we are watching British colonialists defend Queen Victoria's holdings in Africa against a native uprising; on the other, the real action is taking place in the barns and bedrooms of the colony. Before the play is over, almost everyone has had sex with everyone else, irrespective of family ties: husbands, wives, children, brothers, sisters, friends, strangers, sometimes four in a single bed. At the end even the mother wants to get into bed with her children, but she settles, as the play's final image, on making love to herself—or rather to the man who played her role in act 1. So we have a continuing narrative metaphor, similar to Mother Courage's wagon of goods: sexual appetite running rampant against the backdrop of the rape of Africa by Victorian imperialism. One is the same as the other—or rather, both spring from the same political reality. Colonialism, as Brecht would say, is sex by other means.

We may also note that the false-self system, or alienated character portrayal, is once again the primary means through which the play continuously makes its point. The characters, at least those in act 1, are all walking contradictions, or what one might call signifying signifieds.[1] By this I

---

[1] It is of course impossible for a signified to signify something itself without becoming another signifier. I am only suggesting that, as in the case of Escher's *Drawing Hands*, we can pass from one function to the other—or seem to.

mean that Churchill's characterization reserves the privilege of bifurcating the identity of the character, both visually and behaviorally. Clive's wife Betty is played by a male actor; his son Edward is played by a woman; Joshua, the black boy, is played by a white actor. In a sense, this is similar to the Laughton-playing-Laughton idea insofar as the cell division is always in evidence. But it is not the actor who becomes visible in the transaction; it is rather another aspect of the character which can editorialize the character's meaning directly to the audience without really stepping out of character. For example, Betty is a man because she has taken her identity from her husband:

> I live for Clyde. The whole aim of my life
> Is to be what he looks for in a wife.
> I am a man's creation as you see.
> And what men want is what I want to be.

Edward is played by a woman because his father has tried to make him into a man:

> What father wants I'd dearly like to be.
> I find it rather hard as you can see.
>
> (1984, 4)

So Churchill uses the alienation technique (with this difference) in order to dramatize the distance between sexual (or racial) identity and institutional identity. She treats the theme, especially in act 1, as a kind of sexual farce somewhere between the style of Brecht and—given the rapid-fire sexual permutations—the Keystone Cops. Coleridge once defined farce as follows: "Granted, at the outset, an improbability, or even an impossibility, see what wild and outrageous things might follow." It is certainly improbable that a society could be as sexually driven, to the exclusion of almost everything else (except racial aggression), as the society of *Cloud 9*. Yet there is a respect in which our world is dominated by sexual interest, as we see subliminally in the underwear ads of the daily newspaper. Now let us suppose that all this subliminal sexuality, these subtle and not so subtle genderizations of everything we use, buy, wear, or touch, were condensed and summed up in the master activity, sex itself; and suppose that sexuality were additionally enlarged, taken out of its normal context in a restrictive society where, as Freud said in *Civilization and Its Discontents*, we punish perversions of bisexual monogamy, and carried to the extreme of seeming to be the norm, like Brecht's concept of the virtue of warfare—sexual prowess as gestus. That, it seems to me, is the mission of farce and satire, in Coleridge's sense of the word, which we might revise like this: "Granted, at the outset, a single appetite in human nature given its full bent and see what outrageous things might follow." This might serve as a mutual gestic formula for Churchill and Brecht.

As still another variation of the principle, I turn to Peter Handke's *Offending the Audience*, which purports to offer a demolition of mimesis itself. On our chart (dispensable at this point) the first-order signification would be that of the speaker/lecture (signifier/signified). This is a rather crude generalization, however, because the speakers in Handke's play are really condensations of many other languages. The "rules" for speaking include emulating the inflections of such institutional speech as the litanies of the Catholic church, football cheers, debaters cutting each other off, the arrival and departure of trains, speeches from movies, monkeys aping people, and so on. So the lecture takes the form of an incantation delivered to the audience and authorized by a hundred different modes of automatic speech that prompt us, in daily life, into various behaviors and attitudes. All of these voices, as Barthes would say, belong to the culture.

The second-order signification, or metalanguage, is much trickier. It is actually a two-stage affair. Unlike Laughton, in the Brecht system, who continually reappears as Laughton the actor acting, the Handke actor is, in optical and gestural fact, a *disappeared* actor from the "naturalistic" tradition. I am not referring to naturalistic acting "style," only to the primary requirement of naturalistic acting that the actor "become" the character and leave all traces of acting out of the mimesis. Indeed, if anything would undermine a performance of *Offending the Audience*, it is *visible* acting. The Handke actor has the exacting job of imitating a Speaker (in the sense described above), and this involves the same operation of self-suppression that faces the actor in Chekhov. Thus far, then, we are viewing traditional theater. The inversion comes in the content of the actor-speaker discourse. To sum it up: the actors "take hold of" this "already built" set of significations and turn it against the institution of theater in a daring Oedipal inversion:

The Pleasure of the Play

You will hear nothing you have not heard here before.
You will see nothing you have not seen here before.
You will see nothing of what you have always seen here.
You will hear nothing of what you have always heard here.

You will hear what you usually see.
You will hear what you usually don't see.
You will see no spectacle.
Your curiosity will not be satisfied.
You will see no play.
There will be no playing here tonight.
You will see a spectacle without pictures.
. . . .
It may be the case that you expected what you are hearing now.
But even in that case you expected something different.

(Handke 1978, 7)

This is what might be termed the "Judas variation" of Oedipal inversion: the actors are imitating speakers who betray their profession by denying they are actors—or that the stage is a represented world ("These boards don't signify a world. They are part of the world" [9]). And we have the paradox (false) of a playless play without actors, setting, lighting, dialogue, or plot; moreover, a play that is perfectly "classical" because it observes the unities of time, place, and action—or the unities of reality itself. The true plot of the play, however, is the wholesale reversal of the roles of audience and actors. It turns out that at approximately the point in Sophocles' play when Oedipus is hearing the good news from Corinth, *Offending the Audience* pulls its conventional peripety and announces that the audience (in thriller parlance) is the real criminal: "You are the topic. . . . You did not play, you *were* the part . . . You lived your roles. . . . You were a sight to have seen, you ass-kissers" (28–29). *Offending the Audience* is a difficult play to bring off, and it may be that it is ultimately unsatisfying as a play because the schizophrenia of the split signifier has entered a phase of mimetic catatonia. Still the conception is brilliant. What Handke forces a tolerant playgoer to recognize is the role of the spectator in imitation. Beneath its premise of offending the audience is the play's subtler mission of elaborating the master recognition of drama's own hidden secret.

My final example is taken from the work of Harold Pinter. The first-order signification of Pinter's *Landscape* is the language of the reverie or daydream in which people speak their thoughts, either aloud or to themselves. It is probable that people have reveries about their lives, and therefore it is probable that people will make plays about people having reveries. Manifestly, then, *Landscape* is the reverie of a man and his wife in the kitchen of their employer's house following a long illness of the wife. The play deals with their marriage, which has drifted into a state of indifference which the husband, on his part, is attempting to relieve; on her part, the wife remains impassive and withdrawn into a kind of dream world. Duff speaks to Beth "but does not appear to hear her voice." Beth "never looks at DUFF, and does not appear to hear his voice" (1968, 6) But this study of a failed marriage is only the first-order of signification belonging, so to speak, to the *fabula*, or represented content. It is simply what Pinter has "stolen" in the way of a probable situation. The second-order signification is built on this first order and consists in the careful juxtaposition (the *sjuzet*) of the two reveries, which are peculiarly isomorphic to each other. One reverie recounts a set of events similar to the other, but certain fundamental details are different, rather like the Martins' twin children in *The Bald Soprano* (one has a red right eye, the other a red left eye). Thus Duff saw a "man and woman, under the trees, on the other side of the pond" (11) who were conceivably his wife and another man; but Beth's account of the rendezvous with her "man" took place in the dunes on the beach. Moreover, in Beth's reverie, the beach was vacant except for "an elderly man, far away on a breakwater" (22). This could have been Duff, except that Duff's account places him under the shelter at the pond during the rain, and Duff is not elderly. Neither reverie mentions the possibility of the observed people being either Duff or Beth.

One is led to assume, then, that these are two different events taking place at two different times (it isn't raining in Beth's account). Austin Quigley (1975, 238), who takes this view, finds the juxtaposition completely explainable in terms of the human tendency to hear one thing and be reminded of something else from one's private memory. So the points of connection between the reveries are simply points of normal association between two different sets of experiences: Duff's account reminds Beth of her experience, which Duff does not hear. And the play can be explained on purely psychological grounds as dealing with people who are suffering a marital crisis. (If Beth and Duff had had children, perhaps their marriage might have survived, etc.) Thus Quigley sees *Landscape* as the attempt of Duff to bring Beth out of her romantic fantasy. Beth's possible relation with Mr. Sykes (their employer) is seen more or less as a possible (but not likely) sexual affair, or as a weapon Beth uses against Duff's confessed adultery.

But this interpretation doesn't fully account for the odd effect the play has of teasing us into believing we are *also* hearing two versions of the same event, rather than two different events with common elements. What is passed over to the audience is not only a signified/content (concern, possible jealousy, indifference, "interrelational adjustment", etc.) but a form as well—that is, a pattern (much like rhyme or meter in verse) which is a property of the signifying system. The text consciously manipulates the options for interpretation (and coherence) by offering partially conflicting versions of "the truth." This is not like Shakespeare's habit of simply not stating certain facts (Gertrude's part in King Hamlet's murder, Macduff's flight to England, Iago's *real* motive, etc.) and allowing the audience to draw its own conclusion. Nor is it like Chekhov's habit of ironically undermining one character's sentiment with an overlapping conversation in another part of the room. In Pinter, the text actively juxtaposes events—or reveries of events—in such a way as to make the *possible* isomorphism the center of the audience's interest. Of course, one might claim that this is really part of the content, the theme of the play being that there is a "Rashomon" effect at work in our versions of what happens in reality. But the Rashomon idea only suggests that different people will have different perspectives on events and no two accounts are identical (as in Pirandello).

In *Landscape*, it isn't a question of interpreting a single event or of whether one account is false and another true, or of things being different when viewed from different points of view, but of how many events there are and what they add up to. For at the same time the two reveries intertwine, reciprocally attracting and repelling each other, a picture unfolds that seems to promise a causal convergence of the two chains of events. The trouble on this level, however, is that there are at least four possible ways to piece together the evidence of the combined reveries: Beth's man on the beach may have been pure fantasy; he may have been Duff in the days when they were in love (but that all changed when she is told about his casual adultery, thus—perhaps—bringing on her mental breakdown); it may have been a real man who is simply not identified (not a very satisfying option); and (the most coherent—or at least the most interesting—reading), it may have been an actual affair with Mr. Sykes, her employer, who, like Rodolf in *Madame Bovary*, had her and left her and went to Italy or London (why otherwise would she keep banging the dinner gong on that afternoon?). Or, to come back to the first option, her reverie may have been a fantasy of an affair with Sykes with whom she fell in love.

But none of these versions fits completely. As Beth says, in one of those signature speeches Pinter serves one to a play, "Sometimes the cause of the shadow cannot be found" (42). In short, the Pinter text moves persistently from one nexus of possibilities to another, thus giving the text a sense of being deliberately designed to produce a quandary. At each junction of the play, we are faced with something like an Epimenidean paradox: the play invites us, on one hand, to conflate its versions of similar events and to read the play as psychologically straight ("The following sentence is true."); but at the same time it rejects any such conflation because the coin*cid*ence, or isomorphism, is simply *too* coincidental to be explained by human associational powers ("The preceding sentence is false"). As Aristotle said of the wonder-full death of Mitys' killer, "it stands to reason . . . that such things don't happen by chance." And indeed, this is the running peripety of the play: the manipulation points to a textual motive rather than to a motive of the characters. The text, one might say, is a serial confuser that escapes every effort to track it down.

Overall, I would add that Pinter is almost as intrepid a peripetist as the thriller author. Everywhere in his plays the characters are out to out-surprise each other by injecting the unexpected into the conversation or situation. To this degree peripety remains a plot device contained well within the mimetic illusion (again, as in *Oedipus*), the basic weapon for playing what Mick in *The Caretaker* calls "the game." But there has always seemed to me something ventriloquistic (see Chapter 10) in all of this one-upmanship. I have no wish to deny Pinter his due as our specialist in a certain form of schizophrenic experience, but there is a sense in which his characters behave like little authors, or inventors of fiction, in their own rite (or game). My pun is intended to catch the sense in which reality on Pinter's stage seems so often to be an uncanny extension of the ritual of performance itself. Indeed, this imitation of imitation is what deepens his plays and takes them out of the category of naturalistic drama about hateful people trapped in a room.

This point deserves some qualification. Pinter is not a self-reflexive dramatist in the sense that he is calling attention to his own theatrical trappings. But the motivational psychology of his characters involves a similar form of manipulation. That is, the Pinter character is given (for whatever local reason) to what we might call the killdeer principle of feint, or leading the enemy astray, very much as the thriller delights in pulling the rug from under its own established givens (the manor parlor suddenly becomes a theater stage during a rehearsal). The thing about the Pinter character, however, is that he or she creates a fictional self-construction (it is part of the game that everyone *knows* that what the "other" advertises as truth *isn't*), there is finally no real foundation, no *there* there, so to speak—nothing is explained. The feint ends up being the permanent identity and consequently an environmental characteristic of the world as opposed to the particular psychology of an individual. Hence the dreamlike affect in Pinter. Why dreamlike? Not because his people create fictional dreamscapes, but because they are all "wondrously similar," as Maurice Blanchot says of dream people. "In fact, this is their only identity, they resemble, they belong to a domain that scintillates with pure resemblance"—like the separate narratives of Beth and Duff, or the two versions of "Odd Man Out" in *Old Times*. And Blanchot goes on:

> a being who suddenly starts "resembling" takes on a distance from real life [or the illusory "real" life of the play], passes over into another world, enters into the inaccessible proximity of the image while nonetheless remaining present, though his presence is not his own or somebody else's—an apparition who transforms all other presences into appearances. . . . Whom does the resembler resemble? Neither this person nor that: he resembles no one, or an elusive Somebody. (Leiris 1987, xxv–xxvi)

In Pinter's case, we may say that the resembler resembles the unarticulated and inaccessible feint itself, since it is the only public sign of a possible interior.

In any case, Pinter is a characteristic "open" author. I do not know whether Umberto Eco would consider Pinter's work an example of the openness he specifically refers to as a "work in movement" (which seems, for Eco, to include the plays of Brecht), but Pinter has long been treated by actors and directors (not to mention critics) as offering an invitation to fill out the aporia of his text with their own motivations and causal constructions (Who are Goldberg and McCann? What happened in Leeds? Were Anna and Kate lovers?): in short, the actor is obliged to respect the placement of the pauses and silences, but the content *in* the pauses and silences is negotiable and open to artistic mediation. And this is one of the characteristics of the work in movement (and, we may add, of the psychology of appearances): "The author offers the interpreter, the performer, the addressee a work *to be completed*. He does not know the exact fashion in which his work will be concluded, but he is aware that once completed the work in question will still be his own" (Eco 1984, 62). More important for my argument, "The poetics of the *work in movement* (and partly that of the 'open' work) sets in motion a new cycle of relations between the artist and his audience, a new mechanics of aesthetic perception, a different status for the artistic product in contemporary society" (65). Eco is writing in 1979, and we are well into fresh phases of such openness by this time. My point is to give this "new mechanics of aesthetic perception" an Aristotelian origin, insofar as it involves the operation of the principle of reversal identified in only one of its possible forms by Aristotle.

It is important to say that I am not equating these procedures with the language of myth, in Barthes's sense of the term. In fact, as Barthes puts it, poetic language (including its theatrical variation) resists myth, the "language which does not want to die" (1972b, 133). Poetry, unlike myth, is continually attempting "to regain an infra-signification, a pre-semiological state of language," largely through various forms of de-familiarization. Poetry "wants to be an anti-language." That is, poetry seeks, as Victor Shklovsky would say, to make its language "more difficult"—and one way it achieves this end is to "stretch to the limit the link between signifier and signified" (Barthes 1972b, 133). And this stretching is what I am examining here in terms of dramatic poetry's obsession with reversal on all levels of its performance. Reversal is a symptom of restlessness shared by both signifiers and signifieds of drama which can never afford to repeat a precise signification; it is a vital principle of the form to which all possible contents are submitted in the process of imitation.

The Pleasure of the Play

In this respect, the thriller would be the exemplary dramatic form. In fact, as Ionesco's Choubert in *Victims of Duty* puts it, "All the plays that have ever been written, from Ancient Greece to the present day, have never been anything but thrillers. . . . Every play's an investigation brought to a successful conclusion" (1958, 119). Like the tearjerker, the thriller is the genre named after its emotional effect on the audience, which in cathartic terms stresses the goal of *clarification*. As a signification, the thriller seeks clarity (Whodunit and what is the motive?), but what is posited as unclear (the killer's identity) is only an *alibi*, as Barthes might say, erected in order that the audience may endure the delights of confusion among the signifiers along the way. The mortal enemy of the thriller is predictability, a factor that separates it widely from tragedy, which has a strong inclination to emphasize the inevitable through some variation of the Tiresias or oracle principle. As a result, the thriller is vigorously engaged in a process we might call *expectational defamiliarization*, or outmaneuvering the audience's familiarity with the genre. One of the more inventive recent examples, Rupert Holmes's *Accomplice*, even contains a commentary on the problem in one of its own displacements of audience expectation, a theater company discovered in act 2 to be rehearsing the murder we thought we saw in act 1:

BRIAN: Well, as a veteran of the genre, I've learned that no matter how intricately plotted the piece has been in Act 1, this is nothing compared to the plot twists the audience invents during intermission. . . .

HAL: And what do you think the audience will be speculating at *our* intermission?

BRIAN: At *Accomplice*? Well, my guess is that a lot of people will say that Derek's still alive.

ERIKA: Even though they've seen me electrocute him?

BRIAN: Uh-huh. Part of that'll be pragmatic; it's logical to assume that, what with only four actors in the cast, no death is real until at least midway in Act 2.

HAL: Okay, but do you think that they'll get the *real* ending?

(1991, 62)

But the thriller is only symptomatic of theater at large, each genre of which has its own need to keep the audience off the scent and in some state of cathartic alertness. What happens is that any plot form, character type, style—any discrete unit of theatricalization—accumulates in time, as Brecht would put it, an ordinariness or an immediate accessability (1966, 143). It becomes, in his term, inconspicuous, like the face of one's watch. To this degree it resembles myth, in Barthes's conception: (a) its meaning "is exhausted at one stroke" (1972b, 130) and (b) "It has at its disposal an unlimited mass of signifiers" (120) in which to express this meaning for as long as it has validity in the culture. (Myth tends to last longer because it has a certain invisibility, thanks to its way of distorting and hiding its meaning.) Thus, like myth, any theatrical motif would be susceptible to *almost* infinite variation, were it not for the decay of the image into an empty sign, and at some point the profits of investment in variations of the original (long since forgotten), begin turning into losses. And at this point (though it is hardly as specifiable *as* a "point") the need for "something peculiar, striking and unexpected" (Brecht 1966, 143) becomes apparent.

This is not a problem or a "crisis" in art, to use one of postmodernism's favorite words. It is what art is all about.[2] To put it another way, poetic representation may be said to be involved inadvertently in a continual idiom-making and idiom-escaping process, or a natural passage of language out of the fresh metaphorical to the idiomatic or the household; what was "once a trim metaphor" soon becomes a dead metaphor, at which point poetry seeks renewal in some strategy of defamiliarization. So there is always a creeping discontinuity between signs and their referents, but such discontinuity has more to do with the march and exhaustion of meanings than with a "crisis of the sign." In fact, as Adorno has suggested, art is in an eternal state of self-critique or determinate negation: "The truth content of works of art is part and parcel of their critical content. That is why, among other things, they criticize one another. Their continuity consists, not in one being based on another as its model, but in their critical relationship. 'One work of art is the mortal enemy of another'" (1984, 52).

The whole process, in all its countless manifestations, might be referred to as Aristotle's law. I coin this term in the blanket spirit in which we speak

---

[2] This is not to deny that some arts choose to remain "classical" (e.g., Oriental theater) in that they resist change. As Barthes puts it, they become "strongly mythical" in the sense that they impose "on the meaning one extra signified, which is *regularity*" (1972b, 133n).

of the Copernican or the Einsteinian universe—that is, that Aristotle, like Copernicus and Einstein, only partly understood the ramifications of his own discovery. The law is simple and unastonishing: *the interest and pleasure of the audience arise from the gap between the predictable and the unexpected*. This is the case not only within a single work of art but within the tradition to which the work belongs and to the history of art regarded as a continual "self-regulatory" effort to avoid the equilibrium of entropy (see Arnheim 1974, 25).

As an illustration, let us imaginarily demolish the interest and pleasure of Aristotle's favorite play. Let us imagine a version of *Oedipus Rex* in which Oedipus proceeds quite logically and temperately, without hurry or anxiety. Imagine Oedipus as a mature gifted man, a leader (as Brecht might say) with the wisdom of Solomon, the bravery of Caesar, the honesty of Socrates, and the unselfishness of Brother Martin. The scenes with Creon and Tiresias, in which all is revealed, are models of cooperation and trust: like Socrates, Oedipus wants only to confirm Tiresias's soothsaying with clear facts. And so methodically he goes about the business of tracking down his man. He sends to Corinth for the truth of his birth, and in due course it is reported by the Messenger; he sends for the Herdsman, who confirms the Messenger's report beyond a doubt. There is of course a moment of pain as the facts converge. And then, ritually, he blinds himself—or he doesn't. It doesn't matter, either way, because he has lost all interest, he has become a boring figure, like Chekhov's Kulygin, in a boring world.

What is gone from the plot are those countless moments of friction, recursion, and strange attraction, signaled in the seemingly gratuitous occurrence of innocent details that turn out to be less than innocent ("but, see now, he, the king, was killed by foreign highway robbers at a place where three roads meet—so goes the story"), and in the constant suppression of Oedipus's own suspicion under the cover of his violence—in other words, what is gone are all those things, large and small, in which the progress of the inevitable clarification registers itself as an unforeseen feature of the causal order. This, I assume, is what Shklovsky meant by saying that the purpose of defamiliarization is to make poetry "difficult" and to increase length of perception—that is, difficulty as a form of impedance, like air density, that slows down the speed of the event so that it may be savored, at the proper pace of unconcealment, by the play's wonder-wounded hearers.

CHAPTER 8

Character

My revision of *Oedipus* brings us to the subject of character, the topic on which Aristotle is least satisfactory, although in one small way astonishing. Nothing in the *Poetics* is quite so notorious as Aristotle's insistence that character is secondary to plot and that a tragedy might exist without characters but not without a plot. Gerald Else long ago put this matter to rest by pointing out that by *ethos* Aristotle does not refer to dramatic characters or an *essence* of personhood but to a speech form, or an utterance that "makes clear the moral choice(s) of the dramatic person(s)" (1967, 270). In this respect, ethos is to be regarded as parallel to Aristotle's notion of thought, or *dianoia*: both are "joint or reciprocal aspects of *what is said by the dramatic persons in their speeches*" (270).

This is an attractive finding to any reader of Aristotle who doesn't know Greek, but we are still left without a clue as to how Aristotle may have regarded the element of drama that probably most appeals to us since Shakespeare: the affective display of a powerful personality undergoing good or bad fortune. What we get from Aristotle by way of defining the character of characters is four relatively bland principles of characterization: a poet should make the character good (*chrestos*), appropriate (*harmotton*), like (*homoios*—*us-like* apparently), and consistent (*homalon*).

Much more interesting, however, is Aristotle's idea that the tragic hero should be "a man who is neither a paragon of virtue and justice nor undergoes the change to misfortune through any real badness or wickedness but because of some mistake" (sec. 13). What my reconstruction of *Oedipus* does, in effect, is to convert Oedipus into a completely virtuous man whose change of fortune, as Aristotle says, is neither pitiful nor fearful but morally repugnant. However, when you ask yourself why Sophocles' Oedipus appeals to us and why his fall isn't morally repugnant, it is hard to point to tangible things. There are the hamartia, or error, committed unknowingly at the crossroads (outside the play) and the hamartia of marrying the wrong woman, but these errors would also obtain in my reconstruction of Oedipus as a paragon of virtue. So it can't be the hamartia that rescues him in our affections. What we are left with is the rather odd contribution of his violent temper, a trait of character that even Else sweeps away without comment ("Oedipus, the wise, kind, hotheaded, vital king" [1967, 307; see also 385]). I have commented on this matter elsewhere (1971, 53–54); here I want to say only that if you take away Oedipus's temper, or hubris (a term Aristotle doesn't use), you are left essentially with my recharacterization, for the violent scenes with Creon and Tiresias would not have taken place if Oedipus had a less volatile personality. These scenes, and Oedipus's character as a headstrong man—otherwise good, appropriate, like-us (or like other famous heroes), and consistent—mitigate Oedipus's virtue and innocence just enough to place him "between two extremes." Moreover, one might conjecture that the popular and incorrect definition of hamartia as "tragic flaw" got its start from the conflation of hubris and hamartia in the very practice of tragedy, rather than exclusively through the biblical conception of hamartia as sin. In short, tragic heroes tend not only to make understandable errors concerning their possible courses of action (Agamemnon at Aulis), they also tend to make them in a certain headlong way that renders their misfortune affectively, if not morally, acceptable. Hotheadedness on the stage is not wickedness or evil in itself, but it is a dozen times more compromising of a character's visible virtue than a string of murders committed offstage. One might forgive a murderer, under certain conditions, but no one loves a hothead. So we are in the interesting position of observing how a relatively small shortcoming of character can sufficiently right the balance enough to produce the greatest quotient of pity and fear.

Moreover, it would seem that Else is right in claiming that hamartia is really an element of plot, rather than of character, and that Aristotle didn't list it as such (along with peripety, recognition, and the pathos) because it normally takes place outside of the play, as in the cases of Oedipus, Agamemnon, Antigone, and so on (385). Whatever Aristotle may have meant by the "error" of hamartia in relation to Greek tragedy, hamartia remains an enduring element of drama because it is a means, among other things, of instigating the causal chain of the action in an event that lessens the moral damage to the protagonist's character because (a) hamartia is not attributable to wickedness, and (b) it is usually kept outside the play. This is not always the case, by any means, but the *placement* of the hamartia—when it is an operative feature—has a strong effect on the affective appeal of the character. In any case, we see hamartia operating regularly in the drama into the modern period. In Ibsen it is a standard element of the plot: for example, Mrs. Alving electing to follow Pastor Manders's advice (against her better inclinations) and remain with her dissolute husband; Hedda's casual remark about the Falk estate, which causes Tesman to propose marriage; Nora forging the check in order to please her husband; and so on. In Chekhov the hamartia function is less in evidence but, as I suggested in Chapter 3, that is due to the peculiarly nonconsequential nature of Chekhovian action. Likewise, in Pinter and Beckett it is remotely operative, at best, because the action has very little to do with linear experience; if there were an instance of hamartia in the past of a Pinter character's life, you couldn't trust that it was reported correctly anyway. As the narrator in Pinter's *Go-Between* puts it, "The past is another country. They do things differently there," and one of the things they do differently in Pinter country is to do everything in at least two conflicting versions. On the other hand, *Betrayal* might be an instance of a highly original use of the principle, inasmuch as the action moves backward in time to the point of the adultery's origin, which, as an "error in judgment," could probably qualify as an instance of delayed hamartia— hamartia as pathetic event, or as ending rather than beginning. In fact, one can even imagine Ibsen's *Ghosts* plotted in reverse, à la Pinter: the play would begin at the end and move back in time to the moment when Mrs. Alving stands in her living room before Pastor Manders and makes the decision that affects the remainder of the life we have already seen unfolding.

The effect of such a structure, of course, is to produce what we might call a pathos of origins rather than a pathos of consequences. I mention this by way of illustrating that the point of origin of a dramatic situation, often outside the play, is usually the place where character, in our modern sense of the word, and plot intersect and start the ticking of the causal clock. All in all, one might say that hamartia is steadily a feature of what Elder Olson (1966, 45–46) calls the consequential plot form, or the drama in which one thing leads to another. His example of the form, *Macbeth*, offers a textbook illustration of the principle occurring within the play in the first soliloquy in which Macbeth "yields to the suggestion" planted by the "supernatural soliciting" of the Three Witches. The very phrasing, "yields to the suggestion," carries the idea of hamartia as a moment of hesitation (in this case) in which the hero stands poised, so to speak, at an entelechial crossroad and commits the act that will give tragic meaning to his life.

Still, with Shakespeare the nature of the "error" involved in hamartia changes radically, and a strict Aristotelian might object to my use of the term. But I see no dramaturgical difference between the hamartia in *Macbeth* and the one at the crossroads in *Oedipus*. The real difference between them lies in the nature of the deed committed in either case. In *Oedipus*, the moral aspect of the deed is ambiguous, to say the least; in *Macbeth*, there is no moral ambiguity at all. Indeed, Macbeth's deed does not occur until some time after the notion of murder has been put in his head. Students often remark that Oedipus commits a crime when he kills Laius, the idea being that it is wrong to kill another person, for whatever reason. However, judgments of this sort are made from the perspective of modern legal justice and do not consider the mythic status of the ancient stories, which take place, in Macbeth's words, "i'th' olden time, / Ere human statute purg'd the gentle weal" (3.4.74–75). Indeed, the question of whether Greek heroes are criminals is beside the point: they are indeed criminals, and, as Hegel suggests, "One can . . . urge nothing more intolerable against a hero of this type than by saying that he has acted innocently"—or, for that matter guiltily, since they "are quite as much under one category as the other" (1975, 67–71). The point is that the play does not examine the relationship between the deed and the moral or immoral intention behind it, as modern drama tends to do. In Greek tragedy, the act of murder is strangely above and beneath any exercise of will, in any Kantian sense of the term. Indeed, as Kierkegaard put it so succinctly, "Greek tragedy is blind," insofar as murder is often committed without knowledge of who the victim is (Oedipus, Iphigenia at Taurus); hence, "the impression of a marble statue which lacks the power of the eye" (1954, 93).

The question of innocence and guilt is a complicated problem beyond our immediate concern here, but on characterological grounds it is worth our interest in passing. Jean-Pierre Vernant has taken the question well beyond Hegel's notion that the deed and the doer are virtually consubstantial with each other: "Even while to some extent [the crime] becomes identified with [the hero]," Vernant says, "it at the same time remains separate, beyond him. . . . The individual who commits [the act] (or, to be more precise, who is its victim) is himself caught up in the sinister force that he has unleashed (or that exerts itself through him). The action does not emanate from the agent as from its source; rather, it envelops him and carries him away, swallowing him up in a power that must perforce be beyond him since it extends, both spatially and temporarily, far beyond his own person" (1981, 39–40). Thus hamartia, in Greek practice, has about it an aura of suddenness and nonhesitation: the deed simply occurs as a reaction and the causal series is let loose. In the mind's eye, one might see Oedipus "thinking twice" before slaying Laius at the crossroads, out of some moral scruple, but it does not occur to Sophocles to posit such a moment, nor to Oedipus to express any such doubt when he tells Jocasta "the whole truth" of the event. It is simply not a dramatic issue.

Macbeth, of course, is an entirely different story. In Macbeth's case, the soliloquy does two things that are characteristic of Shakespeare's art. First, it raises the horror of murder to the highest power, making it repugnant in the extreme both to Macbeth and to the audience, and, second, it paradoxically elevates Macbeth in our estimation by demonstrating an intense moral comprehension of his predicament. For instance, these lines:

> why do I yield to that suggestion
> Whose horrid image doth unfix my hair,
> And make my seated heart knock at my ribs,
> Against the use of nature? Present fears
> Are less than horrible imaginings.
> My thought, whose murther yet is but fantastical,
> Shakes so my single state of man,
> That function is smothered in surmise,
> And nothing is, but what is not.
>
> (1.3.134–42)

The mind that can conjure such a complex vision of revulsion and enthrallment—is not to be considered as a moral cripple or a man driven by venial motives of ambition and gain. It is not in the least that we approve the murder, either here (when it is still "fantastical") or thereafter. But moral approval or disapproval is not what brings us to the theater. The value of Macbeth as a tragic character lies in his becoming the crucible in which Shakespeare dramatizes the full spiritual consequence of murder, not simply as a crime but as the act through which a man might "Pour the sweet milk of concord into Hell, / Uproar the universal peace, confound / All unity on earth" (4.3.97–99). Even the crime is hyperbolized. Thus Macbeth dooms himself on our behalf. Through the window of his soliloquies we see a quality of mind and character which is, in psychopathological terms, ambivalent, or capable of holding opposed ideas at the same time. The upshot is that there is always a contradiction in Macbeth which disallows a simple judgment respecting his *value* for us. He may murder— and that is categorically wrong—but has he not taken us on one of the most profound psychic journeys to be found in world drama?

There is another factor in Shakespeare's rescue of Macbeth from moral abomination. Curiously, what Vernant says of the Greek hero returns in another form: Macbeth's crime "envelops him and carries him away, swallowing him up in a power that must perforce be beyond him since it extends, both spatially and temporarily, far beyond his own person." In a word, the "thought" of murder has been supernaturally solicited. "Look, how our partner's rapt," Banquo says, as if to tell us that psychology is only one factor in the event. And thus on another ground, the effect of his murder is softened by partially deviating its motive from character to Fate, or entelechial causality. We see Macbeth in the grip of circumstance at the point where he falls irrevocably under the influence of his fate, as Othello does in listening to Iago, as Hamlet does when he stabs Polonius, or Oedipus in the meeting with Laius at the crossroad.[1]

---

[1] An example of hamartia in modern drama might be the scene in *Death of a Salesman* when Biff walks in on Willy and the prostitute in Boston. Given the loneliness of Willy's life on the road, it is understandable why he would turn to such a woman. And it is understandable that Biff would come to Boston. But the secret broods over the whole play, like the scene at the crossroads in *Oedipus*. While we could hardly say that this "error" is what causes the fall of Willy, it is the event that supplies the main tension between Willy and Biff. I find it interesting that in the showdown scene between them the incident is not mentioned, but the insinuation is made and the rubber hose (!) is

Let us return to this scene at the crossroad. Else makes one other reference to the scene which provokes a further observation: "We may debate over which caused the killing of Laius, Oedipus's ignorance [of Laius's identity] or his hot temper, but there can be no argument about what he 'recognizes': it is the identity of the man he killed" (1967, 385). I find little cause to doubt that it was the hot temper that caused the killing. Oedipus confesses that his anger moved him to the deed. Moreover, the ignorance of Laius's identity is hardly a reason for killing him, though *knowledge* of the identity, in this case at least, might have prevented the killing. What is necessary in order to kill someone is a provocation that will be "processed" according to the character of the individual. It would seem, then, that we can also debate the cause of the hamartia's eruption: if it turns out in the end to be a grievous error (and *as* hamartia, it always does), it was brought on by the same character we see displayed in the play proper—for instance, in the Creon and Tiresias scenes, and again in his cruelty to the Herdsman. I point this out not to refute Else—who is concerned strictly with what Aristotle meant rather than with what Sophocles did—but to bring us back to the topic of character, in the non-Aristotelian sense of the term. Character is always a causal agent, among others. If Hamlet had been in Othello's shoes, Iago wouldn't have got to first base with his insinuations; if Lear hadn't been so vain, he wouldn't have divided his kingdom in the first place; Banquo had a completely different reaction from Macbeth's to the Witches' solicitations, as Ismene had to the edict on her brother's burial; and so on through drama. Character, then, is intricately entwined with the causal order, and it does no good to posit incidents of hamartia (as error) as if they came out of nowhere. Hamartia is rather a consequence of something else (character) while, at the same time, causing of the protagonist's active entry into the "field of guilt," in Benjamin's phrase.

A passage from Frye will clarify the point: "What [Adam] does is to exchange a fortune of unlimited freedom for the fate involved in the

---

thrown onto the table with the line, "This supposed to make a man of you!" I leave it to psychoanalysts to elucidate the connections here, but the scene is similar to the Herdsman scene in *Oedipus Rex* in the sense that the play never alludes to the purpose for which Oedipus summons the Herdsman (to clarify the number of robbers who killed Laius). This lapse, of course, provides grist for the well-known theory that Oedipus may *not* have been the killer of Laius after all.

consequence of the act of exchange, just as, for a man who deliberately jumps off a precipice, the law of gravitation acts as fate for the brief remainder of his life" (1957, 212). As we all know, Adam is the first in a long line of sinners and is thus the archetype of the tragic pattern. But despite the absence in Genesis of a motive for Adam's act of primal disobedience, it is impossible to conceive Adam's action as arising without some "corresponding *attitude* that precedes the act," as Kenneth Burke says. Thus "we come upon the need for some such term as Pride," even as we would arrive at the term "humility" if we were naming the attitude that leads to obedience (Burke 1970, 187). And such an attitude involves us in the province of character as a sort of ur-causal agent respecting the deed itself. (Indeed, disobedience in itself is already ambiguously a trait of character.) It is, in other words, the moment of hamartia that *marks*, as opposed to *causes*, the onset of Fate, or the moment in which the hero exchanges unlimited freedom for the gravity of disaster through the manifestation of character.

Character, then, is personal momentum, subject primarily to the laws of probability which obtain in the empirical world. Oedipus's character is not the cause of his fate, for his fate was ordained before his birth. But it is the cause of his possible actions in the field of Fate, and one of these is to rise up in anger and kill an old king. This much is probable, and we may note in passing that some attention has been paid in the play to mitigating Oedipus's guilt in the matter by making the murder a reaction to the anger of the old king (like father, like son) who had attempted to kill him with his "two-pointed goad." I take this as an instance of pure dramatic instinct on Sophocles' part, whereby he balances the forces in play in such a way as to comply with the logic that Aristotle would express in the *Poetics* almost a century later. Small as this detail may seem by comparison (five lines), I would attribute it to the same instinct that causes Shakespeare to give Macbeth a powerful moral conscience, Othello a vivid imagination, and Lear a capacity for feeling that carries him above his own foolishness. Here we perceive a difference between the Greek and Shakespearean examples: Shakespeare's is the tragedy of character not in the sense of flaw, as is sometimes suggested, but of excellence (intelligence, conscience, sensibility). It is, in a sense, through an excess of virtue that Shakespeare's heroes are propelled to their fates. I am not speaking so much of moral virtues as of qualities of mind which are, taken in themselves, positive attributes. What drives Macbeth, for example, is not ambition (a motive that is "mouthed" but given no dramatic actualization) but something spiritually apocalyptic that puts him closer to Raskolnikov among the world's fictional criminals.

In short, Shakespeare's heroes are all, each in their own way, gifted creatures, and it is their gifts that cause their "chief afflictions," as the line in *Timon* runs. Or, as Kierkegaard deftly puts it in his discussion of *Macbeth*, "The more excellent the machine. . . , all the more frightful . . . the confusion" (1954, 238). In *Oedipus*, character is less central, but what character (in the sense of psychology) *is* displayed is hubristic, or visibly "insolent," to use the Chorus's word, and this is the case with Antigone, Electra, and Philoctetes as well. There are no real criminals, in Macbeth's sense, in Greek tragedy—there are only people claiming certain rights in a world where grudges are held for generations and gods are likely to be as hubristic as humans. Hence the need to give character an unpleasant "edge" that will poise the hero delicately between the paragon and the abomination. Such compensations make the actions of the hero understandable, if not acceptable in the moral sense. He is seen to be both innocent (but not quite) and guilty (but not quite). Ultimately, however, these shadings are devices of playwriting, as particular groupings of sound are devices for creating the harmonies of music. And all of them belong to the field of character, seen as the personal behavioral contribution of the hero to his or her entrapment in the snare of Fate. Character is not precisely all there is to Destiny, but it is the part of human nature through which Destiny's work is accomplished.

Of course, as we have said earlier, what is not probable is that the old man at the crossroads would be Oedipus's father, and here we enter the mysterious causal realm assigned to the gods, Moira, Providence, Fortune and, again, the manipulative hand of the playwright. What arranges the symmetrical circumstances that bring on the hamartia cannot be ascribed to character or to empirical logic. The occasion always appears "accidentally on purpose"; as Barthes says, it is "at once indecipherable and intelligent" (1972a, 193). Laius appears out of the blue, as the Three Witches appear, without warning, out of the foul-fairness of "the day of success." Hamartia, then, is a merger in which two fields of causality intersect, one explicable in probable terms and one inexplicable as anything less than an inscrutable principle of order. Without both of them, operating in perfect synchrony, the world order would be perceived as sentimental, melodramatic, or malevolent, as the balance of character in the protagonist shifts in one direction or the other. Aristotle's paragraph on the tragic hero as "median man" hides in its brevity the key to all possible alternatives in the character/fortune mixture. Alter the formula, put an innocent paragon of virtue in the place of the arrogant Oedipus, and/or at the same time elevate the villain to good fortune (where we have villains), and the world order is instantly perceived as malevolent, satanic, or absurd. Punish the villain and rescue the paragon, and you have sentimental melodrama, the form we get more often than not instead of tragedy.

With this introduction, then, I turn directly to character itself. According to Aristotle, the four "parts" of character one should look for in drawing a tragic hero are goodness, appropriateness, likeness, and consistency. These are aspects of character present in the best tragedies. My sense of character "parts," in contrast, relates to what an audience actually sees in the character manifestation, whether the qualities named by Aristotle are present or not.

I suggest that we perceive fictional characters on at least five levels, though this perception obviously occurs as a single and unified impression. For convenience, I will call them the individual, the dialogic, the thematic, the stylistic, and the mimetic.[2] On the individual level, the character is seen as a single person (Oedipus, Ophelia, Macbeth, Brutus, Cassius), or an individual (I, he, she) consisting of a bundle of traits that form a disposition distinct from that of any other character in (or outside) the fiction. Brutus is Brutus and Cassius is Cassius: Brutus speaks Brutus's lines and Cassius Cassius's. Simple, and very much as we perceive individuals in the real world.

On the dialogic level, characters may be said to create each other: in a dialogue, speaker and listener merge and are dependent on each other for life and identity. When Cassius and Brutus argue over what to do about Caesar, they coresponsively create each other's characters before our eyes through the dialogical principle of provocation and response, one provoking the display of emotions, traits, attitudes, and so forth, of the other. At

[2] What follows is a revision and enlargement of a discussion I posed in *Dreaming and Storytelling* (1993), 54–55.

this level, in other words, character (as a dramatic force) has begun to distribute itself beyond the personal phase of the discrete human entity and we begin to see that character is a reactionary formation, not a self-starting autonomous entity. Brutus is now Cassius—and Caesar and Portia and Marc Antony, and whoever Brutus talks to or thinks about—or at least Brutus owes his liveliness to the provocations of these people. One qualification is in order: there are plays, or parts of plays, that are, strictly speaking, monologues, and they display character even so—the First Player reciting the rugged Pyrrhus speech; Chekhov's *The Harmfulness of Tobacco*, certain plays by Samuel Beckett (*Not I*, *Rockaby*, *Footfalls*); Spalding Gray's *Swimming to Cambodia*; etc.). So it is hardly the case that character requires two people in order to manifest itself. But the monologue is dialogic even so, for it addresses itself to an Other, if only an imaginary Other, to which it explains itself. What counts is that we see character forming itself around the armature of an occasion that brings on the speech, justifies it in the here and now. There is always a presumed listener, someone with an interest, whether it be visible like the Auditor in *Not I* (who says nothing), the mythical audience in Chekhov's play, or the actual audience in Spalding Gray's.

On the thematic level, characters begin to manifest a superpsychological cast in that their individual subjective positions, or interpositions, are perceived as part of a larger harmony. For one thing, Brutus and Cassius, unlike us, always talk on the same subject that other characters talk about when they aren't around (Rome, Caesar, conspiracy, assassination), and it never occurs to them that there are other topics in the world, like love, revenge, or ambition, such as obsess Romeo, Hamlet, and Macbeth, who don't care in the least what happened in Rome.

At the stylistic level, as T. S. Eliot said of Shakespeare, character and author speak "in unison" (1954, 34). If characters are each different in their own way, there is the imprint of another individuality in them, and it is that of their author who endows all of their speech and actions with the characteristics of a single individual style. And style, as Mikel Dufrenne has put it, is "the locus in which the artist appears" (1973, 105). At this level of perception we may say that Hamlet is Brutus, Romeo, Cassius, Macbeth, and others, and all were "fathered" by the same creator. As an illustration of the stylistic principle, imagine yourself standing at the fringe of a family reunion. Here grandparents, parents, grandchildren, and even great-grandchildren are having a picnic. You watch and listen, and soon you fall into a metaphorical trance in which you begin experiencing déjà vu: motifs and continuities announce themselves among the family members. You see where the grandson got his slouch, the daughter her wide forehead and freckles, the father his stentorian voice, and how a fondness for fatty meats runs in the family. As you notice all this you begin, inaudibly, to laugh—not at the family but at the fact that these people *constitute a family*. In each member is inscribed a genetic proposition, though you would be hard-pressed to say what this proposition is. Behind what each person is, is something he or she cannot help being. It is a variation of Bergson's mechanical encrusting itself on the living, of the humor theory of self-repetition, of metaphor itself, which is always faintly funny, and finally of archetype, which is, after all, nothing more than a metaphor that doesn't know when to stop. This is basically a comic perception of the world, and you would have to be in a strange state of alertness to see it in the theater or in reading, but it is there if you happen to think about it. The best way to experience it directly is to open a volume of the works of Shakespeare, or any other dramatist, to a randomly selected page. Put your finger to the text, read a speech or two, and repeat the operation at another randomly selected page in the book; you will eventually get the feeling that you are trapped in an invisible metaphor.

At the fifth level of perception, which I will call the mimetic, characters are seen not simply as belonging to the Shakespeare or Beckett or Chekhov family but as fictive creatures—in effect, as having about their appearance before us an aura of intentionality. Vaguely speaking, characters have been *created* for our benefit; they are signs of something, different in kind from anything you are apt to confront in the world of real people—or in the people of your dreams. For example: in the dream something happens to this "nested" relationship of perceptual planes. Perhaps the main thing is that while the characters of a dream (and its world) are created by the dreamer, the dreamer is now inside the world as an inhabitant and the activity of observing no longer takes place from a superior standpoint. Indeed, from a purely phenomenal perspective, creativity does not take place at all: it is a reality that unfolds before the dreamer's eyes. The dreamer, for instance, is no more conscious of theme than Brutus and Cassius are conscious of being bound by the theme of conspiracy or by an awareness that they are creatures in a play by William Shakespeare. As a consequence, any anticipations the dreamer may have about how things will "turn out" have only to do with personal expectations and nothing to do with aesthetic pleasure. Moreover, the dreamer does not perceive other characters in the dream in any such perceptual depth—or even a gestalt of this depth—as I have outlined here: characters are simply others in the same world, and it is a world without theme or style, a world in which, like the waking world, anything may happen to you, but you will always react "in character."

These, then, are the perceptual levels on which we detect character. It should also be said that everything that occurs or is present in a play has character. Character is an adjectival, or modifying, phenomenon: the sofa is "run down, fatigued by decades of use," the room is "cheerful," "through the window one can see frozen barren trees, their branches grasping greedily at the windows," and so on. All worlds are characterized by character of some sort, and one way to understand this is to imagine any stage setting as having an imaginary window through which you can gaze at the world beyond. Some settings do have windows, of course, but the window I have in mind is like the two windows in Beckett's *Endgame*: you can't see anything through them—except in the mind's eye. And what the mind's eye sees is an extension of the world on the stage, not in the literal sense of seeing more and more sofas, chairs, and tables, but a world that is a qualitative continuation, to return to Sparshott, of all the images that pass in the course of the play, and usually within the first ten minutes in which world-quality is established. Try as you will, you can't imagine a bustling village or a beach filled with bathers through the blind skeleton eyes of Beckett's *Endgame*. But this notion of character is remote from our central interest here, which is the character of the characters who inhabit the world. I turn to this subject in the following chapter.

CHAPTER 9

The Anatomy of Dramatic Character

Very little in the study of the drama is as difficult to pin down as character. Character is both cause and effect, both the fuel that drives the plot and a kind of emanation given off by it. Again, Henry James: "What is character but the determination of incident? What is incident but the illustration of character?" (1948, 13). How can we possibly disentangle character and plot in an exchange such as this:

> . . . what can you say to draw
> A third more opulent than your sisters? Speak.
> Nothing, my lord.
>
> (*Lear*, 1.1.87–88)

Any attempt to isolate Lear's and Cordelia's characters from the event in progress will simply convert them into abstractions. Plainly, one can no more conceive of character without action than one can conceive of gravity without seeing objects falling through its field.

For reasons of this sort, fictional character (and nonfictional as well) has for some time been undergoing a strenuous critique from poststructuralist writers. The general argument is that those who assume there is such a thing as character, or self, are holding an "essentialist" or naive "humanist" view of human nature. The truth is—so the argument runs—character is unreliable as a concept primarily because it is in itself an illusion. To take one of the most recent and vigorous arguments in this vein, Hillis Miller suggests that "character (in the sense of self) is never

136

present. It is always over there, somewhere else, pointed to by characters (signposts) that cannot be followed to reach an unmediated access to what they indicate" (1992, 94)—that is, "a fluid assemblage of fleeting catachreses" as opposed to "a fixed personality" (117).[1] I make the point here, first, because it affords an opportunity to discuss this very quality of character—its fleetingness—and to set out my belief that character (literary or dramatic or, for that matter, real) is no more "over there" than narrative or theme or thought. Reading, one might say, is being continually "over there," being led on by "signposts" called words. And as I have tried to show in my discussion of time, there is nothing "fixed" in the theater, and it is precisely the flux, the specious quality of its composite present, that characterizes its mode of appeal. The Aristotelian notion of a change of fortune pertains not only to a certain arrangement of events in a plot but to the human condition of temporality which, to quote George Steiner, "is made concrete by the overwhelming truth that all being is a being-toward-death" (1979, 106). It seems a reasonable postulate that, without the fact of death, our drama—including comedy, farce, and biography, not to mention a great deal else in life that has little to do with death—would take very different forms (for instance, retirement plans). But it is impossible to conceive a world without these mutual endings.

So character (and the self) is an illusion within an illusion, as far as fictional forms are concerned. Moreover, the notion of a "fixed self" or a "fixed character" is a patent absurdity at any behavioral level. A fixed character, in the sense in which Miller apparently conceives it, would be as useless to a human being (or a character in a play or novel) as a bicycle with a fixed front wheel. This is not to deny that there are vestiges of the fixed self notion in our thinking. Indeed, a good deal of the world's business gets conducted on the assumption that selves are in certain respects fixed.

Take the standard letter of recommendation. To write such a letter is to create a kind of metaphorical figuration similar to that of writing a character into a novel. That is, there may be a real person to whom the letter pertains, but my description of that person is not essentially different from an author's fictional description of a character, except that my letter will be much briefer and, apart from an illustrative example or so, non-

[1] My response to Miller's argument appears in "The Mirror and the Labyrinth: The Further Ordeals of Character and Mimesis," *Style* 27, no. 3 (Fall 1993): 452–71.

mimetic. Both kinds of descriptions are products of the observation of human beings in the real world, the main difference being perhaps that the fictional author might deal more generally (or compositely) with human behavior than a letter writer who has a specific instance in mind. In any case, both descriptions are fixed in the sense that they are directed simplifications of behavior which stand, like the ingredients of the Eucharist, in the stead of a metaphysical complexity. I hope that what I am saying in the letter will be verified in the person's future behavior. In other words, I want to assure potential employers that Mr. Parsons has qualities that are attachable to certain business projects, such as reliability, diplomacy, and so on. I would certainly not help Parsons get a job if I suggested that these qualities stood under the jeopardy of reversal or dissolution (which I realize is quite possible), or that although Parsons will reliably show up for work his character may not. So I don't mention such things, knowing that whatever I say about anything in a letter for Parsons will reflect contextually on Parsons's character. Even my tardiness in supplying the letter may be taken as a sign that Parsons is not worth hiring if he is not worth writing about.

So, altogether, I want Parsons to live up to my expectations about him, if only for selfish reasons. If an employer happens to write me, later on, and says, "You were right about Parsons. He is very industrious and intelligent," the character in question is no less a fiction because the employer is employing signs, or signposts, to refer to an absent object, a certain zone of reliability that seems so far (knock on wood!) to attend the performance of this temporary cloak-bag of biochemicals who goes under the name of Parsons. Moreover, the employer is restricting his estimation of Parsons to the "plot" of business life (god knows what Parsons does after hours). If, soon thereafter, the employer should write me that one afternoon Parsons ran amok, put a ring in his nose, and insulted the manager of the firm's largest account, I would be shocked because that simply isn't like the Parsons I knew. Now that I think about it, though, in my mind's eye I can see Parsons running amok in that office. I wasn't there, but I can imagine how he did it. By this I mean that, if Parsons were to run amok, he would do it *in character*, just like the Parsons we all knew and once relied on: if he was Parsons when he was reliable, he is also Parsons when he is unreliable, fixed in his unfixedness, you might say. That is to say, even though his behavior shocked me, I wouldn't doubt for a minute that it was Parsons who was running amok—Parsons's voice,

Parsons's peculiar way of coming at you with that fixed-from-under stare like a charging bull (a little like Lord Jim), Parsons's slight nervousness, Parsons's—yes, my god! Parson's tendency, now that I think of it, to brook no interruption with anything he set his mind to, whatever it might be, that quality I described as doggedness in my letter, a quality that (looking back) often asserted itself in our conversations as an insistence on pursuing his point over any question or remark I might want to interject. Indeed, I confess that there were times I didn't really like Parsons much. It wasn't doggedness at all, or, if so, a doggedness that, under extreme pressure, crossed a behavioral line of some sort and became—I know not what. In retrospect, I should probably have seen the signs. They were certainly there. But of course Parsons wouldn't have got the job if I had reported them in good character.

My sense is that Miller wants to throw character out with the bathwater of the "fixed self" myth. But the thing about people is that they can undergo an event, or a profound change, that will irrevocably convince them there is no such thing as a fixed self, or an unvarying identity, and they will go to work the same morning and behave reliably. Or, they may run amok or throw it all up and go to Tahiti, or to law school. But whatever they do, they will carry a good deal of what they were with them, from habits of mind to preferences and dislikes, convictions about morality, right and wrong, and other people (based on readings of character). More particularly, they will retain an elusive dimension of personhood for which our best word is probably "personality." Of course, this too may undergo change, in certain radical cases become unrecognizable, but personality is more perdurable than ideas a person (or a literary character) may hold about politics, gender, society, or selfhood.

So when I refer to character and attempt to break it down anatomically in what follows, I am always assuming a good deal of behavioral slack, in life as in fiction, together with a good deal of self-repetition. For, even though character may seem to be always "over there," there is another respect in which it is always "all here and now." I can best illustrate this with a speech of character from Shakespeare. This is the response Hamlet makes in act 1 to his mother's question respecting his unusual grief for his father, "Why seems it so particular with thee?"

> Seems, madam? Nay, it is. I know not 'seems'.
> 'Tis not alone my inky cloak, good mother,

> Nor customary suits of solemn black,
> Nor windy suspiration of forc'd breath,
> No, nor the fruitful river in the eye,
> Nor the dejected haviour of the visage,
> Together with all forms, moods, shapes of grief,
> That can denote me truly. These indeed seem,
> For they are actions that a man might play;
> But I have that within which passes show,
> These but the trappings and the suits of woe.
>
> $\qquad\qquad\qquad\qquad\qquad$ (1.2.76–86)

Much like Hamlet speeches elsewhere in the play, this passage is a discourse on what Hamlet isn't. Let us put aside the possibility that Hamlet is dissembling before this politic convocation of enemies. As a speech of sheer self-characterization, it throws up a smoke screen of conventional mourning actions that seemingly denote true grief—but don't. And the *true* source of Hamlet's grief disappears into "that within" which finally has no name at all. Thus Hamlet escapes through a crack in the floor of character itself. Finally, as in all the other Hamlet speeches in the play, we haven't the slightest notion of what bothers him except what we knew at the outset—that he feels his grief, or whatever is "within," is unnameable in its depth. All in all, the speech is a perfect instance of how character is "always over there, somewhere else, pointed to by characters (signposts)"—Hamlet in this case—but not available for inspection, much less definition.

It would be an odd reader, however, who, having read the rest of the play, couldn't see how consistent this passage is with everything that passes Hamlet's lips, in public or in private, in all the "over theres" of his stage life. To name the qualities, or traits, the speech expresses would only be to offer my own misreading of the character. The point is not to specify Hamlet's traits or an overall description of his character; the point is, rather, that whatever his character is—for Johnson, Coleridge, Bradley, Knight, or Calderwood, it is all of a piece, as far as "nature," "character," and "mind" go; that is to say, it is bound by a certain repetitiveness of nature that accumulates in all Hamlet's scenes (and references to him by others), though each of us will have our own readings of what makes this repetitiveness repetitive. For instance, no one would be deceived into thinking that Claudius, Laertes, Horatio, Fortinbras, or any other character in fiction could have spoken these lines. If readers from different historical periods have widely different ideas about Hamlet's character, they all respond to the same character construction that must have struck Shakespeare as being adequate, in 1600, to communicate to fellow-Elizabethans some sense of self-continuity in the part Richard Burbage eventually bent his considerable human actuality around. The fact that estimations of Hamlet's character change through the years has nothing whatever to do with the province of character as an affective locus of literary energy. We may go even further and add that someone coming upon Hamlet's "seems" speech for the first time, without knowing the rest of the play, would have some sense of the character of the speaker of the lines, from the lines alone, some idea of what *kind* of person was speaking the lines, and the description would be accurate enough to coincide to some degree with the character demonstrated in all the lines to follow. All the parts would form a whole, a coherent portrait of a virtual human being—always over there, always all here and now.

The most useful way to perform an anatomy of character is to examine it from an etymological perspective. Since we cannot usefully separate character and plot, we might consider how our words for character illuminate distinctive sectors of the phenomenon which stand in need of identification, like the various kinds of snow in the Eskimo's world. I have selected three terms that always seem to recur in discussions of character, three keywords, as Raymond Williams might put it, that may constitute a working anatomy of character if we treat it as a structure of complementary parts. Such a structure will help us decompose character and see more clearly how it behaves in plays—to identify what it is, in fact, that develops or changes when we sense that such things are happening to a character. The terms, then, are Personality, Character, and Identity.[2] Immediately, I am in the awkward position of having to use the word

---

[2] I will use these three terms throughout as both proper and common nouns. As proper nouns (Character, Personality, Identity), they refer to my own formalistic definition as applied to the anatomy. As common nouns, they refer to more general or prior conceptions of their meaning. I will sometimes use "character" as a shorthand term for the Character/Personality complex. I trust the context will make clear what I mean in each case. It occurred to me, at one point, that I might avoid confusion by using the Greek word "ethos" for what I call Character. But this turned out to be too confining, even more confusing (with its Aristotelian implications), and a little pretentious.

"character" to define itself. This is unavoidable, however, since "character" is at once our generic word for the *dramatis persona*, the aggregate of his or her personal traits, and, as I will treat it here, a specific dimension of the character's nature. In other words, a character in a play has a character, and he or she also has Character.

Let us begin with Personality, the most palpable level on which character asserts itself. The word is primarily derived from the Latin *personalitas*. In its earliest meaning, common until the nineteenth century, personality referred to "the quality, character, or fact of being a person as distinct from a thing" (*OED*). In this sense of the word, Personality is the host, or pure being, of dramatic character. It is the person we recognize as Oedipus each time he appears: the Oedipus-body (on stage the actor, in the text our mental image of the man) who keeps saying "I" in reference to a self that persists. It is what Heidegger might refer to as the "who" of *Dasein*: that "which maintains itself as something identical throughout changes in its Experience and ways of behavior, and which relates itself to this changing multiplicity in so doing" (1962, 150). If this *material cause* of character seems self-evident or incidental to a discussion of interior character, I should point out that just this persistence, or sameness, of a character's person makes possible the cathartic effect of the ending. At its deepest and most ironical base, drama arises from the reappearance of "something identical" in the character which survives the flux of dramatic life. Oedipus's "All brought to pass!" speech is moving because it is spoken by the same being who, two hours (and a lifetime) earlier, spoke the words, "I Oedipus whom all men call the Great."

The more recent understanding of Personality is a direct outgrowth of this earlier, literal meaning based in the distinction between persons and things. We now conceive Personality as "that quality or assemblage of qualities which makes a person what he is, as distinct from other persons; distinctive personal or individual character" (*OED*). In short, Personality has become for us the quality or style of behavior that distinguishes one person from another, rather than a person from a thing. Thus we have a whole lexicon of Personality adjectives—unique, weak, overwhelming, offensive, charming, explosive—most of them referring to the kind and level of energy emitted by the individual.

This is an appropriate point to begin making some distinctions between Personality and Character. It is impossible to abandon the synonymic aspects of the two words (as seen in the definition above), or to pin either one into a narrow range of meanings. Indeed, they sometimes collapse into each other (as when we say that someone with an outrageous Personality is "a character"), and writers commonly shift from one term to the other simply to avoid repetition. What seems to draw the two terms apart in our collective usage is a need to account for two different kinds of possessions or attributes of the individual: those given by society and those given by nature. No one would deny that Personality is powerfully influenced by social life and Character by natural endowments (as Richard Crookback is quick to point out), but the possession of Character is what joins a person to the enterprise of maintaining an orderly society (or, in the case of "bad" character, endangers the enterprise), and Personality is what sets the person apart from other men and women.

The original meaning of Character (coming from *caract*, *characte*, *caractere*, etc.) was drawn from the graphic arts: an impression or impressing instrument, "a distinctive mark impressed, engraved, or otherwise formed; a brand, stamp" (*OED*). Shakespeare uses the word primarily in this vein, as when Viola says, "I will believe thou hast a mind that suits / With this thy fair and outward character," or when Claudio says, "Our most mutual entertainment / With character too gross is writ on Juliet." We have more or less lost this usage of the word and have replaced it with the modern term "personality." Here we arrive at the leap in the meaning of character which corresponds to the evolution of the meanings of personality. It is illustrated by the definitions of character in the *Oxford English Dictionary*: character, for example, is "the sum of the moral and mental qualities which distinguish an individual or a race." This moral notion of character goes back at least to Aristotle and is one I wish to retain as the principal area of difference between Personality and Character. Still, we use the word character in a sense very different from Aristotle's definition of ethos in the *Poetics*. For Aristotle, as we have seen, ethos is one of "three objects of imitation," the other two being plot (mythos) and thought (dianoia). Today, however, we think of character in a more encompassing sense, although it remains primarily ethical or moral, and only secondarily "mental" in most of our usages.[3] We would find charac-

---

[3] One might argue, of course, that Aristotle was thinking of moral choice in a somewhat broader sense than our modern usage suggests. For example, O. B. Hardison: "The term 'moral' enters the definition [of ethos] for the simple reason that most of

ter in the parts of a play where Aristotle would find only thought—those passages when someone sets forth an opinion, tries to prove something, or states a general principle. For example, we would see Creon's defense of the principle of obedience to state, in *Antigone*, a clear instance of thought, as a mark of ethical character: specifically, evidence of Creon's growing insecurity as his position regarding Antigone comes more and more into civic question. In this modern sense, one can scarcely write a scene, much less an entire play, in which the characters do not exhibit character.

To sum up, I would describe Character as something lying back of, or beneath, Personality. Personality is born with the person, whereas Character is formed over time, as we say, in "the fires of experience," or "the school of hard knocks." Children have Personalities long before they have Characters. They are, in fact, little Personalities waiting to be filled with Character. Thus Character is the deeper (if later) part of the person, his or her value sphere as defined within or against that of society, while Personality is his or her distinctive way of being himself or herself. It would be absurd to suggest that Personality and Character are two different things or that they exhaust, between them, the contents of human nature. Character is not simply the moral part of nature in the narrow sense of the word, but rather that whole system of internal self-government which Shakespeare often likened, in its complexity, to a state or "little kingdom." Thus I would subsume concepts like Freud's ego, id, and superego, the instincts, repressions, unconscious, and the like, under Character. The psychologist, who rarely uses the word character, would put them under personality, which in psychology refers to the whole psychophysical system. But psychologists are not dealing in fictional characterization, and such constructions of the mind are not a part of dramatic character but are derived interpretatively from the behavior of characters, as when we say, "Unconsciously Oedipus knows he is the killer," or "Macbeth is caught between the demands of the superego and the id." In other words, as they relate to fiction, these are thematic or hermeneutic categories, not constructional or anatomical ones, as in psychology. If a dramatist wrote an

---

what would now be called psychology was included by ancient and renaissance thinkers under the heading of 'moral philosophy'" (Aristotle 1981, 124). In any case, this interpretation of the term "moral" is consistent with my usage in this chapter.

allegorical play with a character named Ego, Ego would not have an ego but an egolike character, though a clever psychoanalytic critic might come along and discover an id lurking beneath Ego's ego.

A dramatic character is, first and foremost, an intensified simplification of human nature: he or she is a Personality with a Character—someone who appears and behaves in a certain way and carries within him or her a certain ethos or disposition with respect to moral conduct and choice. This disposition may be shallow (Charmian) or complex (Cleopatra), but apart from maids carrying drinks or extras swelling a crowd, it may be seen in any character the dramatist has bothered to make an important agent in the action.

Returning to our distinction between dramatic and real character, let us imagine an absurd hypothetical situation. Suppose it were possible for a human being to walk through a magical screen into the world of art and turn into a character. What would have changed? First, he would discover that his range of behavior—the way he walks, speaks, his moods, even his facial manipulations—had radically shrunk, as though his entire expressive system had become impoverished. He would now have one tic, not three or half-a-dozen. He would do infinitely fewer things, but all would somehow be done more purely. Like Sartre's waiter in the cafe who is "playing at being a waiter in a cafe" (1956, 102) by restricting his behavior to waiterly movements, he would find himself "playing" at being himself, or some distilled essence of himself that had always been diluted in the endlessly shifting demands of daily life. All told, he would be reduced to a gestus of his former self. Second, his moral nature, his entire relation to the sphere of value (what is good, what is bad, what is prized, and what is valueless) would be intensified. For every situation he faces in this new world requires that his essential moral self accompany him ostensively as the directive force of all his acts. In brief, he would find himself efficiently designed to play a role.

Thus we arrive at a proposition: character is to role as plot is to action. It breaks down like this:

1. Character expresses itself in events.
2. Plot is the arrangement of the events.
3. Action is the indwelling form of the plot.
4. Role is the indwelling form of character.

Role, then, is the trajectory of character, its path to destiny, just as action is the trajectory of the plot. These two trajectories are ultimately one and the same, for the play's role-trajectories feed into the overall action-trajectory, somewhat like a shower of arrows. We see now why character is not simply a passenger in the action. Aristotle likens the plot to the soul of a tragedy, but might we not go a step further and speak of the plot as having a soul—that is, as having the vital energy of character designed specifically to make the plot possible, complete, and morally intelligible—to make it, in other words, an action?

To see fully how dramatic character becomes this purposive driving force, the concept of Identity must be brought into the discussion. Before leaving the Personality-Character complex, however, I want to touch on another problem that bears directly on the major reason for drawing such a sharp distinction between these two areas of the character phenomenon. Our use of either term points to the particular way in which an individual persists and coheres in the unstable narrative of life. In his essay "The Inside and the Outside," Jean Starobinski refers to the skin of the organism as that sensitive frontier of the self which is the contact surface between the inside and the "hazardous outside." Skin is "alike the place of exchanges, of adjustments, of sensory signals, and the place of conflicts and wounds" (1975, 342). In a metaphorical sense, Personality is the skin of the Character, the "place" of exchange between inside and outside. It is worth recalling, however, that one of the roots of the word "personality" is the Latin *persona*, meaning mask and/or actor: buried in the word and the concept of personality is a Janus-faced ambiguity. Taken in one direction, personality becomes synonymous with "role" or "part" or "guise," in another it becomes synonymous with the substance of the self. While it is indeed a skin, containing and defining the person, it is also a mask, obscuring the person, disguising it, becoming what Wilhelm Reich calls "character armor."

Hence one of the fundamental problems of human "exchange" is that of knowing what is inside the outside. Can the mind's construction be read in the "fair and outward character"? It is the ever-present possibility of this duplicity (in people or events) which gives us much of our drama, this art of unconcealment whose mainspring is the principle of reversal. For as we see beginning with Clytemnestra and coming up through the tribe of Iago and Edmund, it is possible to smile and murder while one smiles, and much of the drama of seeming-and-being between Shakespeare and Harold Pinter runs on this theme of a breach between Personality and Character. Hamlet himself becomes a complex character by virtue of something unarticulated "within" that passes the show of his public behavior, consternates the court, and provides work for the critic. In Pinter, finally, Character is almost entirely usurped by Personality, or at least has been submerged so far that it can only be felt as an upsurge of malice, what Gothic fiction would call a "nameless vice." The Pinter play is a dance of Personality in the ruins of an accountable moral world.

Let us shift our perspective for a moment and think of our two terms as artistic principles rather than as properties of individual characters. In other words, let us shift ground from the psychology of character to the psychology of characterization. We have noted that, even in Aristotle, there is an affinity between character (ethos) and thought (dianoia), for it is primarily these two qualities of the person that incite the action and determine the outcome. Adapting Aristotle liberally, we might say that character speaks through thought, and through thought the play speaks its theme, a problem I will examine in the following chapter. A similar affinity seems to exist between what I have called Personality and what Aristotle calls *opsis*, or spectacle, whereby the visible appearance and (I would add) the behavior of the characters constitute the *objects* of our interest.[4] Following this idea further, one might say that the affective power of dramatic character runs on an axis from ethos to opsis, from moral code to personal manner, or (in Horatian terms) from the useful (*utile*) to the delightful (*dulce*). What plays allow us to see, then, is an intensification of the inside and outside of the human being, our moral and mannerly possibilities carried to extremes. Putting aside the obvious possibilities of spectacle and theme arising from plot (mythos), diction (lexis), and song (*melos*), we may say that a dramatist or dramatic tradition

---

[4] For example, Gerald Else on opsis: "I follow Bywater in referring this term (*opsis*: 'vision, sight, appearance') to the appearance of the *persons*, i.e., their masks and costumes, rather than to the stage setting in general" (Aristotle 1967, 90). Whether Aristotle intended this definition or not, I am suggesting that opsis can be broadened even further to accommodate the manner of the persons' appearance, or the spectacle of their personalities in action.

manipulates the Personality/Character complex in a variety of ways to produce spectacle and theme. Primarily, the dramatist may choose to emphasize either the thematic aspect of Character or the spectacular aspect of Personality. Finely balanced plays like Shakespeare's probably derive as much of their interest from one as from the other: Personality is an extravagant force in the Shakespearean spectacle, yet it remains closely, if ambiguously, linked to the moral idea (with a heavy emphasis on antinomies like *fair* and *false*). But a drama highlighting the principle of ethos, or Character, would place a very high premium on moral utility, the confirmation of our value system, what we should be for and against—behavior as conduct. At this extreme, we would locate morality plays, allegorical drama, sentimental drama, and other such forms in which the characters are little more than spokespersons for an ideology. Other examples might be symposium drama and certain heavily cerebral plays from the existentialist period which focus on the problem of freedom and choice, self-authenticity, and the search for value in a godless world. These are odd fellow travelers, perhaps, but I am not lumping plays into an eccentric category so much as seeing how ethos adapts itself to various projects. Personality does not disappear in such projects but rather becomes a host for Character, a translucent skin through which we see, as it were, the beating ethical heart.

At the other extreme, then, we would find a drama that capitalizes on the spectacular potential of Personality. Here the assumption is that the display of behavior is more interesting than the questions of right and wrong it provokes—or more typically, wrong behavior is usually more interesting than right. Bad people are simply more fun to watch, and if you crowd enough interesting moral delinquents on the stage, moral questions become somewhat beside the point. The play may still mean something, but whatever it means is less interesting than what it is doing. Jonson, for one, was forever insisting that his plays were moral object lessons, a sentiment that reminds one of Gertrude's line, "The lady doth protest too much, methinks." For in a kingdom of thieves, we will simply cheer for the most competent thief. To give Jonson his due, however, it is possible to see his humor play—especially his bestiary play *Volpone*—as a dystopic, and therefore thematic, vision of the world.

A better example of the spectacle of Personality can be seen in the Restoration comedy, which has always puzzled us because we cannot agree on whether it was endorsing its immorality, satirizing it, or simply making money with it. The problem arises from the virtual absence of an ethical awareness in most of the characters, and when it is present the character is usually boring. Here again, one is reminded of Pinter, whose plays are equally based in the game of Personality and wit—if one can be said to be playing a game when the game is all there is to life. The best example is probably *No Man's Land*, which, in point of its ornate language, reminds one of a Congreve play set in Eliot's wasteland. Pinter's world may be far more ferocious than Congreve's, but success and failure rest on the same base as expressed in Wildean doctrine—in matters of grave importance it is style, not sincerity, that counts. As Spooner says at the end, "All we have left is the English language," and as a consequence Personality voraciously incorporates the melos and lexis of poetry into its spectacle.

Another form of Personality drama is one we might refer to as the "007 plot" in honor of its most spectacular form, though it has been copied in principle a thousand times over, chiefly in the cop and detective movies. Here the moral and ethical motives of the hero are taken on faith, as is the evil motive of the villain. We assume that James Bond is motivated by patriotism and a desire to rescue the world from evil, but this is something of a granted premise. The entire emphasis is thrown onto his personality and consists in his doing with panache and ingenious technology what Pinter's and Congreve's people do with language—coolly surviving the rigors of an endlessly menacing world that exists precisely to display his personality.

These are only samplings from the extremes. Most plays are probably closer, on this ground, to Shakespeare's balanced drama than to *Everyman* or *No Man's Land*. Moreover, I have dealt with only one set of extremes. One can probably reverse the polarities and speak of plays based on the thematics of Personality (*Peer Gynt*) or the spectacle of Character—the panache of extraordinary virtue (*Cyrano de Bergerac*) or the shock and delight of ethical paradox (almost any play by Shaw). In many cases, it is probably a question of where one wants to locate the emphasis.

A more challenging application of the principle arises with today's performance theater and the theater of images. While this theater resists reduction to a genre, it does seem legitimate to ask how my scheme of character anatomy might apply to a theater that deliberately abandons a mimetic representation of human beings. Until recently, we have been comfortable with the assumption that the unique thing about drama is that everything in it must pass through the characters. Yet it is now clear that the medium of theater (its material cause) is not necessarily the actor playing a character who has Character and Personality. Still, I doubt this represents a rejection of artistic principles so much as a new mode of defamiliarization. In performance theater, the thing traditionally allocated to dramatic character is dispersed into the physical universe of the stage— that is, into any element of the production (light, sound, projections, montages, images, puppets) through which the performance achieves its meaning, even if the meaning is only an emotional experience for the spectator. Anything can be a character as long as it does the work characters are supposed to do, and this work is primarily thematic and spectacular: nothing fundamental has changed.

In her essay "The Politics of Performance," Bonnie Marranca claims that such a theater "displaces . . . character with personality" (1981, 62). What she means by personality is not made clear but makes sense, in my terms, if we consider the strong optic affinity between Personality, as self-presentation, and performance, as the display of the actor's virtuosity. Thus, as Xerxes Mehta says, "the performer is the solution to the 'problem' of character" (1984, 195). The "problem," basically, is that character commits the theater to a representation whose moral and spectacular energy is limited by the motives of the human body. One of the solutions of performance theater is to replace the logic of character motives with a logic of audience emotions. To put it another way: connotation displaces denotation. As a simple illustration, take the following statement: "The red book is in the library." Here, in miniature, is the traditional text-bound play that writes the "sentence" of its meaning mimetically in a plot with two characters (book and library). But if we reconceive the statement thus—

red   read   book   library

—we enter the world (or at least the logic) of performance. *Red* is not a modifying adjective; it is a character in its own right and the source of all that follows. Here we depart from *red* by a kind of punning (red / read), pass transitively from verb to object (read what? book), and arrive at a metonymy or synecdoche (book = library)—a "sentence" constructed not in the logical order of probability and necessity but at the level of the Lacanian unconscious, which is structured like a language. We needn't even go that far, for the Freudian unconscious performs the same sort of work insofar as it is the starting point for the associative process that, I take it, energizes performance art. In any case, it is all brought about by play rather than linear causality—that is, by permitting play to become the subject rather than the medium *for* a subject, a variation perhaps of the Oedipal inversion I discussed in Chapter 7.

Indeed, the best analogy, again, might be that of the dream, that central art form of the unconscious. As dreamer, I invent a world that I experience as a protagonist, as if it were coming *to* me rather than from me. Essentially, dream is the process by which we cycle emotions into images. The dream is the ur-dramatist: I pour my desire or terror or joy into a mailbox, an animal, a mountainous sea, anything that wanders into the environs of the dream. These are all characters in the dream, but they are all played by one Character (the dreamer), who may discard any of his or her (its?) manifestations at any moment and take the form of something or someone else. Performance theater would apparently reverse this process, putting the dream on stage and hoping that its images will become the spectator's emotions. Since Strindberg, we have been trying to perfect this process, albeit with limited success, as everything depends on how well a waking audience can be taught, so to speak, to dream someone else's dream.

In any case, the dream shares certain fundamental characteristics with performance theater. For example, Nerval's idea of the dream as "a second life" might apply as well to performance theater. Both are "actuals," in Richard Schechner's well-known term, in that they minimize the distinction between real (actual) space in the world and the theatrical and fictional space of a stage. The dream, of course, achieves this end through the physiological process of REM sleep, whereas performance theater, however much it may resemble actual environment, is a deliberate aesthetic process.

I turn now to Identity, which I have set apart because it does not belong to dramatic character in the way that the other terms belong. One does not seek, or strive to maintain, one's Character or Personality, and here lies all the difference. Like my other terms, Identity has undergone a metaphorical evolution out of its original Latin root in *idem,* or "the same." Philosophers treat identity as a serious problem and endlessly debate the question of whether something can remain absolutely itself. (For example, if you completely disassemble a car in Philadelphia and reassemble it in Chicago—or even in Philadelphia—will it be the same car?) Literary critics, on the other hand, have a softer concept of the word and write about identity as a theme in literature, principally, as the quest for self. The philosophical question of identity is not relevant to my purpose here, except as it touches the base from which all metaphorical usages of the concept spring: the possibility of self-repetition, or continuity in time. Likewise, the literary or thematic idea of identity represents only a narrow, and comparatively recent, vein of our preoccupation with the identity concept. If identity is to be at all useful as a characterological principle, it must have a general application. Clearly Character and Personality do not cover the whole realm of behavior. They pertain primarily to the sphere of *being* or *having*. It is true that Personality, as the sector of visible behavior, belongs also to the sphere of doing: smiling is, after all, as much an act as murdering. But we need another principle if we are to see how these "possessions" come fully into the sphere of doing, how they are energized by the world, and there is, in Identity, an intentional thrust not carried by the other terms.

This implication cannot be found in the dictionaries, for we have only recently amended the meaning of identity—given it, in effect, a mystique—and we have done so because it is identity that is so endangered by modern life. Consider the unlikelihood of a statement such as "I have found my character" or "I have found my personality." Yet to say "I have found my identity" is to imply that one has been seeking it in a precarious world. All around our contemporary notion of identity is a sense of *being* expressing itself in *doing*, in being for something, not simply (as in modern literature) a goal or a lost state, but a natural channel of action in which one's Character and Personality are given meaning and direction. Identity has become synonymous with that continuity of purpose which gives being a meaning in time, and in this general sense it is the best term through which we can examine the contribution of dramatic character to mythos and praxis.

In the drama, whose subject matter is the conflict of self and world, or self and other, Identity is what often gets people of good Character in trouble and makes people of bad Character dangerous. Identity is what attaches person, Character, and Personality to the world, like the foot of the mollusk. Thus Othello's Identity cannot be summed up as easily as one might sum up his Character or Personality. For in order to be brought to the paradox of killing the thing he loves, Othello must be planted in the world as someone with a particular Identity. This Identity begins in the Othello pride, confidence, and masculinity, the soldierly power that Shakespeare concentrates in such lines as "Keep up your bright swords, for the dew will rust them." As the play opens, all of this history and "occupation" have been newly identified with the love of Desdemona, distilled in the gift of the symbolic handkerchief. Only gradually does Iago bring this extravagant energy to bear on a new Identity, that of the cuckold whose single task is to avenge his betrayal. It is this veering of the Othello energy from its noble moorings that arouses our pity and our fear.

So at each of these points Othello's character condenses itself into one project.[5] In this same vein, there is the case of Timon of Athens, who begins his drama as a man "born to do benefits" and ends it on the side "opposite to humanity," or Romeo, who is all Rosalind, until he meets Juliet. In each of these cases, Shakespeare has carefully established protagonists whose particular Character and Personality are expressed in a certain stance toward the world, until he submits them to the machinery of reversal, which is substantially composed of the Identity-projects of other characters. "I did never think to marry," Benedick says to himself, and in that statement we hear the voice of all dramatic characters whose life currents are abruptly altered by the unforeseen. Identity must now redirect itself. What is amusing, pathetic, or tragic here is the persistence of person, Personality, and Character in the context of a new thrust into the world of action.

---

[5] I am using the word "project" (*projet*) in Sartre's sense: "Our being is immediately 'in situation'; that is, it arises in enterprises and knows itself first in so far as it is reflected in those enterprises. We discover ourselves then in a world peopled with demands, in the heart of projects in the course of realization'" (1956, 77). In her translator's note, p. 806, Hazel Barnes suggests that "project" is one's choice of the way of being in the world, expressed in action in the light of a future end.

Perhaps I am doing violence to the first meaning of identity: "the sameness of a person or thing at all times and in all circumstances." Let us bear in mind, though, that change as considered above is not inconstancy or flux. Identity, while it lasts, is directional or intentional behavior and, like anything else, subject to mutability. I am trying to capture the sense of doggedness and momentum in human behavior, though these terms may be too aggressive to suit drama's more gentle characters. Still, can we not speak legitimately of the doggedness of Chekhov's characters? And cannot one's momentum, like that of Hamlet and Vladimir and Estragon, take one in circles as well as in straight lines? Identity, in this respect, may be defined as the attachment of one's energies, voluntarily or involuntarily, actively or passively, consciously or unconsciously, to an enterprise. Identity differs from the gross sum of traits we call Character or Personality in roughly the same sense that a final cause differs from an efficient one. The mind, Aristotle says, "always does whatever it does for the sake of something, which something is its end." Identity, then, is one's end: it may take the form of an obsession, an *idée fixe*, a sustained exercise of will, a passion, a humor, a status, or a passive satisfaction or dissatisfaction in being what one is.

There is no doubt that the conversion of Identity is an essential force in the drama, from the spiritual conversions of the morality play to the secular conversions of comedy and sentimental drama. However, I would not suggest that Identity is necessarily a shifting phenomenon, for as often as not, it seems to remain as steady as the North Star. Crisis in drama comes normally from the conflict of individual identities that refuse to "give." For example, in Aeschylus's trilogy the spectacle of generational sin derives its pathetic force from the fact that each succeeding agent, from Atreus through Orestes, is obsessed with retaliation. It would be hard indeed to imagine characters with Identities more stubbornly focused toward a single end. This is, of course, Hegel's major point about Greek tragic character: Greek heroes adhere "irrefragably" to their projects. They "also no doubt [like modern heroes] act in accordance with their particular individuality; but this individuality is necessarily identical with an ethical pathos which is substantive" (1975, 84). Hence the peculiar sculptural, or "blind," quality of Greek characters, the impression that there is no auxiliary nature beyond the drive toward the deed. The Greek (and Aristotelian) concept of character permits a virtual collapse of our three terms into one: ethos, which is expressed only in moral choice. As Kierkegaard would say, to exist is to choose, and no other sector of characterization is needed. Thus the absence of a "ravaged interiority" (Barthes 1972a, 63) in Greek characters, at least until Euripides, and thus Aristotle's idea that as tragedy became more modern (and presumably more detailed and realistic in its characterization), it became more "characterless," that is, more displaced into subjective states of will.

The characters of comedy, particularly farce, are almost constant in their Identities. The point about the comic character is, in fact, that he or she is a kind of hedgehog who knows, or wants, only one thing. We might say that the comic character *is* an Identity whose dogged appetite is the guarantee of a certain predictable mirth, and out of Theophrastus's small book of vices you can virtually get comedy's entire arsenal of walking jokes. Obviously such stereotypes occur in tragedy as well, but, Shakespeare's genius for individuation aside, their presence (when not confined to the making of "comic relief") tends to undercut the tragic point by reminding us that self-repetition is basically a comic theme. Comedy, in general, requires the stereotype as the basic material out of which it builds a world that, above all else, is instantly recognizable—in Albert Cook's terms, "probable" as opposed to tragedy's "wonderful." Comedy depends on our recognition of causal absurdity as these probable Identities interact and create the improbable, whereas tragedy capitalizes on the consequences of individual choice—that is, on how the "single and peculiar life" (as Rosencrantz says) makes its peculiar motion, unleashes the causal chain, and in turn is itself changed, at least in Shakespeare. The difference between Falstaff and Hamlet is not that Falstaff is a comic stereotype and Hamlet a character of great depth. The difference is, rather, in the nature of their Identity projects: Hamlet's is basically an evolving search for commitment in a world made sterile by the outbreak of corruption; Falstaff's is basically one of self-repetition, emphasizing the gluttonous conversion of the world to his own value system.

Character, then, is a certain form of self-consistency in behavior within the field of change. The proper characterological alternatives are not "fixed personality" versus "fleeting catachresis" (or self as illusion), but something quite observable between the two extremes. We should take James quite literally here. Character is what determines incident, and incident is an illustration of character. Events, then, have character ("a brutal blow," "a gentle breeze"), and character is an event because it cannot be perceived unless in the form of an event (of speech, of motion). Character (and I am using the term here in its total sense), then, is neither a determinate dormancy or a floating essence but a performance grounded in what Erving Goffman calls a "person-role formula" (1986, 269–70).

Even so, from all of the person-role formulations that attend a given individual's social and private life—including those of characters in plays—there does emerge a common denominator or likeness that allows us to sense a certain coherence in behavior. In life we may on occasion be shocked by a friend's behavior (as Desdemona is shocked by Othello's). The odd thing, however, is that we, as audience, are not shocked by this same behavior, because it is embedded in a consistency (Aristotle's term) that has been established in Othello's repetitive behavior. And so in all drama: we are rarely surprised by character, because the perceptual code through which we view it in action precludes significant change. Even so, this mimetic restrictiveness applies primarily to the sector of Personality. Morals may change under the pressure of events or a conflict of roles; honorable men and women may be driven to desperate terms; and their Identity projects may shift radically. But Personality—with its inevitable basis in the physical person—is our bond of recognition with the character. Even a "good" character driven to murder commits a "good" murder—that is, he or she murders "in character."

So it is not so much change that occurs in the drama as fulfillment, an ideal projection of *being* into *doing*. The most appropriate word for this movement is "destiny," the shape given to the character's life by the interaction of nature and experience. Destiny, unlike Identity, is always a one-to-a-customer proposition. It is impossible, for instance, to imagine Macbeth returning to any sort of quotidian existence, not because he has murdered and must pay the price, but because that would be a meaningless repetition. Moreover, it is hard to think how he might live another life differently in the light of his knowledge about what his own has led to. In this he is like all dramatic characters: he *is* what he has done.

CHAPTER 10

Thought as Ventriloquism

In this chapter I am concerned with the topic that Aristotle most closely treats as thought, or *dianoia*. As I have noted already, Else calls attention to the "close affiliation between character and thought" as devices for revealing what is on the characters' minds, or in their souls (1967, 270). The concept of dianoia, it goes without saying, has been lavishly expanded to include the entire dimension of meaningfulness in a literary or dramatic work. Dianoia can be construed as meaning or as theme, and theme, as Seymour Chatman suggests, is "narrative content seen under its aspect of unity" (1978, 161); it is "a concept of a high degree of generality extractable from the work of fiction and relatable to coded human experiences, experiences of other real and fictional worlds" (164). Anything you can derive from a poetic work in the way of significance, then, is covered by the principle of dianoia. The Aristotelian idea that comes closest to this new investment of the term is his statement that "poetry speaks more of universals," unlike history, which speaks of "particulars." But Aristotle's example of a universal is simply, "what kind of person is likely to do or say certain kinds of things, according to probability or necessity" (sec. 11). In short, Aristotle hasn't the least interest in any metaphysical meanings a poem may contain (Else 1967, 306).

My specific interest in thought here centers not in metaphysical meanings so much as in the means or agencies through which meanings of various kinds are expressed by the play and in turn interpreted by the reader or viewer. For this particular purpose, I follow Aristotle rather than, say, Chatman. Hardison defines thought as "the objectification in language of reasoning and feeling" of the characters (Aristotle 1981, 244). I would broaden that definition in a dramaturgical direction as follows: Aristotle maintains that "the things [tragedies] imitate are three (plot, characters, thought)" (sec. 9). From an audience perspective, the *thing* that tragedy, or drama, imitates is really *one*—a character doing something or thinking thoughts (aloud). And how can one finally separate the doing from the thinking? For example, is Richard II pondering the nature of time in his cell in Pomfret Castle simply thinking? Does he only begin to *do* something when he lifts his sword to kill his assassin? In which instance is his character revealed more clearly? In short, I would treat the three parts as one object united by an overall objective that derives finally from the thinking of the author, for it is the author who causes the characters to do or say or think the things that give the play possible meanings and significance. In a sense, then, I am looking at the author-character relationship, the conduit through which meaning is conducted, somewhat as I looked at the actor as the conduit of our overall response to the play in Chapter 1.

By the author-character relationship, I do not mean the biographical presence of the author in the character (Shakespeare and Hamnet in *Hamlet*), but the conditions under which character is a product of manipulation. I would look at character, in other words, as a particular affective "construction" that appears in and is bound by a frame composed of other affective constructions (environment, behavioral limitations, other characters of the same "species," etc.), all of which constitute the "as if" world of the play. Each fictional world would be different from every other fictional world, though one would expect that all of the worlds created by a single author (say, Shakespeare) would have more in common with each other than with a world created by any other author (the stylistic level of perception). Moreover, any fictional world is different from the world of real experience in being a consequence of the elaborate "editorial" process called writing, or poetic composition (the mimetic level).

It might be useful, in advance, to examine briefly what this difference between worlds involves in terms of artistic process. I am drawn particularly to a discussion by Wolfgang Iser. In any act of fictionalizing, Iser suggests, we become involved in the realm of the imaginary through the artistic process of selection and combination. The imaginary is normally experienced "in fleeting impressions [fantasies, daydreams, reveries] that

defy our attempts to pin it down in a concrete and stabilized form."
Fiction is not "identical to the imaginary . . . ; [rather, it] endows the
imaginary with an articulate gestalt":

> Just as the fictionalizing act outstrips the determinacy of the real, so it
> provides the imaginary with the determinacy that it would not otherwise
> possess. In doing so, it enables the imaginary to take on an essential
> quality of the real, for determinacy is a minimal definition of reality. This
> is not, of course, to say that the imaginary *is* real, although it certainly
> assumes an appearance of reality in the way it intrudes into and acts upon
> the given world. (1993, 3)

The virtue of this distinction, or double process, is that it explains how
fiction occurs in a "space" known to every child or adult through fantasies,
dreams, and daydreams, yet one that carries with it, unlike these "dreamy"
realms, certain characteristics of empirical reality, such as determinacy or
objective availability. To return to our discussion in Chapter 1 of the Lascaux cave paintings, fiction occurs in a space equidistant between reality
and the imaginary: in fiction "extratextual reality merges into the imaginary, and the imaginary merges into reality"—precisely Merleau-Ponty's
point seen from a different perspective.

The author-character relationship is a reduced version of this double
process of "boundary crossing." We are constantly aware that a character
is both real and imaginary. But a character is real only according to standards established by the work, and not by standards of probability im-
ported from our own world. The behavioral determinacy of character, as
of everything else in the work, has been altered by a process we may call,
after Aristotle, *selective* probability and necessity. This is, obviously, what
makes it possible for Superman to fly faster than a speeding bullet without
raising our skepticism, but it is also what makes it impossible for the
Prozorov sisters to buy a ticket and go to Moscow. One might say, "Well,
they could if they really wanted to," and that may be true respecting
possibilities of economy and travel in Chekhov's world, but it is not true
with respect to the world-rules of the Chekhovian universe. Just as the
world-rules of Superman make it unnecessary for him to rely on trains and
buses (when he is in costume), so the world-rules of Chekhov make it
unlikely that anyone will resort to transportation as a way of getting

somewhere or making a dream come true. Transportation in Chekhov, as it turns out, is available only to people (Astrov, Vershinin, the Ranevskys) who are *leaving* the play-world, never to be seen again. Apart from the initial arrival of the outsiders, all travel in Chekhov occurs on a one-way street.

What we would be looking for, then, is the sense in which character, beneath its liveliness, is also an artificial construction made out of strategic forces that obtain only in the fictional world, however much this world may, in certain respects, remind us of possibilities in our own. As Iser puts it, "If we are to uncover the intention of a text, our best chance lies not in the study of the author's life, dreams, and beliefs but in those manifestations of intentionality expressed in the fictional text itself through its selection of and from extratextual systems" (6). In short, we would study the lingering evidence of absent authorship, or the sense in which characters are made to say and do things because an absent author has willed it, or, to put it another way, the sense in which the author sends messages via the characters with or without their psychological complicity. We might think of this approach as submitting character to a kind of lie-detector test, intending lie, in this case, to refer not to cheating on the part of the author (though there is often that as well) but to the author's way of telling certain truths through the licensed equivocations of illusion.

I can find no better model for this process than that of the ventriloquist and his or her doll. Here the "author" is right there before us, manipulative hand hidden in the doll's clothing. But this visible apparatus is part of the effect and purpose of such playing—the seemingly telekinetic endowment of the doll with an autonomous life and character by a one-armed person standing right there, halfheartedly pretending to have nothing to do with it. Such ventriloquism has its parallel to the creation of dramatic character in that part of our interest in the character always derives from its known artifactuality, which is precisely the source (among other things) of our neutrality toward the character's predicament. For instance, in real life we would deplore the behavior of an Iago, but the same behavior on the stage fascinates us because we know that, behind everything we see, it is only Shakespeare throwing his voice into the actor-puppet.

In its grossest sense, ventriloquism is the impression we sometimes have of a character mouthing the ideas of the author. More broadly, ventrilo-

quism is the very modus vivendi of dramatic (or any other) characterization, but we become aware of it, usually, only when we sense a forced
complicity or (in M. M. Bakhtin's term) a "double-voicedness" (110–31),
emerging in the speech. One might liken the effect to feedback distortion
in a sound system that reprocesses the echo of its own output as input. It
is hard to find examples that would be agreeable to everyone, because
character itself is a historically specific phenomenon. For example, a medieval moral allegory would probably not have struck its intended audience
as particularly ventriloquistic, because the line between mimesis and
theme was relatively narrow by generic expectation. Which is simply to
say that in certain forms and historical periods characterization itself is
expected to carry heavier, or at least different, cultural burdens than in
others, and liveliness may take the form of ideological or moral vitality, as
it does in a somewhat different sense in the sentimental drama of the
eighteenth century. In today's highly secular world, moral allegories of the
medieval or the sentimental kind would strike us as poorly disguised
sermons. However, we have our own livelier variety of the same genre in,
say, the detective movies in which vitality takes the form, on one hand, of
the hero's extraordinary skills in endurance and intelligence pitted against,
on the other, an "ambidexterous" villain every bit as evil (and as thinly
motivated) as the medieval Vice. It scarcely occurs to us that this is a
morality play, because our interest is focused on ingenious sleuthing,
weapon technology, and the spectacle of violence—things that must surely have had their equivalent in medieval realism. Moreover, the fact that
the cop-hero kills for a good cause is usually muted by his laconic manner
and the self-sacrificial sentiment that "killing may be bad, but someone
has to do it."

Another problem is that character is an extremely unstable construction, and one of the more difficult aspects of character study is that its
province does not stop with the characterization of people. Everything on
a stage has a character (the setting is gloomy; the day is bright and
cheerful), and everything is in character with the overall thematic character
of the play. One might even say that the characters of a play are complex
condensations, or personifications, of the scene itself, scene taken in the
larger sense of play-world. But sometimes this unity of impression gives
way to a monologic shift, or breakdown, in which the voice of the character seems to be usurped, or "possessed," by that of the author (who else?),

and we momentarily see through the rigging of the illusion to what we might call the thematic agenda behind it. Two simple examples are Madame Irma's closing speech in Genet's *The Balcony* and Charlie's choruslike requiem speech in *Death of a Salesman* ("No one dast blame this man . . ."), both of which seem aimed directly to the audience, as if the character (and the author) couldn't resist telling us what the play means. Yet, both of these instances are fully consistent with a certain expressionistic liberty the plays have earned for themselves (rather like moral allegories). Such liberty is itself part of the phenomenon of ventriloquism which may be said to range from the Aristophanic parabasis, to the epilogues of Renaissance to eighteenth-century plays, to Brechtian songs and Shavian monologues, to the most common examples of characters advancing opinions assumed to be held (or had better be) by their authors, such as (to take safe examples): it is wrong to steal from the poor, to kidnap children or to torture kittens; it is right to deplore racism, dictatorship, and arson. So ventriloquism is not necessarily a negative thing we are dealing with. To one degree or another it is always in play, characters having after all no more life of their own than Charlie McCarthy had without Edgar Bergen.

There are several kinds of ventriloquism. One kind occurs when we get the impression that an author is voting for or against something through a character, or is inclined to favor one moral or ethical option over another. Another occurs when the author needs something to happen in order to get on with the story, or to close it, and so we get an event that seems fortuitous or strained in its motivation or causality, but absolutely necessary to the plot. Examples of this type might be the poisoning of Gertrude in *Hamlet* and Edmund's last-minute confession in *Lear*. Then of course there are the dei ex machina of comedies (the sudden conversion of the villain, the arrival of a twin brother to fill out a hopelessly stalemated triangle of lovers, and so on). But these blend directly with a third type of ventriloquism which occurs when the genre or the audience requires a certain kind of conventional development from the author, such as the pathos scene in melodrama or the high-speed auto chase in modern police films. All of these levels of ventriloquism pervade dramatic composition and quite often blend into each other; all are aspects of representation in which the manipulative hand of the author comes into view, for better or worse (depending on the skill and the agenda of the author). Finally, there is also the ventriloquism of the stage director who sometimes gets obsessed by a concept, or as we say an "interpretation," that converts the play to a "mirror" reflecting a current social problem (*Titus Andronicus* set in Miami, *Richard II* timed to coincide with the Essex rebellion).

Obviously, a whole book could be written on artistic manipulation. Here I am mainly interested in characterizing the phenomenon through samples, not for the purpose of discrediting playwrights—all plays are manipulations—but of observing them at work. Without further preface, let me offer an example from Ibsen which has fascinated me for a long time. I choose Ibsen for several reasons: he happens to be the most classical (Aristotelian) playwright of the modern period, and he, more than anyone else, taught us how to use characters as tools of "clarification" under the illusion of lifelikeness. If Aristotle's linguistic conception of dianoia is to be found anywhere in modern drama, it is in Ibsen or in fellow "playwright-thinkers" (in Eric Bentley's term) such as Pirandello, Shaw, Genet, and Sartre. My example, however, is quite unspectacular, and it may even be a better example of the second level of ventriloquism than the first, but I think it inevitably feeds into the ideological point Ibsen is making in an interesting and subtle way. In act 3 of *Hedda Gabler*, directly following Tesman's return from the party at Madame Diana's, we have this exchange:

TESMAN: Were you worried about me, Hedda, eh?

HEDDA: That would never occur to me—I asked if you'd enjoyed yourselves?

TESMAN: Yes, we really did, Hedda. Especially at first—you see, Ejlert read me part of his book. We got there quite early, think of that— and Brack had all sorts of arrangements to make, so Ejlert read to me.

HEDDA (*Sits at right of table*): Yes?—Well?

TESMAN (*Sits on a stool near the stove*): Hedda, you can't conceive what a book it will be! I believe it's one of the most remarkable things that has ever been written. Think of that!

(Ibsen 1957, 400)

The question is, on what level do we accept Tesman's recognition that Lovborg's book is "one of the most remarkable things ever written"? Seeing the scene in the theater, you probably wouldn't doubt that Tesman is capable of making such a judgment. For one of the dividends of liveliness in the theater is that the actor's physical presence tends to conceal the seams in characterization. (Ibsen, we've always said, plays better than he reads.) In short, presentation in the theater detextualizes, or "real-izes," a play, and one of the consequences is that the actor's realization (in human form) upstages much of our skepticism respecting the likelihood of certain developments. What seems forced in the bare text through the perceptual weakness of textuality is obscured in the theater by the undeniable fact that it is happening before us. (For example, examine the lyrics of a popular song *without* the musical accompaniment, and the rhymes—devotion, ocean, emotion—become absurd.) On the other hand, as I noted in Chapter 2, when "thought" of any kind becomes too complex, too leisurely, too informational, too much its own end, the life-giving presence of the actor becomes an embarrassment of neglect. Then too, by this point in the play the overall *style* of representation would have gradually become invisible to the eye and inaudible to the ear—a good deal like getting used to the light of day when you wake up. So our awareness of style comes and goes at best, depending on one's mood of perception.

My own reaction seems to shift between extremes. On one hand, I think, "Yes, Tesman *could* feel this way. Why not? Why couldn't he be impressed by Lovborg's book?" and (my pupils thus dilated) I think about finding a better example of what I *want* to talk about. Then, on the other hand, it occurs to me that Tesman is really carrying an idea that doesn't belong to him—or one that seems to fit him like an oversized suit. Could this man, who could not have conceived such a book himself ("I should never have thought of writing anything of that sort" [act 2]) be expected to recognize the merit of a book so far from his presumed reading experience? Of course, there is no rule of psychology that says someone must be able to write a certain book in order to read it appreciatively. But what has Ibsen given us in the way of Tesman's capacities of appreciation or judgment? Ibsen's point all along has been to develop the difference between Tesman's pedantry and Lovborg's undisciplined genius, and one would think that among the things this difference might include would be Tesman's inability to understand what Lovborg is trying to do. Indeed, Ibsen himself notes the irony of Tesman helping to piece together Lovborg's book from the scraps of notes surviving its auto-da-fé, and that irony is sharpened to the extent that Tesman is seen as a boy sent to do a man's job. We could list, by way of further character evidence, Tesman's judgments about his wife and other people in the play, all of which are completely wrong. All of Hedda's innuendos respecting the narrowness of his specialty, her attitude toward his family, her clear fascination with Lovborg, Brack's sudden friendship, and so on, pass over his head without the slightest notice. There is not much evidence that Tesman is even aware that tension exists in his marriage: for example, he doesn't appear to hear Hedda's line, "That would never occur to me"—an awful thing for a wife to say to her husband. And if he is smart enough to see that Lovborg's book is "one of the most remarkable things ever written," a book apparently on the cutting edge of historiography, why can't he see that his wife detests everything he is or does? So, even if it were hypothetically possible for such a man to appreciate an intellectual achievement like Lovborg's, Tesman's character, as dramatized, seems incapable of any such recognition of genius. Tesman's primary stance in the play is to remain stupidly oblivious to everything that goes on around him—with this one curious exception.

So here is this judgment of Tesman's, ambiguously suspended between mimesis and editorial. It isn't firmly one or the other, but a kind of rabbit/duck proposition that varies according to the way you look at it. In any case, the passage contains, for me, the quintessence of Ibsenism, everything that Ibsen is as a rabbit/duck maker of character, and to be detained by it, as I have been here, is simply—and artificially—to arrest a smooth stylistic performance at one of its barely noticeable seams of emergence. I admit that you have to look hard to see it, but once you have the range you begin to see how it pervades Ibsen's style of characterization and the sense in which he is continually requiring that his characters see or do not see, and do or do not do, things according to his thematic plan. For beyond this instance, one could as well ask why Lovborg would bother to read his book to Tesman in the first place. We know what he thinks of Tesman ("—how could you throw yourself away!" he says to Hedda in act 1), and yet he has specifically brought the book with him in order to read it to Tesman, as if he valued Tesman's judgment. Here again, psychological consistency seems stretched to accommodate the act's convenience to the plot. For Ibsen's theme requires that Lovborg's book be read or heard by someone in the play in order to increase the significance of its loss, and thereby the enormity of Hedda's deed. There is no one else in the play in a position to hear it, short of Judge Brack, and his interest in history, or the future, seems to begin and end with his plan for Hedda's afternoons. Indeed, what are we to make, ventriloquistically, of the two closing lines of the play—Tesman's "Shot herself in the temple! Think of that!" and Brack's "Good God—but—people don't *do* such things!"—except that such drastic specificity on the instant of a violent event, before shock could conceivably give way to hermeneutics, seems less attributable to normal human response than to its role in closing the dialectic Ibsen has all along been advancing between convention and self-integrity.

My purpose is not a criticism of Ibsen, who fascinates me immensely, but an attempt to isolate a certain level at which we receive character as a construction owing to the author's real purposes in writing. It is precisely the falsity of character that is my focus, and I use the term "falsity" in the sense of Iser's notion of the necessary lie on which all fiction is founded. But in order to see such falsity one must, like a defense lawyer, suspend one's belief in the innocence of the illusion and the artist's right to a perfectly necessary duplicity. Moreover, all of these events can be explained in one way or another. For example, one might argue that Lovborg needed the assurance of *someone* at this point (things being as desperate as they are), and like most of us he sought the nearest ear—the only fellow historian in town. Why not? And this is certainly a reading a good actor could convey in performance. So the point is not to discover inconsistencies in characterization, but to see that inconsistencies—or forced consistencies—are precisely what makes a character *a certain kind* of character rather than any old character, a real person, or a being from the world of fiction rather than the empirical world. One could run through Shakespeare and find similar seams in character and event, or telltale places where we see the thinking playwright at work, but such places would be different in kind from those in Ibsen (or anyone else), owing primarily to the different assumptions about what constitutes theme and to what end thought is put.

Merleau-Ponty tells us that the eye of the painter "sees what inadequacies [*manques*] keep the world from being a painting" (1964, 165). Translated into character formation, the idea might read, "The dramatic poet sees what inadequacies keep real people from being characters, and one of these is that real people are not bound in a thematic context: they get to do pretty much what they want to do or are used to doing." In real life, a Tesman might say to his wife, "Eilert's book is interesting enough. He's a smart man. But I don't think many people will care to read this sort of thing." That wouldn't do at all in an Ibsen play, if only because the speed and rational unfolding of his plot makes such personal detours into jealousy, self-doubt, rationalization, and so forth, irrelevant. In another play (e.g., one by Chekhov), these might be central qualities of behavior. At any rate, the best place to observe character construction is just in these textual seams, for it is only in the gap between character speech and authorial speech—when you can locate it—that character tips the author's hand before the interpretive act of an actor covers up the traces. And here is an essential difference between Ibsen and his contemporary opposite, Chekhov: in Ibsen the sphere of causality is intimately fused with the sphere of comprehension, or what is perhaps better referred to as clarification in view of the tenacity with which the Ibsen play gives birth to its idea: the event unfolds only to produce the ideational consequence. An almost self-parodic example occurs at the very end of *Enemy of the People:*

DR. STOCKMAN: . . . I have made a great discovery, you see.

MRS. STOCKMAN: Not another, Tomas, dear?

DR. STOCKMAN: Another, yes—another! Yes. (*Gathers them around him, and speaks in a confidential tone*) And I'll tell you what it is: the strongest man in the world is he who stands alone.   (1957, 255)

This final line has the quality of a syllogism closing on itself, and it is a perfect instance of Aristotelian thought as a discrete unit of rhetoric. For it is symptomatic of Ibsen's people to have thoughts of just this sort. Recognitions, large and small, are as indispensable to Ibsen as the ostrich syndrome is to Chekhov. They occur every time a new character enters the room, and there is rarely an instance in Ibsen in which the audience knows more than at least one of the characters on stage. Behind the alertness of the Ibsen character—at least of the protagonist and the antagonist—is a litmus sensitivity to the slightest change in comportment, and as a consequence the interest of the Ibsen play is chiefly that of the conversion of events into symbols:

> BRACK: Cheer up! Your wedding trip is over now.
> HEDDA (*Shaking her head*): Not by a long shot. No, we've only stopped at a station on the line.
> BRACK: Then the thing to do is to jump out and stretch oneself a bit, Mrs. Hedda.
> HEDDA: I never jump out.
> BRACK: Why not?
> HEDDA: There's always someone there waiting to—
> BRACK (*Laughing*): Stare at your legs, you mean?
> HEDDA: Precisely. (1957, 375)

Here is the texture of innuendo that Ibsen will pass on to his student, Harold Pinter. Here dialogue, conversation itself, is a conscious evolution of strategies, a speaking in tongues that preserves the requirements of manners at the same time that it bespeaks another language of intimidation locked beneath it, like the weasel under the cocktail cabinet, in Pinter's own metaphor. In both playwrights, the act of conversation, especially between antagonists, is itself a mimesis of comprehension, of meaning being made, or of experience being constituted only by meaning and intentionality, as if conversation were not a quotidian situation that is taking place but Destiny itself. To confine our focus only to Ibsen, however, here the psychological and the thematic levels are fused, thus giving rise to (among other things) the high frequency of oracular statements by the characters, that peculiar attraction of the Ibsen character, at least the unconventional ones, to the symbolic order ("I'm burning your child, Thea!"), or:

> HEDDA: . . . Well, at least I have one thing to amuse myself with.
> TESMAN (*Beaming*): Thank heaven for that. What is it, Hedda, eh?
> HEDDA: (*At center opening—looks at him with suppressed scorn*):
>   My pistols, Jörgen.
> TESMAN: Your pistols!
> HEDDA (*With cold eyes*): General Gabler's pistols. (1957, 370)

Even the ignorant characters in Ibsen have a knack for making the apt trivial remark that feeds the idea ("That's a very elegant hat you've treated yourself to"). In Chekhov, such a line would belong at most to the order of phatic conversation, or the conversation that covers silence with human noise; nothing would come of it but further silence and our awareness of the arbitrariness of the content in most Chekhovian speech and objects. Imagine, for instance, an Ibsen character getting birthday presents, like Irina's silver samovar and a high school yearbook, whose meaning was exhausted in their inappropriateness.

There is an exception to this point, but one that will better illustrate the difference in technique and world view between Ibsen and Chekhov. As an Ibsenian moment in Chekhov, consider Olga's remark about Natasha's belt in act 1 of *Three Sisters* ("You're wearing a green belt! My dear, it's not right!" [Chekhov 1977, 117]); and in act 4, under reverse circumstances, Natasha returns the favor to Irina ("My dear, that belt doesn't suit you at all. . . . It's tasteless." [156]). This is rather like Aunt Juliana's new hat in the sense of the first reference being a "plant" for the second, though in Chekhov the second shoe is almost a whole play in falling. But if you look at what is made of the plant in either case, you see that Ibsen uses Juliana's hat to illustrate Hedda's revulsion toward the family she has inherited through a casual conversation that led to her marriage. Beyond that it figures prominently in the whole question of woman's options in the world, represented, on one hand, by Aunt Juliana and Thea Elvsted who are, so to speak, wearing the hats of feminine self-sacrifice throughout the play. So the hat is attached fore and aft to the play's master argument. Without much trouble, one could condense the whole dialectic of *Hedda Gabler* into the symbolism of the hat and the pistol, which are the options available to a woman with Hedda's problem—feminine servitude or suicide.

It is harder to say what motivates the belt business in Chekhov. I can't see that he is using Olga's snobbishness to make a thematic point, or at least nothing comes of the snobbishness. One could scarcely say that if Olga and her sisters were more tolerant of the lower classes (Natasha), their course of life would have been different. To put it another way, if the Natasha principle triumphs over the Prozorov principle in the end, it has nothing to do with social attitudes.[1] One doesn't have the sense that Chekhov is loading an argument or a dialectic between two positions; the episode is just his means of reminding us punctually who is now in control of the house. In Ibsen, on the other hand, something will come of everything. The hat is instrumental in setting up the Ibsen dialectic; as a consequence, character psychology can no longer be confined in the limits of behavioral consistency. Or rather, behavioral consistency is coterminous with thematic development.

In Chekhov, however, the only truly functional dialectic runs between *any* and *all* spoken philosophies or principles of existence, on one hand, and, on the other, a causal series unleashed by an author irresistibly drawn to the impasse, if not the dead end of living. And through this technique Chekhov was, in a manner of speaking, free to do something with character that Ibsen wasn't: to create the most lifelike of all stage characters whose primary duties in his plot were to enter the room on the slenderest of pretexts ("Where are my galoshes?") and, once there, to be devastatingly themselves. It is in the entrance or the exit of the character (e.g., Vershinin's first entrance in *Three Sisters*, Astrov's exit at the end of *Vanya*) that the main plot function is served; what the characters talk about while on stage is, at best, a temporary alleviation, or a refreshing variation in the "persistent low-keyed unpleasure" of life, in David Riesman's apt phrase. Thus Chekhov is the master of "plotless" or situational drama in which nothing happens but a predictable escalation of human possibilities from bad to worse. Chekhov's world is dominated by the principle of randomness; but this does not mean that his plays are disorderly. The randomness is a mask worn by a brutal form of causality that is as orderly as a surgical procedure. We do not meet Chekhov's like again in the theater until midcentury when Samuel Beckett, having perfected the novel of progressive self-deterioration, decided to try his hand at plays.

But one might ask, what of ideas in Chekhov, of which there are plenty? I can only come back to Francis Fergusson's statement that Chekhov's

---

[1] More to the point, we may note that Chekhov is generally fastidious about the symmetry of his beginnings reappearing in his endings; that is, in leaving his people more or less where they started (only far worse off), and the belt business, as a framing device, fits right in with the repetition of the firing of the guns and the military band that both open and close the play. This neatness of design (the *plus ça change* principle) in Chekhov marks the evolution of the fateful process of dispossession.

plays "predicate nothing." I doubt one could improve on this basic perception. Search as you will in Chekhov's plays for evidence of a thesis, you will not find *his* thesis in positions taken by the characters. If there is a thesis (and this would be stretching the notion of theme in an odd direction), it must be found in the plot itself—that is, in the arrangement of the events, rather than in a debate or a progressing dialectic in which characters serve as more or less conscious carriers of ideas. For in a sense, all plot arrangements might be said to prepare a thesis in the author's more or less conscious manipulation of events to a certain inevitable conclusion. It is Chekhov, finally, who gives Lopakhin the money and incentive to buy the Ranevsky estate. The Soviet interpretation of this event may be that Lopakhin has the right attitude toward work and industry, whereas the Ranevskys have the wrong idea. But one doubts that this is what Chekhov meant by the transaction, or at least that this is all, or centrally, what he meant by it—which is not in the least to say that the play can't be made to mean that. One of the most interesting things about Chekhov, and for me the thing about him that is most like Shakespeare, is his remarkable ability to draw flawed people without blaming them or bringing the house down around them because they aren't perfect.

In Chekhov, ideas have a peculiar impotence; however much Chekhov may privately share a belief in certain ideas advanced by his characters, they always seem to emerge directly from the character's psychology, much as ideas do in the real world. Without knowing anything about Chekhov's personal philosophy, we could probably assume that he endorsed the idea of work, as opposed to daydreaming or philosophizing, simply because most of us would take the same position; but those who preach the philosophy of work in his plays are usually sitting down when they do so. In short, "We must work!" usually has the character either of a self-admonition or a *plan* for distant action, something we needn't do today. In his ironic manner, then, isn't Chekhov lamenting this very thing in his people—talking about work rather than doing it? Possibly. But is this lament something his plays say or something a reader assumes they say, as we assume that Chekhov wouldn't agree with Solyony about frying and eating children? Those who do work in Chekhov (the doctors, estate managers, schoolteachers, and servants) are in no sense shown as better off than those who preach the work ethic. Thus work, as a possible solution to life's ills, is given the character of a chore, as opposed to a pride of achievement or what people unavoidably, if not cheerfully, do in order to fill their days—as, for instance, certain characters profitably do in Tolstoy, where the smell of new-mown hay is thematically equated with the breath of God. Working does not seem to make life any better in Chekhov: you will inevitably catch the virus of *nastroenie* whether you work or not.

But, one might ask, what about Astrov's philosophy of ecological destruction? It is well known that Chekhov often gives his own ideas and habits (Solyony's cologne) to his characters, and we know that Astrov's lament for the vanishing greenbelt is Chekhov's as well and that one of his purposes in having the good doctor offer a speech on this theme was very likely to make Russians aware of the problem he had himself tried to confront on his own estate at Melachivo (Simmons 1962, 270–71). But *Uncle Vanya* is not a play about this problem, and the lecture's main function is to serve as an excuse for Yelena's inquiry about Astrov's intentions toward Sonya. In short, Astrov's lament has about as much to do with any idea being explored by the play as the harmfulness of tobacco has to do with the theme of Ivan Ivanovich Nyukhin's lecture on "the terrible poison" that has made his life so miserable. The entire motif, sincere and important as it may be in Astrov's (or Chekhov's) mind, is, as it were, divested of thematic significance by the very casualness and inconsequence of its appearance. It is an idea without the teeth of its author's dramaturgic backing. It is not debated or countered by another idea but by a circumstance of life. One might claim that the theme of the destruction of the forest parallels the destruction of human hopes in the play, but this is not an analogy that Chekhov pursues very far. It is probably not a wrong reading of the play, but to make much of a thematic predication of it is rather like reading Kafka as an admonition against paranoia.

How can one tell when the author is putting his or her themes in the mouth of the character, ventriloquistically? Suppose one character says to another, "The weather is beautiful today. I don't know why my heart's so light!" How is the author speaking here? Well, it is after all the author who is making the day beautiful, and in this sense the character is perpetuating a condition the author has deliberately created. Weather, in plays, is usually thematically appropriate. But we are not likely to think of it as the author's doing; if we do, the entire play will end up being spoiled for us, because there will be nothing left to accept as part of the freedom of the characters, and the illusion itself will disappear. We are more likely to see the character as reacting to a condition that in some way we accept as part of the play's "given," rather than as the author's ulterior point. That is to say, if there is to be a play, there must be weather, environment, and such elements as go into the making of a world, and today it happens to be "beautiful." So the nice day is a detail much like the "once upon a time" that initiates the telling of the story.

Now suppose a character says to another character, "Not only in two or three hundred but in a million years, even, life will be just the same as it was; it doesn't change, it stays constant, following its own laws, which are none of our affair." Is this Chekhov speaking, in some other sense than he was speaking Irina's line above? It is certainly an idea, of sorts. But our interpretation of its status must be determined by the manner in which the play manipulates and disposes of it. For one thing, in this scene the speaker, Tusenbach, is debating the question of human happiness with two other characters, Vershinin and Masha, both of whom advance different ideas about the issue. Here, then, we do have a genuine debate, but the ideas being advanced come to the same fate as the idea of the vanishing forests in *Vanya*. They are simply the materials out of which the surface texture of the play is constituted. There is no reason to assume that Tusenbach is advancing Chekhov's preferred opinion, though it is possible to see the argument itself as a typical Chekhovian one. (One can't imagine Ibsen's people sitting around "philosophizing" like this.) Moreover, a student of Chekhov's work in general might make a convincing case for locating his real sympathies with Tusenbach, as opposed to Vershinin or Masha, by showing through personal letters, pronouncements, and the rest of the oeuvre that Chekhov continually prefers this notion in subtle or deliberate ways. I am not claiming that he does, but literary criticism spends a good deal of time converting texts like Tusenbach's into manifestations of an author's system of values. And when you can prove that an author shares an idea or a position with a character, then you would seem to have a smoking gun that suggests a palpable ventriloquism at the ideological level.

But this is not at all the case. When an author's self-declared philosophy appears in a play, it is not necessarily an instance of ideological ventriloquism. A good case in point is Georg Büchner's nihilistic philosophy of "must" that one finds in his letters. Here is a belief that Büchner must have held, and he thought enough of it to put it directly into his protagonist's mouth in *Danton's Death*. Moreover, Danton is one of those literary characters, like Hamlet, that you feel must have been written from the inside, that is, out of the author's own being and character. How else could anyone probe such dark subjectivity without having lived it, been in those shoes? Still, Shakespeare isn't Hamlet and Büchner isn't Danton, and the "must" sentiment isn't one of those lines that strikes you as overtly ventriloquistic, or as something Büchner *wants* you to believe in the sense, say, that you suspect Arthur Miller wants you to believe that Willie Loman shouldn't be blamed for what the capitalistic world does to him.[2]

But I would argue that the only way you can detect true ventriloquism is through matching the ideological statement against the conduct and outcome of the plot, as opposed to the real world on which it is more or less based. No doubt all these ideas have something to do with Chekhov's system of values, though it would be difficult to determine how they bear on that system. The more likely possibility is that an author may—at least until such opinions become more and more strident and "authorial"—be using his or her own ideas to a dramatic rather than to an ideological end, much as an actor might use to advantage a long and ungainly nose that embarrassed him or her so much in real life.

Where, then, would we locate ventriloquism in Chekhov? The obvious parallel to my Tesman passage from Ibsen would be the Olga-Tusenbach-Chebutykin exchange discussed in Chapter 6 as a variety of irony. Except in the ubiquitous stylistic sense, Chekhov's voice is not to be heard in the voices of his characters, nor are his characters instruments of clarification in the sense that Tesman frames Lovborg's achievement for our benefit in order to maximize the symbolism of Hedda's burning of the manuscript. In Chekhov the characters say nothing that could be attributed to the author in the sense that it had to be got into the play if the theme is to be articulated; they remain perfectly bound by their own likelihoods (nothing un-characteristic, or strained, is said or done here). As long as Chebutykin and Tusenbach said something *like* what they say, something *antiphonal*, the purpose has been served. And here again, we are at the very base of character construction where we can see the vast difference

---

[2] The scene in Howard's office, for instance, seems clearly designed to serve this function. Why else is Howard, the one example of capitalism in the play, depicted as so insensitive to Willy's frustration?

between the Chekhov and Ibsen dialectics at large. The Ibsen dialectic is formed out of opposing versions of thought and action: the Gabler versus the Tesman principles, the conventional life versus the daring life, feminine self-sacrifice versus masculine professional rivalry (with Hedda poised androgynously between the two), and so on. The Chekhov dialectic, on the other hand, occurs *between* character and world, not between ideological positions held by the characters in the world.

The key to Fergusson's idea that Chekhov's drama "predicates nothing," then, lies in the fact that Chekhov doesn't conceive his characters as integers in an ethical or an ideological equation. There is a presumption in Chekhov that the ethical speaks for itself and that ideology, as a vehicle of ethics (i.e., what's wrong with society?) has very little to do with life at the level at which Chekhov is observing it. Ideas in Chekhov are not *causal* factors in the plot; nor are they reactions to immediate effects in the causal series (as they are, for example, in Pirandello, where a surprising peripety will unleash an elaborate philosophical explanation you're certain Pirandello himself believes in); nor, finally, are they a running translation of the action into a conceptual sphere (as they are in Sartre or Shaw, where a character's actions or reactions to a dilemma work hand in glove with the author's thematics). Ideas in Chekhov have the status of conversations aboard moving trains: they may express truths or conflicting viewpoints about life that Chekhov may or may not have believed, but the direction and speed of the train is in no way altered by them. Thus thought, judgment, and recognition are peculiarly isolated from any possible technique for living life more pleasantly. Typically in Chekhov, ideas or attitudes expressed in the course of the play become, if anything, simply intensified at the end, and they pass without change from one character to another, like a flu virus. It is not that the character has been influenced by the attitude. No one says, "I've been thinking about Colonel Vershinin's philosophy of the future life, and it is beginning to make sense." Rather, the philosophy has simply been passed along, absorbed through a kind of genetic osmosis, out of sheer repetition. As a consequence, one can scarcely claim that the ideas arrived at are either the seed or the fruit of new possibilities or that they represent on the verbal level what has been learned from what has passed in the action. What the three Prozorov sisters have to say about work and the future life at the end of act 4 springs from the same psychology of deferral that leads doomsday societies to set a new date when the world fails to end on the day they have scheduled. Compare such speeches to the endings of any Ibsen play—which bristle, in Dr. Stockman's word, with discovery and resolution—and you see how speech and action intersect in one instance (Ibsen) and how they follow parallel paths to infinity in the other (Chekhov).

I am not in the least claiming that Ibsen's meanings are clearer or more obvious than Chekhov's. My comments have strictly to do with the face of character which comes forth in each case and how character behaves in relation to thought. I don't have any clearer sense of why Hedda burns Lovborg's manuscript or shoots herself than I know why the Prozorovs let Natasha dispossess them of their property. So it isn't a matter of Chekhov being "deeper" than Ibsen or of Ibsen being "clearer" than Chekhov. If one has the impression that Ibsen is more explicit than Chekhov or more parliamentary in his conduct of the argument, it arises not from the answers he supplies (none) but from his way of putting the questions.

We are led to the conclusion that ventriloquism occurs along a spectrum from objective to subjective. In any case, the subjective presence of the ventriloquist is always felt stylistically, though the subjectivity of style may also be that of a historical period (naturalism) or a poetic tradition (Gongorism). Beyond style, however, there is sometimes the pronounced subjectivity of an ideational agenda springing directly from the author. Objectivity, on the other hand, does not imply that the author has an objective view of the world at large or that the view can't be called pessimistic or optimistic by the audience, only that the view is, so to speak, the given from which an investigation follows. We begin to sense objectivity when an author knowingly or unknowingly sets up structures or options that debate each other within the dimensions of a topic or theme. Objectivity begins to fade into subjectivity as one of the voices in the structure wins and the other loses, giving the impression that the theme is becoming a thesis.

For example, a scientist investigating the causes and behavior of a plague would certainly do so objectively, but one could hardly say that he or she was pessimistic or cynical in choosing the plague as a topic of investigation. The plague is simply something that is *there* and must be dealt with scientifically if any good is to be done. Poetic themes are no different, though it is probable that poets are led to certain themes on rather different incentives than scientists are led to study the plague. Still, what is there is there; what occurs in the world of human psychic or social action needs poets to deal with it, though the curative results of art are not the same as those of science, assuming the investigation is successful in either case.

Thus Chekhov, Beckett, and Kafka are sometimes called depressing or nihilistic or negative about human possibilities. But such opinions are less important than that such "depressing" visions are legitimate assessments of the world (insofar as they are convincing) and that Beckett and Kafka examine the grounds for holding them in an objective manner. Consider, for instance, how Kafka's world of "atrocious institutions" (Borges's phrase) and psychic paranoia might be expressed by a hack who was out to prove that things are this bad or who threw his hands up in despair, like one of Pirandello's *raisoneurs*. One has the feeling in reading Kafka's version of the world that the drive or motive of the work is to offer a thorough description of the condition as perceived. Hence in the bleakest pages of Kafka (or Beckett), one senses a *reserve*, or a holding back—not, by far, of the extremity of the condition itself but of emotion (despair, for example)—respecting how one faces the fact of the condition. Ventriloquism of this sort isn't selective; it doesn't manifest preferences, it manifests an equanimity of mind and a levelheaded curiosity that doesn't blink at anything. It says, in so many words, that to have gone less far would be to speak an untruth, to have biased the evidence. Indeed, it is to say what Shakespeare puts in the mouth of Edgar: "The worst is not, so long as we can say, 'This is the worst'" (*Lear*, 4.1.27–28). In short, when the poet is caught saying, or thinking, "this is the worst," the voice loses its authority in the self-pity of its conviction.

As I write, David Mamet's play *Oleanna* is being widely discussed. It is concerned with sexual harassment, one of the most powerful themes in present society, and it will doubtless provoke strong arguments pro and con as to which "side" Mamet has taken, that of the female student or the professor. No doubt a director could project either view in a theatrical interpretation. What makes this possible, in part, is that Mamet has maintained a remarkable degree of what I have here been calling poetic objectivity. You may disagree. But I can think of any number of ways he might have altered his case to gain or reduce sympathy for one or the other of the two characters. As the play is written, however, the fault seems to me equally distributed or at least to arise, on either side, out of a complexity of understandable reactions as the play progresses. The real theme of the play is not who is in the wrong, or where the wrong rests in social terms, but how wrong and misunderstanding arise reciprocally in situations of this sort—this is "the kind of thing that *can* happen," as Aristotle would say. The play is thus an anatomy, a certain *climate* of fear, rather than an accusation or an exposure of a unilateral source of that fear. It allows you think, rather than doing your thinking for you. But precisely because of the play's balance, it is open to manipulation, in either direction, to a degree that thesis drama normally is not.

Some years ago, we got the idea, mainly through Jan Kott, that *King Lear* was an absurdist play, a dark endgame of the world in which innocence is the victim of a malevolent world order. One can grant that Shakespeare may have been in a darker mood in *King Lear* than he was in *As You Like It*, or even in *Hamlet* or *Macbeth*. But we might think of a poet's change of mood as less a shift in belief or loss of confidence in the human race than as a consequence of a directed curiosity. Scientists who specialize in turbulence tend to learn more and more about turbulence. Poets who write tragedies tend to learn more and more about what tragedy is. They achieve this by exploring the possibilities of the genre, and their advances over time tend to lead them in directions they haven't been, if for no other reason than that self-repetition is the deadly enemy of art. What the absurdist view of *King Lear* requires, of course, is that certain features of the play be squinted out, beginning with Shakespeare's manner of balancing his vision so that waste and value are held in a typical Shakespearean equipoise, as I have suggested blame is held in Mamet's play. What triumphs in *Lear* is not the "good" or the "bad" but the voice of a poet who understood the mechanism of how one is revealed in and by the other. Unfortunately, such points of balance are easy to overlook in a play when you are reading out of a frame of reference that is itself unbalanced. In such cases, one might say that it is the reader, or the age, that ventriloquizes the play, and all ages do this in their own way. Galileo was condemned, Umberto Eco tells us, "not for logical reasons (in terms of True or False) but for semiotic reasons—inasmuch as the falsity of his factual judgments is proved by recourse to contrary semiotic judgments of the type 'this does not correspond to what is said in the Bible'" (1984, 85).

And so it works out that we "condemn" Shakespeare, or any artist, to our own meanings by making semiotic judgments of his work he could not possibly have understood. This is not a reason to reject interpretations like Kott's as incomplete but to see them as unavoidable readings of our own culture, rather than as Shakespeare's reading of his own.

CHAPTER 11

Tragedy Today

It doesn't seem likely that if Aristotle's lost poetics of comedy had survived we would be debating whether comedy is any longer possible today. However, I suspect this to be the case with his *Poetics* on tragedy. It is not strictly that the *Poetics* is the *cause* of our debate on the death of tragedy, but most flourishing conceptions of tragedy as a genre or a structure go back to Aristotle (the philosophy of tragedy is something else), and in most cases they go back directly, bypassing interim revisions along the way (i.e., neoclassicism, romanticism). Brecht is an altogether symptomatic case in point. "The principle of imitation," he writes, has been replaced by the "gestic principle":

> This marks the great revolution in the art of drama. The drama of our time still follows Aristotle's recipe for achieving what he calls catharsis (the spiritual cleansing of the spectator). In aristotelian drama the plot leads the hero into situations where he reveals his innermost being. All the incidents shown have the object of driving the hero into spiritual conflicts. . . . The individual whose innermost being is thus driven into the open then of course comes to stand for Man with a capital M. Everyone (including every spectator) is then carried away by the momentum of the events portrayed, so that in a performance of *Oedipus* one has for all practical purposes an auditorium of little Oedipuses. (1966, 86–87)

So we are essentially back where we began: the spectrum of possibilities for drama runs a course between Aristotelian and non-Aristotelian. And as we move to the latter extreme, the possibilities for writing tragedy become slimmer and slimmer. Thus, in a subtle process through which the theory and practice of drama have become equated, we have effectively decided that tragedy is dead because we are no longer writing according to the Aristotelian formula. Tragedy and Aristotle have become synonymous.

The debate itself has been a frustrating and sentimental affair, in Schiller's sense that we are outside looking nostalgically back at something apparently lost to us, something practiced and experienced simply or naturally by others who shared beliefs different from our own. The question is, what is supposed to be lost—the genre or the vision, or both? Thomas Van Laan suggests that the two are inseparable: "Tragedy, I presume, cannot exist without the tragic vision, and I also presume that the tragic vision can exist only through and because of tragedy" (1991, 29). I am in general agreement with Van Laan (against the arguments of Joseph Wood Krutch, Lionel Abel, George Steiner, and others) that tragedy survives and that it does so, and will probably continue to do so, through all cultural change. But there are some implications in Van Laan's remark which call for a closer look, not as a critique of Van Laan but as another way of conceiving the problem.

Van Laan seems to be saying that tragedy and the tragic vision are two distinct things with a symbiotic relationship to each other. One is not the other, but one is impossible without the other. But how are they different things? Do they have the relationship of, say, form to content, product to process, representation to theme, poem to poet (or seer)? I assume he means that the tragic vision somehow depends upon tragic poems, plays, and novels as its (more or less) material foundation. But there are testaments of tragic vision in philosophy which barely mention tragic works, either as products of the vision or as a necessary source of its appearance. Even if this weren't the case, however, it is quite possible to develop a tragic theory of human experience without much, or any, reference to tragedy itself. Surely, then, we must assume the possibility that there are people in the world who are what Murray Krieger would call "tragic visionaries" even though they have never read or seen or written a tragedy.[1] Improbable perhaps, but something to consider.

---

[1] For Krieger, the tragic visionary seems to be the protagonist, not the author. For example, if an author "becomes one with his tragic visionary, he so cuts himself off from

Perhaps Van Laan's statement is better taken to mean that tragedy can exist only through and because of the tragic vision in the sense that it is the vision that determines the nature of the work. The visionary artist "sees" the world tragically and then imitates what he or she sees in a work we would call a tragedy. Still, this reading isn't adequate either, because it suggests that all works legitimately called tragedies are necessarily informed by a tragic vision, or, taking visionary in Krieger's sense (and perhaps Van Laan's), that all tragedies have tragic visionaries as their protagonists. It is relatively easy to accept either of these notions in the cases of certain (but by no means all) tragic works by Aeschylus, Sophocles, Euripides, Shakespeare, Racine, Dostoevsky, and Thomas Mann; but the notions become questionable when applied to Kyd, Jonson, Corneille, or Dryden, who wrote tragedies that do not seem, on the whole, to inspire reference to a tragic vision or to have protagonists who could be called visionaries. Finally, to take the case nearest to us, *Death of a Salesman* seems in every respect a "true" tragedy, if only because its author deliberately set out to write one and has as much right to the term as the authors of *A Yorkshire Tragedy* and *The London Merchant*. But something about the play suggests that Miller's vision, not to mention Willy's, is far from what one might call tragic—at least in the sense that we say Sophocles or Shakespeare or Dostoevsky or Thomas Mann, in their foremost tragedies, see the world tragically. This has nothing whatever to do with the quality of *Salesman* as a play, but with the modesty of its conception of the origin and metaphysical depth of human catastrophe. Indeed, I wonder if any *deliberate* attempt to write tragedy, in modern or any other terms, can spring from a truly tragic vision. The very premeditation of such a project implies *some other* kind of orientation (social, aesthetic, reactionary), something, in short, like Maxwell Anderson's attempt to bring verse back to tragedy, because "it is inescapable that prose is the language of information and poetry the language of emotion" (1947, 50). Can one imagine Kafka saying, "It's time we wrote about angst," and sitting down to write *The Trial*?

This is not the issue I want to discuss here. My feeling, however, is that

---

man's communal need that, in surrendering to moral chaos, he surrenders also the only possibility left him to impose aesthetic form" (1960, 19). I am using the term throughout to refer to the tragic author or philosopher of the tragic vision.

tragic visionaries are not produced by social or aesthetic motives and that they occur more or less as the great comic, epic, and religious visionaries occur—rarely and in single numbers. I think we are inevitably forced to disengage, or at least loosen, the bond between tragedy as a genre and tragic vision as a philosophical or a thematic standpoint. The two do not *necessarily* occur together, though they are apt to be co-present and indistinguishable in many of the works that make up the canon of the world's great tragedies. All that we can say with some assurance is that something about the tragic form invites tragic vision, and something about tragic vision moves some of its visionaries, some of the time, to write tragedies (while others write music or paint, others do philosophy, and still others simply carry on with what Miguel de Unamuno called a tragic sense of life). But there is also something about the tragic form that invites the melodramatic "vision" (the strong organization of human energy into good/bad polarities), the satanic, the didactic, the ethical, the sentimental, and the pathetic, all of which *might* serve as a perspective from which to write a tragedy and yet have little to do with a fully tragic vision.

For example, I might try my hand at comedy, but the result, though recognizable *as* a comedy, may get a few laughs but be far from comic; and one of the deficiencies may be precisely that I have no comic vision but know only how to string a few jokes together. The same is true for certain writers of tragedy who knew only how to string a few deaths together. In the 1620s, William Rowley wrote a play called *All's Lost by Lust*, which contains so many gratuitous murders and suicides in the last act that you are reminded of Monty Python. To say that Rowley wrote a tragedy seems unavoidable; to claim that he was animated by the tragic vision is to make a visionary of every hack who has ever cashed in on the tragic form.

Of course one might say, "Yes, but isn't an assumption of vision and high seriousness implied in our use of the term tragedy? Don't we *know* a tragedy from a goat-song?" This seems to me the main problem: we have given tragedy an honorific status in confusing it so easily with vision. This is why we cannot decide whether tragedy is dead or alive: something *like* it is still around, but it doesn't come in the right shape. In my own view, I. A. Richards is right in saying that tragedy, as a coalescence of vision and form, is one of the rarest things in literature (1961, 246). At any rate, four-fifths of the plays that go under the name wouldn't make it to the quarter-finals of a contest in Tragic Vision. Only by drawing a distinction between practice and vision can we see that the whole death-of-tragedy debate is based on a questionable premise that equates the tragic vision *with the form taken by past tragedies*. (This point, of course, was made long ago by Morris Weitz [1956].) If, like George Steiner, you believe that Shakespeare and Racine are the last genuine tragic visionaries, you will in all likelihood locate the characteristics of tragic structure and effect in some sort of a composite form based on everything up to your cutoff point.[2] If, like F. L. Lucas, you believe that tragic vision implies only a "serious and true" reading of life, then the form tragedy may take will be virtually open-ended and include everything that is serious and true, whatever you mean by that (1962, 66). In any event, as long as vision and form are considered as aspects of the same thing, past models of tragic structure will always dictate one's conception of tragic vision itself, and vice versa—a kind of procrustean bed whirling in a hermeneutic circle.

Another corollary to this problem is the high risk that any commentary so derived will equate the tragic hero and the tragic visionary, as if the protagonist were the direct extension of the artist's tragic vision;—thus when heroic and visionary protagonists fall out of the picture, high tragedy becomes impossible. Among other things, such a conflation leads to judgments that ignore the cathartic influence of artistic formulation itself, irrespective of the vision of the protagonist. So we find sentiments such as, "If Pirandello [or Beckett or Kafka or Chekhov] believes life is that bad, man that poor, why did he bother to write?" These sentiments ignore the possibility that the representation of suffering may, in certain hands at least, constitute a cathartic and artistic revenge on the condition itself. Thus there is an entire dimension in which the value of tragedy and the tragic vision, when they coalesce—or when the vision coalesces with something else—lies not in the message of the expression or the size of the tragic hero, or in some precarious balance between the ethical, the religious, and the tragic, but in the power of the artist to evoke the tragic condition, however darkly perceived, as unflinchingly as possible. We hear

---

[2] For example, "Man [must be] ennobled by the vengeful spite or injustice of the gods. It does not make him innocent but it hallows him as if he had passed through flame. Hence there is in the final moments of great tragedy, whether Greek or Shakespearean or neoclassic, a fusion of grief and joy, of lament over the fall of man and of rejoicing in the resurrection of his spirit. . . . From antiquity until the age of Shakespeare and Racine, such accomplishment seemed within the reach of talent. Since then the tragic voice in drama is blurred or still" (Steiner 1968, 10).

a great deal about how despair has ruined tragedy, but this belief seems to me a variation of the old argument between the pot and the kettle. If the tragic vision was capable of dealing with the deaths of Lear and Cordelia it should have no trouble dealing with the more recent death of God and all the despair that followed that event. Why should we not extend to modern tragedy—or, again, certain instances of it—the same motive and cathartic power that we extend, say, to Matthias Grünewald's *Crucifixion*, which paints Christ and the world in which he dies in gruesome detail? Is it our belief in Christ's heavenly transcendence which overpowers such dark realism? Or could it be Grünewald's own vision—which is to say, his insistence on looking so precisely, so darkly, on the event?

It is clear that we need some sense of what the term "tragic vision" means. The problem, as always in these matters, is that so many people have attempted to define the tragic, and I would like, if possible, to avoid privileging one view over another. Moreover, deriving a definition of tragic vision from past formulations amounts to spinning in the same hermeneutical circle I have just described. My (partial) solution to the difficulty is to look for a tendency, based on philosophical formulations, that might be helpful in differentiating tragic vision from, say, the religious, ethical, and satanic visions, which I take to be tragedy's nearest visionary neighbors and the grounds on which most of the intermingling takes place.

Here I am making a subjective judgment already, but I am guided less by a thesis than by a curiosity about what a tragic vision would be if we were to determine it on a comparative visionary basis and without the influence of tragic practice. In other words, one can assume that plays, even those we regard as examples of the highest tragedy, are conditioned by, even generically contaminated by, a complex cultural motivation that springs from a number of imperatives. One doesn't write a play (or a novel) in order to demonstrate the tragic but to say something about the face of disaster in a *specifically* tragic world. To come back to religion, there is the religious vision and then there are Protestant, Catholic, Jewish, Muslim, and Buddhist faiths, all of which are concrete instances of a universal that differs in its local directives. The question, then, would be, what constitutes the universal of the tragic vision before it gets put into tragic works written in and for specific societies? At the risk of being rather bland—or procrustean—I will suggest two foundational propositions that, in one way or another, are not accommodated by any other vision. The formulations are not my own but persistently underlie conceptions of the tragic since Schelling, if not Pascal. They are also deducible from many plays, but that is another matter.

I assume, first, that a tragic vision is an extreme view of human experience. And by extreme I mean having no further extensibility—if you will, an end-of-the-road conception. Here Northrop Frye's idea that "the basis of the tragic vision is being in time" might serve as a bottom line. Unfortunately, one might also say that the basis of the comic (or any other) vision is "being in time," since *being* and *time* are pretty much all we've got. But what we mean by the phrase—or what Frye means by it—is the "one-directional quality of life . . . [wherein] all experience vanishes, not simply into the past, but into nothingness, annihilation" (1967, 3). Or, as Camus's Caligula simply puts it, "Men die and they are not happy." The not-happiness may vary in intensity from David Riesman's "persistent low-keyed unpleasure" to Munch's shriek, but it is not the consequence of a lack of comfort or security in the social world, something somebody *does* to you or something that could be repaired if taxes were lowered or there were equal opportunity for all. The tragic view of being-in-time springs from an awareness that time and value cannot be called back and the belief that Being has no "other" except Nothingness. I do not take this as a cynical, pessimistic, or, in Murray Krieger's word, "demoniacal" postulate.

But why so bleak? Because such a view is the only extremity to be weighed equally against its non-tragic antithesis: the possibility that there is a next life or some form of redemption for this one. Otherwise, what need would we have for fictions or philosophy grounded in the confrontation with death and the conspicuous absence of redemption? Why the ongoing debate about whether *The Book of Job, The Eumenides, Oedipus at Colonus,* or *Faust* is guided by a tragic vision, on one hand, or by some sort of a philosophy of deliverance, on the other? In short, in the tragic view something tugs us toward the *terminal realization* that nothingness is the likeliest of two possible extremes in any dialectic on human destiny. Anything else could easily be contained within the religious or some other redemptive vision, and although such visions often participate in the tragic, they avoid the extreme consequence of tragic understanding, which is (as Yogi Berra would say) that when it's over it's over.

As a corollary to this first point, I should add immediately, via Max Scheler, the sense of an absolute indifference in the causal order toward the order of human value. Here George Steiner has it absolutely right: tragic catastrophe is irreparable, inexplicable, and has nothing whatsoever to do with justice or injustice, either human or divine (1968, 8). If there were a direct relationship between causality and human value, if there were a clear sense in which we all get what we deserve in a world with a dependable set of rules, there would be no need for tragedy and nothing in life to arouse a tragic vision. But this is far from the case. As Scheler puts it, "The simple fact that the sun shines on the good and bad alike makes tragedy possible" (1954, 184). And, we might add, inevitable as a vision and indispensable as an artistic form.

The second extreme proposition of a tragic vision is that the visionary accepts this basic condition of our "thrownness" into an indifferent world without the least suppression, subterfuge, or whimpering. In the tragic view, as I. A. Richards puts this point (in a passage quoted by Van Laan), "The mind does not shy away from anything, it does not protect itself with any illusion [of heaven, hell, or God], it stands uncomforted, unintimidated, alone and self-reliant. . . . The essence of Tragedy is that it forces us to live for a moment without them" (Richards 1961, 246). The moment any of these various subterfuges appear, we leave the tragic vision and enter the religious, the mystical, the pathetic, the ethical, or some other sphere.

These seem to me the two fundamental and categorical characteristics that form the ground of a tragic vision. Beyond them, we may mention at least two auxiliary refinements that derive from this base and indeed take us closer to the actual practice and form of tragedy itself. First, human beings have a tendency, through desire or fear, through a kind of self-momentum (that tragedians eventually call hubris or hamartia) to create situations in which they inadvertently radicalize the destructive power of the causal series, thus distributing the responsibility for the tragic condition between individual and world. This balance is implicit even in Aristotle, and without it the tragic vision immediately becomes indistinguishable from the satanic (whose main postulate is that the world is malevolent, as opposed to indifferent). In short, it is a tragic truth that we do, in part, author our own fates, and this is one of the factors that allows us to resist giving the name of tragedy to natural disasters, to casual or mass slaughter, or to most naturalistic plays and novels with social agendas. Second, as a consequence, the tragic vision, like tragedy itself (usually), implies a certain factor of recognition or awareness—if nothing else, an awareness that each single and peculiar life, despite the indifference of the causal order, has, after all, its own entelechial shape.

Many theorists who claim that tragedy is dead associate this recognition with the principle of "affirmation" and cite its absence from modern works as evidence for the death of tragedy; but like Van Laan, I can find no quality of affirmation in the most profound tragedies—and no reason for assuming it should be part of a tragic philosophy. Concomitantly, I suggest that one of the main differences between classical and modern tragedy is that the latter is more often than not written from the standpoint of recognition (or, if you prefer, self-consciousness) rather than that of causality, and this may be one reason that modern tragedy's patron saint is Prince Hamlet. However, the principle of affirmation, as usually elaborated, seems to me another subterfuge for whistling ourselves through the graveyard.[3] But let us not confuse affirmation with nobility in the tragic protagonist. Dying well (with honor, courage, dignity) is certainly admirable in life and a desired ingredient in the tragic hero, but it doesn't change the consequences of tragic fate itself. When Horatio speaks of flights of angels singing Hamlet to his rest, we take it as a metaphor for Hamlet's value to him (and to us) rather than as an expression of real possibility. Even if Shakespeare personally believed that angels exist, he kept the belief out of the play, and in this respect his vision was tragic rather than Christian. In any case, affirmation seems as poor a word for what arises in tragic catharsis, on the optimistic side, as Schopenhauer's resignation is on the pessimistic. Whatever else tragedy may teach us

---

[3] If we are referring to affirmation in the sense used by Hans-Georg Gadamer, I have little trouble with the term: "The spectator recognizes himself and his own finiteness in the face of the power of fate. What happens to the great ones of the earth has an exemplary significance. The tragic emotion is not a response to the tragic course of events as such or to the justice of the fate that overtakes the hero, but to the metaphysical order of being that is true for all. To see that 'this is how it is' is a kind of self-knowledge for the spectator, who emerges with new insight from the illusions in which he lives. The tragic affirmation is an insight which the spectator has by virtue of the continuity of significance in which he places himself" (Gadamer 1985, 117).

The use of the term I find cloying is the one suggesting that the hero is somehow morally bigger than his or her fate by standing up to it "nobly," and that fate (if it were possible to personify it) would go skulking offstage in shame. In sum, tragedy does not *contain* an affirmation, it *is* an affirmation in the sense that tragedy is an insight into the "metaphysical order of being that is true for all." What else is art itself but such an affirmation?

about our virtues and capacities, the perception it gives us in the full embodiment of tragic vision is apocalyptic, or the feeling, as Richards puts it so beautifully, that everything is "right here and now in the nervous system" (1961, 246) and that becoming itself has ceased to be a matter of concern. For affirmation, then, we might substitute Shakespeare's "readiness" or "ripeness," words that catch the precise sense of the finality of our fall from the tree of experience.

I do not expect every reader to find this description agreeable. But I know of no other way to differentiate tragedy as an aesthetic form from tragic vision as a philosophical outlook than to make an assertion along some such lines. I have tried to be at once as basic and radical as possible (in the sense of following implications to the end of the line), and my design was not to prepare a measuring instrument that will allow me to prefer some works over others according to how well they fulfill my criteria (though that is indeed possible). As I say, mine is an extreme view of the tragic condition itself—the ground of its discontent, one might say—and not necessarily a view that all tragic visionaries follow to the end of the line. We glimpse it briefly, however, in phrases like Lear's "unaccommodated man," Hamlet's "quintessence of dust," and the Greek refrain "Count no man happy . . ." This is not to say that *King Lear* or *Hamlet* themselves are so unrelievedly dark, only that the pure tragic condition is that of a world in which we have no compensation, beyond the life lived, for the descent into the dust. Indeed, I think it is essential to get over the notion that tragedy is somehow privileged over other forms, or that it has to be either present or absent. Tragedy is not so much a category to put things in (or exclude them from) as a noun that is always modified by at least one adjective, the adjective standing for the standpoint from which the visionary views the condition. There is even a sense in which one might say that we make art, in all its forms, in reaction to this condition. However, I do feel that such a scheme, even if you wish to alter particulars or change the emphasis, has certain advantages. For one thing, it gets us past the habit of identifying works as tragic only if they are *called* tragedies and follow recognizable (i.e., traditional) tragic form. We are faced with a seeming paradox that is really no paradox at all: a dramatist who possesses a tragic vision does not necessarily write tragedies in the formal sense of the term, and a dramatist who writes tragedies does not necessarily possess a tragic vision.

In some respects it is unfortunate that the word "tragic" must be used to describe tragic vision, because the word implies a derivation (in more than the etymological sense) rather than an affinity. The central quality of a tragic perspective, in its most extreme manifestation, is that it differs from the ethical, moral, religious, and satanic perspectives (in *their* pure or extreme assertions) in its dual relation to being and catastrophe. By this I mean simply that if ethical, moral, or religious violations and assertions instigate a tragic situation (and they usually do), they have only secondarily, or "adjectivally," to do with the thematic that emerges from the experience (as one might speak of Ibsen's *ethical* tragedy, Chekhov's *pathetic* tragedy, or Strindberg's *psychopathic* tragedy). I am not suggesting that Ibsen, Chekhov, and Strindberg should automatically be classified as tragic visionaries. The question would be, at what point does the adjective (ethical, pathetic, psychopathic) overbalance or offset the tragic substantive and become the substantive itself, with respect to thematic emphasis? The answer will always depend on one's interpretation. Chekhov's is perhaps the most debatable case. David Magarshack finds Chekhov's plays positive and forward-looking in their endings (1960, 262–63). F. L. Lucas, on the other hand, finds "no more really tragic ending in all drama" than the ending of *Three Sisters* (1962, 66). Finally, in a devastating essay titled "Creation from the Void" Leon Shestov argues that Chekhov is "a sorcerer. . . , an adept in the black art [with a] singular infatuation for death, decay and hopelessness" which would seem to place Chekhov securely in the category of the satanic (Shestov 1966, 23).

As for Ibsen, he is the only one of the three who seems comfortable in the Aristotelian tragic form. But it is possible to argue that ethical concerns sometimes get the upper hand in Ibsen and obscure the tragic implications (*Pillars of Society, A Doll House, Enemy of the People*), or that death itself, when it occurs, seems a statement made about a world that is potentially curable, or tragic only because people "do such things," as Brack says, and not because existence itself is tragic. Finally, much the same might be said about Strindberg's sexual vendetta. I offer these quibbles, however, not to determine who's in and who's out, but as illustrations of combinatory possibilities. In practice, the tragic vision necessarily accommodates itself to terrestrial concerns, often to the point of losing the terminal edge I have tried to describe here. This is not ground for saying that one dramatist is inferior to another because less tragic, but only that dramatists have different goals, thanks to which we have an infinite variety of forms and visions. Pirandello, to offer a somewhat different case in point, sees the world as irrevocably tragic in condition (doomed to the communal lie, reciprocal deceit, falsity of language itself, etc.), but chooses to write humorous plays in which the protagonist (a distant relative of Prince Hamlet) is aggressively out to prove it to everybody, including the audience. What, then, are we to call Pirandello—a polemical tragical-comedian or a comical-tragical polemicist? It is all a matter (as I will suggest below) of artistic imagination operating according to what Darwin would call the principle of divergence of character, which is the means by which species proliferate the variety of forms in response to conditions in their environment.

At any rate, as the substantive perspective, the tragic always leads beyond its social origin in empirical life to the confrontation with nothingness—otherwise one could explain *King Lear* as a play deploring filial abuse of the elderly and *Macbeth* as a moral injunction against manslaughter. If you find God during tragic disaster, or if God finds you, or if you die standing up for your rights or the rights of others or some other construction of the superego (such as saving the community water supply), your fall isn't tragic—on that account anyway—but something closer to divine comedy or heroic or polemical drama. George Steiner defines tragedy as "that form of art which requires the intolerable burden of God's presence. It is now dead because His shadow no longer falls upon us as it fell on Agamemnon or Macbeth or Athalie" (1968, 353). I am not sure how metaphorically Steiner intends this statement, but if the idea is that there must be an operative God or gods in tragedy—of a different order from, say, Lukács's "spectator" God—and that when there are none about, tragedy becomes impossible, then it seems to me another of those sentimental claims that ties tragedy once again to the historical cycle: no gods, no tragedy.[4] In most cases the damage directly rendered by the gods

---

[4] As an argument to the contrary, I think, offhand, of Büchner's tragedy, *Danton's Death*, mentioned only briefly by Steiner as a youthful, experimental play that "renews the possibilities of political drama" (271). To my mind, it is a strange political play that calls into question the motive of politics itself and views history as an accidental and godless rampage of human appetite as uncontrollable as the volcano to which it is likened. Perhaps for these reasons Steiner would not call it a tragedy, though in connection with *Woyzeck* he does speak of Büchner's "radical extension of the compass of tragedy" (272).

I hope it is clear that I am not throwing religion itself out of the tragic experience or

in tragedies could as easily have been rendered by human beings. As for their being *indirectly* responsible, Shakespeare speaks interchangeably of the gods, God, Fortune, and Providence, and it isn't clear from the plays what role any of these things has in the tragedy. The damage is all done by people who have good or bad intentions, and the gods are usually brought in as a kind of hyperbole for maximizing the scope of disaster, rather like metaphysical swearing. And when daemonic power *is* clearly present—as in *Macbeth* or *Death in Venice*—we are not quite sure whether it isn't a metaphor for human daemonic power, or a way of confusing the distinction between the psychology of the protagonist and something infinite, or at least unlocatable, outside of him or her.

However, the moment gods appear on the stage, as they do in Euripides, the metaphysical air goes out of the balloon, and I take this as an indication that gods are more believable in tragedies when they stay at home and spectate, or work through other mortals like priests. Visible or invisible, though, I can't see how god-power differs, in purely tragic terms, from the power unleashed, for example, by Claire Zachanassian in Dürrenmatt's *The Visit*, who is after all a very rich lady who knows human nature very well. There may be good reasons to argue that *The Visit* isn't a tragedy, or tragic, but the absence of God's shadow doesn't seem a convincing one. Anyway, it is simplistic to claim that modern gods are no longer divinities but diminished forces like money, greed, jealousy, corporate business, and social phenomena of this sort, and therefore tragedy is not possible. For all practical (i.e., destructive) purposes, the same forces are operating in Shakespeare's world, and if one simply drops all the references to the gods or Providence or Fortune the consequences would still be wholly believable in terms of human appetite. The point, anyway, isn't who or what causes the catastrophe, but that it is inevitable and answerless. God-power, as conceived by creative human playwrights, is designed to enhance both effects.

In his final paragraph, Van Laan introduces what he calls a countermyth as a way of freeing tragedy from the myth of its death so that it may

---

vision. I agree with H. A. Mason's view that "the world's greatest tragedies are soaked in religion." My argument here respecting the ethical, the satanic, and other such perspectives is precisely that, "in entering tragedy, religion loses its absolute rights, and submits to the laws of poetry" (1985, 192).

"become available for reasonably objective study" (1991, 29). The proposal is offered tentatively as an extension of Murray Krieger's notion that modern tragic vision perceives the "Dionysian without the Apollonian" and views life as "unalleviated, endlessly and unendurably dangerous, finally destructive and self-destructive—in short, the demoniacal" (1960, 10). Van Laan sums up: "It is but a small step to use [Krieger's] analysis to conclude that traditional tragedy always fell short of the potentialities of tragedy and that instead of dying out with the advent of the modern era tragedy was not actually born until then" (29). This seems a questionable claim, but it does clear the slate in a Draconian way. I would simply propose a *semi*countermyth that does not require throwing out history, like the baby in the adage, with the death-myth.

Once we are rid of the notion that tragic vision depends on the tragic form as its host—that is, once we cease associating the tragic with what amounts to a historically derived model (the mythic "median" hero, hubris, hamartia, reversal and recognition, and, above all, death itself as a consequence of "all of the above")—we have no cause to say that tragic spirit is dead or dying or less valuable or less cathartic than that of earlier tragedy. For one thing, there is a good possibility that what purists admire in Aeschylus or Sophocles or Shakespeare, and find deficient in modern works, has less to do with tragic vision, per se, than with a variety of other factors such as aesthetic pleasure and the always tempting notion that the grass is always greener elsewhere. For example, you might prefer Shakespearean poetry to modern household prose, or Greek monumentality to living-room realism, but account for the preference by claiming that one was more tragic than the other, when what you really mean is that one is more sublime. Again, tragedy tends to be the magic word for "high seriousness."

The main idea I want to advance, however, is that art undergoes its own biological evolution as a matter of historical course and that to pronounce a part of it dead or moribund is rather like claiming that natural selection is killing off a species that is only undergoing an adaptation for its own good. It is really a matter of seeing the adaptation in terms of what Darwin referred to as the law of the conditions of existence, which, he maintained, was a higher law than that of unity of type. The latter law refers to "that fundamental agreement in structure we see in organic beings of the same class"; the former refers to the adaptation of "the varying parts of each being to its organic and inorganic conditions of life;

or [to] *having [been] adapted* . . . during past periods of time" (1897, 260–61; emphasis mine).[5] If we can think at all in biological terms about species of art, it is surely safe to claim that tragedy has always been an evolving form, as Hegel's comparison of Greek and modern tragedy will serve to illustrate. Not being a naturalist, however, Hegel was unable to see wherein such modern parts as the emphasis on the subjectivity of the hero, ethical relativity, or the rise of guilt as a causal factor may have been advantageous tragic responses to conditions of life in the Renaissance. Suffice it to say that the "falling off" between *Antigone* and *Hamlet* must have been as radical for Hegel as the falling off between Shakespeare and Pirandello was for Joseph Krutch and the "tragedy is dead" group.[6] It seems to me that this evolution should be seen in its full implications as just that—an evolutionary continuity as opposed to a series of deaths and births.

To apply Darwin's law, analogically, to modern tragedy, what modern conditions of existence seem to have required, as a probable consequence of the naturalistic and expressionist revolutions, was a new "radical of presentation" (in Frye's term [1957, 249]; that is, a form which did not call for a flawed or excessively committed hero exposed to his or her enemies and driven to the point of death (which is also the point of recognition). This, we might assume, had become an outmoded form, suitable only for expressing aspects of "being in time" that had since been modified by modern life or, more likely, were no longer able to produce energetic variations. And where art departs from biology is in the persistent *social*

[5] I trust I am avoiding the application of the evolutionary metaphor in the senses discussed by René Wellek and Austin Warren in their critique of Ferdinand Brunetière and John Addington Symonds in the nineteenth century. Brunetière, for example, taught that literary genres strive toward a perfection and, on achieving it, wither and die. Wellek and Warren argue, quite rightly, that "the evolution of literature is different from that of biology, and that it has nothing to do with the idea of a uniform progress towards *one* eternal model." On the contrary, "the historical process will produce ever new forms of value, hitherto unknown and unpredictable. . . . The series of developments will be constructed in reference to a scheme of values or norms, but these values themselves emerge only from the contemplation of this process" (1956, 257).

[6] An interesting social parallel to my Darwinian argument is offered by Eva Figes in *Tragedy and Social Evolution*. Tracing tragedy (or tragic-tending drama) from the Australian aborigine tribes, Figes arrives at a position that resembles Van Laan's in some respects: "Perhaps we have reached a stage of evolution where we must accept, once and for all, that there is no reason for suffering, that pain and misery is [*sic*] arbitrary and not a punishment for wrong-doing. Perhaps we have left the world of the nursery and finally grown up" (1976, 163).

demand for new variations that will prevent the disappearance of its types into the unity of overfamiliarization, or (again) what Brecht called inconspicuousness.[7] Thus Darwin was right in using the law of the conditions of existence to refute "the belief that organic beings have been created beautiful for the delight of man" (251). But Samuel Johnson was equally right in saying that the drama's laws are given by the drama's patrons; and we might infer that a degree of restlessness must have been setting in among artists and audiences at the century's turn with regard to how intrepidly the dramatic form was consuming the *same kinds* of human experience.[8]

Perhaps the most notable sloughing off of parts was that death—the oldest and most venerable fixture of tragedy—came gradually to be regarded as supererogatory to tragic vision, since the subject was now the *condition* that emanates in death rather than the progress toward it through a series of contingent and peripetous events.[9] (Thus Shaw argued that *Hedda Gabler* would have been more tragic had Hedda lived on.) How, in short, was it possible to deal with the matter of "how it is" (in Beckett's phrase) if one's available model is designed to demonstrate "how

[7] A useful perspective on this aspect of artistic evolution is found in Rudolf Arnheim's *Entropy and Art: An Essay on Disorder and Order*, which deals with two "fundamental processes" that contribute to entropy in a system: the *catabolic* process, which "grind[s] things to pieces . . . by removing constraints and thus enlarging the range of tension reduction, which increases entropy by simplifying the order of a system" (1974, 28); and the anabolic process, which "contributes . . . the structural theme of a pattern, and this theme creates orderly form through interaction with the tendency to tension reduction" (31). It is the anabolic principle that "establishes 'what a thing is about,' be it a crystal or a solar system, a society or a machine, a statement of thoughts or a work of art" (49). I am suggesting, then, that even in the sphere of public reception the progress of artistic form (and theme) is governed by an "anabolic" response to the continual threat of "catabolic" tension reduction, a simpler word for which might be *boredom*. The survival of the species, in short, depends on the right degree and rate of differentiation and variation.

[8] I am of course not implying that old forms ever die out. We see their continuation in such present-day features as pyramidal structure and the well-made play. The species of drama, like organic species, seem to undergo divergence of character whereby, to continue my Darwinian theme, "the more diversified the descendants [of a modification] become, the better will be their chance of success in the battle for life" (Darwin 1897, 161). Stephen Kern has chronicled the turn-of-the-century revolutionary scene in *The Culture of Time and Space, 1880–1918* (1983).

[9] This was already implicit, however briefly, in Shakespeare's *Hamlet*, the archetypal grandfather of modern tragedy. This point was most recently brought home to me in the staging of the duel as a farcical game in Franco Zeffirelli's film version of the play.

things come about"? A related shift (that might have pleased Hegel) involved the decline of guilt, as Dürrenmatt put it, as "a personal achievement [or] a religious act" on the part of the protagonist (1982, 255; see also Lukács 1965). When it was relevant at all, guilt was either collective (the "guilty society") or, as in the case of Kafka, an inescapable part of the private condition. There are many other variations, of course; I concentrate on death and guilt (including its variant, hubris) because they are the forces between which traditional tragedy works itself out.

Such profound shifts, however, should be regarded less as an alteration in vision than as a means of permitting the vision's gravitation to new aspects of experience which had been disclosed by (among other things) the evolutionary advance of art itself. I am not suggesting that the tragic vision remained unaltered in this evolution, only that it remained, by definition, a *terminal* view of existence. What constitutes a terminal preoccupation is bound to vary with each era and to be intimately bound in the progress and capacity of art to render it without iterating itself to death. Natural selection, Darwin said, "acts exclusively by the preservation and accumulation of variations, which are beneficial under the organic and inorganic conditions to which each creature is exposed at all periods of life" (1897, 151). Or, to put the same idea in the language of modern chaos theory, art and language are "engaged in a feedback loop in which articulating an idea changes the context, and changing the context affects the way the idea is understood, which in its turn leads to another idea, so that text and context *evolve* together in a constantly modulating interaction" (Hayles 1990, 128; emphasis mine). Thus you can't tell a tragic vision by a checklist of known characteristics, any more than you can bind the principles of reversal and recognition to Aristotle's specific variations. We must assume, rather, that vision is always adaptable to the changing human scene. It is itself, one might say, a shape-shifter, such as Proteus in the ancient world or the cybernetic robot in the postmodern. But tragic vision has one constant preoccupation: the extremity of the human situation.

The most wholesale mutation of dramatic tragedy in the modern period is obviously its so-called merger with tragicomedy—or, as many would have it, tragicomedy is what replaced tragedy on its demise: the king is dead, long live his jester! Unfortunately, the assumption usually follows that tragic vision was itself lost in the process and what emerged was an alloy that thematically supercharged the comic and emotionally diluted the tragic, weighing in equal scale delight and dole, as Claudius might say. In any event, here was a new way of looking at existence and it undoubtedly produced a new strain of drama, in many (if not most) cases. But that does not prove the point. I could cite many examples of tragicomic form that remained tragicomic in vision, or at least nontragic, but such a list would only parade my own opinions and provoke argument on what I consider an irrelevant ground. So I will illustrate the point by citing what I take to be the central instance of dramatic tragic vision in the post-Ibsen to postmodern era.

I refer to Samuel Beckett, and most especially (for me) the Beckett of plays such as *Krapp's Last Tape, Not I*, and *Rockaby*, the trilogy, and in a more discursive way the critical work, *Proust*. I choose Beckett primarily because he is the quintessential case of modern extremity, and the theater has not yet caught up with him. What Beckett has managed is nothing less than a dissolution of the dialogic form of drama; in his work it is no longer possible to make clear distinctions between the lyric, dramatic, and narrative voices. This is not an achievement in itself, but it is what gave Beckett access to the deepest privacy of mental experience, nuances of thought that were not possible in the Shakespearean soliloquy but may, for all that, have been going on in Shakespeare's own mind. In any case, it is not a matter of arguing that Beckett's plays are tragedies. But to call his a tragicomic vision because he is a "stoic comedian" or has called one of his own plays a tragicomedy is, I think, a confusion of form and vision.[10] It would be hard to find anybody, including Shakespeare, who has stared

[10] I am not the first person to make the claim for Beckett's tragic vision. See, especially, Normand Berlin, "The Tragic Pleasure of *Waiting for Godot*" (1986). For example, "But when a dramatist writes a play that does not provide any screen for his audience to protect itself from a perception of itself, when a dramatist brings us as close to that abyss, when a play elicits the kind of emotions one feels when experiencing traditional tragedies, then Beckett's own balanced classification [that *Godot* is a tragicomedy] should be questioned—not an unreasonable thing to do because Beckett seems to want us to question everything" (56). Berlin takes issue throughout with the notion of a tragicomic vision. Then there is Theodor Adorno's estimation of Beckett, written before many of the later plays: "His plays are neither tragedies nor comedies, let alone tragicomedies, as a scholastic aesthetician might like to believe. What they do is consummate the negative judgment on the utility of those very categories. . . . In accordance with modern art's tendency to focus on inherited aesthetic categories through self-reflection, *Godot* and *Endgame* for instance in the scene where the protagonists make a decision to laugh—far from being comedies, may be said to be plays that give a tragic account of the fate of comedy as a genre" (1984, 466).

with greater equanimity into the abyss than Beckett has. Unlike any other modern dramatist, Beckett went for "the thing itself," in Lear's dreadful term, rather than one of its social or psychopathic derivatives, and that is why his is the most radical vision of the postmodern era. It is also why his vision seems the darkest. In Beckett the protagonist is no longer defined by deeds or by social status (high, low—*any*!) but by what may be called the act of being conscious. His people are postexperiential, all *anagnorisis*—wide-eyed awareness bumping up against its "other," against the "not I," as the narrator of *The Unnamable* puts it. No reversal is necessary because reversal is strictly a function of social experience, or of the deed coming full circle. No death because death is the point of deliverance from both the social and the tragic life. More relevant, death is the point where the pen stops, and the problem is to "say" oneself in words "as long as there are any" (1965, 414). Life in society is somebody else's responsibility: Beckett's topic is the tragedy of *vagitus*, or (as he might have put it) of *is-ness*.

On the occasion of Beckett's death, the *Los Angeles Times* (December 27, 1989) spoke of how his "bleak poetic and darkly comedic works etched the pessimism of the human condition" (1). Beckett died, the article went on, of "respiratory failure," a phrase that got my instant attention. I had not known about Beckett's illness and, like everyone else no doubt, I was stunned to think what it must have entailed, in simple sentient terms alone, and to realize that Beckett (whose mortality some of us had doubts about anyway) had finally met the thing he had been anatomizing in "words" all his life, respiratory failure being only another word for what he called the "time cancer." At any rate, I think Beckett would have appreciated the expression "respiratory failure," even as applied to his own case. It is one of those scientific phrases he liked so much because they carry both a precision of meaning and an unintentional lilt of poetry—surgical words, you might call them, that cut without clotting the wound with sentiment. You can imagine Krapp hearing the phrase "respiratory failure" on one of his tapes, dividing it into syllables, and reveling in the sound.

And that is really the point of my anecdote: this reveling in the sound of words or finding a surreptitious beauty in the names of ugly things, or in mundane and obsessive habits (like the mathematics of stone-sucking), rescues his vision from "the pessimism of the human condition" and gives new proof to Eric Bentley's claim that "all art is a challenge to despair" (1965, 353), as opposed to an indulgence in it. For Beckett, words were blocks of timelessness, a means of making something slightly extratemporal out of the symptoms of the Time cancer, something slightly more immune to the cancer than life itself, something, above all, that belongs not to time but to consciousness itself. So if you put your own fibrous degeneration or respiratory failure into plays (as he did), it is being put to some use; you haven't *beaten* the Time cancer, but you have, in our reporter's word, "etched" your understanding on it, as on the urn that will eventually contain your own ashes.

Unfortunately, the grimness of Beckett's subject tends to obscure the lucidity and wit with which he examines this enduring condition of existence. Many people wish he had been more cheerful about life, and I think we tend to flaunt his political activism in the war as a kind of assurance that, despite everything, he supported good causes. That apart, however, I can't personally see how anyone could read the last ten pages of *The Unnamable* or witness Billie Whitelaw in *Rockaby* or *Not I* and claim that tragedy is dead in our time, that this experience is less compassionate and terrifying—less cathartic—than the death of Lear. It is one thing to write depressingly about depressing things, as the naturalists did, quite another to look at them without consolation, though with a little wink, and try to see what they add up to—"Not count!" as Rooney says, "One of the few satisfactions in life!" (Beckett 1984, 30). The main idea is what Beckett called "getting it right," and getting destiny right has always been the mission of the tragic visionary—getting right things that come up in the evolution of a species incapable of leaving any extremity unexamined, and worrying about the form only to the extent that it is the most advantageous one to suit the experience. If there is any merit in Van Laan's premise that certain potentialities of tragedy are only now being born, it seems to me that the Beckett variation is, at least temporarily, the most extreme. The problem, of course, is whether this particular variation can survive, in any adapted form, the death of Beckett himself. Even if not, its appearance should be cause enough to review our conception of the tragic and how it continually adapts itself to the conditions of experience.

CHAPTER 12

The Pleasure of Pain

On the afternoon of June 23, 1925, a section of earth about one and one-half miles long, a mile wide and several hundred feet deep detached itself from the slope of Sheep Mountain near Jackson Hole, Wyoming, and slid into the valley below. On the ridge opposite a young cowboy happened to be passing on horseback and watched as the mountain slipped toward the Gros Ventre river bed, reached a narrow spur of rock on the north side of the river, and was divided into two forks, one swelling up into a narrow canyon, the other up the river itself for a half mile where it formed a permanent 235-foot dam. The entire event took approximately two minutes and is said to be one of the most spectacular landslides ever witnessed by a human being. O lucky cowboy, to have seen what he had seen! O unfortunate angler to have been fishing the river below!

Since I have been dealing throughout the book with the powers and limitations of the stage, I want to close it in kind by looking at a play that holds the mirror up to the theater process in an unusual and exemplary way. The play is Samuel Beckett's *Catastrophe*, and in view of what I said about Beckett in the last chapter, it may seem perverse to choose a Beckett play that probably isn't an example of his tragic vision. But *Catastrophe* offers compensations even more relevant to my subject. First, it is a play about a tragedy in the making, and from what we see of the tragedy, in *Catastrophe* itself, it is a very Aristotelian one, even to having its protagonist mounted on a Greek plinth, a kind of Oedipus for all seasons, the incarnation of bad fortune. More important, *Catastrophe* is a play about the art of preparing a catastrophe for the audience: in effect, the play "sculpts" the catastrophe before our eyes and then unveils it for our approval and pleasure. The problem *Catastrophe* raises, essentially, concerns the pleasure we receive from the pain of tragedy. Its text might be Aristotle's own: "There are things which we see with pain so far as they themselves are concerned but whose images, even when executed in very great detail, we view with pleasure" (sec. 6). Aristotle's answer, of course, is that pain depicted in mimetic works is pleasurable because it teaches us something about life and because mimesis itself affords the pleasure of purification. *Catastrophe* is a metacommentary on this paradox. It is the nearest thing I know in drama to a critique of theater's own function as a mimetic art, and this is made even more interesting by the play's political theme—the last sort of theme one would expect from Samuel Beckett.

Catastrophe is dedicated to Václav Havel, and it premiered in 1982 during Havel's imprisonment in Czechoslovakia for "subversive activities against the Socialist state." In the political sense, the play is about the making of a Havel—that is, a dissident, or, as Peter Handke might put it, a man who speaks by being made to not speak. Curiously—no doubt in respect to Havel's silenced craft—Beckett links the theme of human victimization to the theatrical business of preparing unpleasant subjects for the pleasure of the audience. The result is far from a simple advocacy of a cause in which we all believe. The play is not one of those written for an audience of the already committed. In *Catastrophe*, Beckett went beyond his wish to honor a courageous fellow-artist to a critique of the artist's weapon. In short, he introduces the question of the *means* into the pursuit of the well-justified end.

Even apart from its political timeliness, *Catastrophe* is an unusual Beckett play. The setting is an explicit place, a theater stage, and, though in Beckett's theater the stage tends to become "all the world," and vice versa, in this case the setting advertises itself as little more than a theater *in* the world on the evening of a dress rehearsal. The characters—all but one— are gainfully employed, in good health, and unacquainted with the metaphysical. To this degree, the play is realistic. Reading it quickly, you might miss Beckett entirely; in fact, in view of a certain stiffness in the style, you might think the play had been written by an amateur (nine in ten students find it a bore). On closer reading, however, one sees that it is unmistakable

Beckett. The absence of the muckheap, the void, or the terminal room in the ex-world is all an illusion for the unwary eye.

Catastrophe is a play that can best be studied through its language. For one thing, it has an almost biblical economy: nothing in the play serves only a local or a descriptive purpose; everything calls into play its mirror other, thus allowing us to speak of there being two plays in one (just as we can eventually speak of two audiences). More specifically, the play is a dialectic between language as speech and language as gesture. Words, in this play (as so often in Beckett), refuse to settle into a servitude to purely semantic meaning. Words carry worlds in their sounds. A word such as "plinth," for instance, is a quintessential Beckett word (like "spool" or "viduity" in *Krapp's Last Tape*): the sound of it gives away the Beckett space, like water dripping in a deep cavern. The assault on the soul here, then, is logo-rhythmic—overall, an odd syncopation of exoteric and esoteric language. On one hand, there is an idiomatic strain consisting of slang or trade language: "Step on it . . . No harm trying . . . Bless his heart . . . Every i dotted to death . . . Get going! . . . Is Luke around? . . . Where do you think we are? In Patagonia? . . . In the bag . . . Lovely . . . Terrific! He'll have them on their feet. This is "urban contemporary." Taken by itself you would think you were hearing Neil Simon dialogue—or, since it is a little antiquated, Kaufman and Hart. Here, however, speech is not atmospheric but a particular species of vocality. Idiomatic speech, for all its local color, is impersonal speech, the speech of the "others" into which "one" disappears. It implies the security of class membership. To say "lovely" or "terrific!" (at least here) is to be in possession of one's world. And I assume that what Beckett was aiming for in such crass nonspeech was the extreme linguistic opposite to the silence of the Protagonist, something that bespeaks the behavioral ideology of the modern world, and in particular that of its commercial theater, or our clichéd idea of it. The Director who speaks these lines, for example, wears a fur coat and smokes a cigar throughout—yet this fountain of clichés is not himself a cliché but an invincible institution.

Beneath the idiomatic, on the other hand, are two related forms of esoteric speech. The first consists of words drawn from the vocabulary of science and formal discourse: *plinth, night attire, moulting, fibrous degeneration, caucus, cranium, explicitation*, and (perhaps) *more nudity.* The overall effect of this language is to lend a clinical objectivity to the rehearsal proceedings. The creation of the catastrophe is all business, all precision of nuance. Hence the science of the theater project—rendered so innocently in our expression "laboratory theater"—comes to be metaphorically identified with certain experiments "performed" in the medical theaters of the prison camps. The medical problem might be stated as, what effect is produced if you do such-and-such to the human body, freeze or burn parts of it, expose it to rays, etc.? In theater terms, what, precisely, do you have to do with the actor's body to produce a certain effect? How does one maximize a theatrical prop to achieve a maximal emotion from the audience? Science proceeds from cause to effect, theater from effect (desired) to cause (how to get it):

D: . . . The hands, how are the hands?
A: You've seen them.
D: I forget.
A: Crippled. Fibrous degeneration.
D: Clawlike?
A: If you like.
D: Two claws?
A: Unless he clench his fists.
D: He mustn't.
A: I make a note. [*She takes out pad, takes pencil, notes*] Hands limp.

(1984, 298)

One procedure is much like the other. Thus the subtext of the play continually whispers that art is achieved by the same patience that characterizes science (as systematic brutality). Scripture, you might say, is quoting the devil. Here, in Freudian terms, we can clearly see the manifest and the latent contents of the play. On one level, all of these effects occur as simple "notes" given (presumably) to the actor: "Don't clench your fists. We want a clawlike effect." On the other, the notes constitute the accumulation of data and control procedures. In short, fibrous degeneration can be achieved either by proper makeup and use of the hands (chironomy) or by careful supervision of diet, the administration of drugs, or other forms of sensory insult. The play never, for an instant, breathes a word that it has anything to do with this second, latent content.[1] It is strictly about theater (as *Godot* is strictly about waiting for a man and *Krapp* about listening to old tapes). The action concerns only the preparation of the tragic victim for opening night—except that a number of routine elements of the rehearsal process are oddly missing: the actor never takes a break or drops character: the director and his assistant never address the actor but rather speak, like physician and nurse, "across" the patient (or like the two warders passing the knife across K in the final scene of *The Trial*); and, finally, where is the rest of the play? Everything leading up to this denouement, if it can be called that, has been suppressed. All details are centered on making the catastrophe (how the creature became one we aren't told) as pathetic as possible: a stationary human sculpture placed on a plinth in a space normally given over to movement, sequence, and dialogue. Beneath the two plays, then, there is a fundamental contradiction between medium and content, and in its own way the play offers another variation of systemic peripety, as discussed in Chapter 6.

But the technical vocabulary is only the surgical edge of a more pervasive quality of style. Even on first reading, it strikes one that there is something archaic about this contemporary play. The language has, at times (particularly when the Assistant speaks), that awkward efficiency of speech spoken by someone for whom English (or French) is a recently acquired tongue: "To have him all black . . . Unless he clench his fists . . . I make a note (eight repetitions) . . . Sure he won't utter? . . . Down the head (two)." Actually this is vintage Beckett (see, especially, *Endgame*): speech from which everything wordy or semantically adventitious has worn away, leaving (so to speak) the grunt of thought. Despite the mod-

---

[1] However, there are subtle hints. As another instance of words that carry worlds in their sounds, consider the value of the word "caucus" ("Step on it, I have a caucus."). Not a producers' or a board of directors meeting, but a caucus; the term is heavily political or governmental in its connotations. Thus the Director is subtly aligned with the party in power, and the entire rehearsal proceedings are again implicated in the punishment of dissidents. As still another world held in the suspension of a word, it is hardly accidental that the lighting man's name is Luke and that he is the only character given a name. Departing from this and other clues, Antoni Libera (1985) makes a case for the play as an allegory that takes place in hell. Shannon Jackson offers still another view, in many ways complementary to my own, that investigates the play as "a commentary on power relations, linking those which operate in the theatrical arena with those exerted in the political arena" (1992, 23).

ern idioms, this is not finally a world made of speech or speaking—such as Ionesco's, or indeed Havel's—but a world in which speech is merely a way of pointing to meanings already understood. For all this "business" is the ageless procedure of rehearsal. Preparing the catastrophe has its own mystery and tradition, just as torture does. Hence the strong catechistic strain:

A (*Finally*): Like the look of him?
D: So So. (*Pause*) Why the plinth?
A: To let the stalls see the feet.
  (*Pause*)
D: Why the hat?
A: To help hide the face.
  (*Pause*)
D: Why the gown?
A: To have him all black.
  (*Pause*)
D: What has he on underneath? (A *moves toward* P.) Say it.
  (A *halts.*)
A: His night attire.
D: Colour?
A: Ash.

(297)

All of these decisions are correct, in advance. They are the theatrical principles of victimization, as passed down from the Greeks. In tragedy, the world (with help from the playwright) perfects the victim by giving him just the right degree and kind of hubris, room for error, just enough rope to hang himself. He is aesthetically "groomed" to be the best possible victim. Tragedy is like the crucifixion, perfect in every detail ("Why the crown of thorns? To show their scorn, his pain."). Why the plinth? ("To elevate the misery, to display the example; to put it all in the old 'marble' world."). These are also the ingredients of political misery which must be abject, must show the invincibility of the power that produced it: the perfect victim would be docilely miserable, beyond lamentation; his (its) eyes would be shadowed (for, as the window of the soul, the "I" itself, the eyes are the only dangerous organ). Above all, misery "mustn't" be gagged ("this craze for explicitation"); the victim, as we see shortly, must worship his torturer. As it turns out, of course, the Assistant—as assistants will be—is overzealous: she would pull all the stops, o'erdo Termagant. Fortunately, the Director—like Dr. Mengele and all good stage directors—is a connoisseur of pain: he knows when enough is enough. And he knows what sells.

And of course we have been sold the product. The question is, what have we bought? Ostensibly, we are watching the dress rehearsal of the final scene of a hypothetical play. We are seeing how directors work with actors and assistants, how they treat actors as properties and assistants as dirt, how meticulous are the preparations behind the effects we take for granted in the theater. But beneath this innocent plot, we quickly recognize the metaphor of theater-as-laboratory, the place where biology is altered, the place of victimization. It is like so many modern plays, from Pirandello forward, in which theater cunningly curves back on itself to perform a metasemiosis. Through the miracle of its unique lifelikeness, theater can always become "the thing itself," as Lear says. But *Catastrophe* goes one further step—further than, for instance, the examples discussed in Chapter 6. It sneaks into play an even more basic assumption of theater: from an aesthetic distance it is pleasurable to see and participate (voyeuristically, of course) in the pain of others. "And pat, he comes," Edmund says of his wrecked brother, "like the catastrophe of the old comedy." Here the word "catastrophe" is used in its original sense (in Greek, overturning): the crowning moment, what we have come to see, the destination of all plays, and the entelechial principle of drama itself. Thus the title *Catastrophe* has a double insinuation: it is at once beautiful and ghastly. Somewhere in the oscillation of the two meanings, the play asks, where, and what, *is* the catastrophe? What is this empathy with the victim, this pleasure in the victim's pain? Why is catastrophe—in nature or in the theater—such a mesmerizing, pleasurable thing to behold?

When he left prison in 1983, Havel wrote a play in response to Beckett's, called *Mistake*. Roughly equal in length to *Catastrophe*, Havel's play is about how prisoners in a cell, without realizing it, set up a replica of the oppressive system that has imprisoned them. "In its modest way," Havel said of the play, "it is meant to warn against the ubiquitous danger of the kind of self-imposed totalitarianism now present in every community in the world, large or small."[2] I have no idea how *Catastrophe* may have influenced this quite realistic play, beyond the act of thanking Beckett. But it is curious that Havel, in response to Beckett, would write of the flaw in the prisoner rather than the horror of the prison (which goes without saying). For this is what, in effect, I feel Beckett did, beneath everything else, in *Catastrophe*; and I wonder if Havel may not have understood that Beckett was really writing about the enemy within, or at least a form of what the enemy relies on—that is to say, the snag in our perception of theatrically induced pain. And what is the snag but the lively torpor of play watching? For however exciting, however angering theater may be, it produces, in its very act of being, a loss of the power of action (*vide* Brecht: empathy-apathy). Like the Porter's drink, the play provokes and it unprovokes: it provokes emotions but it takes away performance. Or rather: to have one form of gratification—a good play—we anesthetize the portion of feeling that is outraged by bad acts, or even the image of bad acts. We consent to watch abominations under the aegis of *utile et dulce*.

But one wonders if the idea that theater *is* useful (as well as pleasing) is not invoked more as a casuistry than as a belief. In any case, we scarcely debate the question, what does this emotional trade-off actually involve? Are we better prepared to recognize outrage by watching it? Do we become inured to what we see "in jest"? Does custom, as Horatio says of the singing gravedigger, make viewing pain a property of easiness? Might there be at the bottom of theatrical make-believe something slightly immoral, even obscene? So we attend this new play by Samuel Beckett, in whose work we are naturally interested, and we watch a man being complacently, as a matter of business, stripped of his humanity, made into a *thing* before our eyes for our pleasure and instruction, whatever that may mean. But then Beckett overturns his catastrophe—overturns the overturning—and poses the real question: *are we to applaud his play*? What are we applauding if we do? The ending is a cul-de-sac. It has us trapped (if we are attentive) in a recursive bind:

---

2 *Index on Censorship* 13 (February 1984): 15. The text of *Mistake* appears in this same issue of the *Index* along with that of *Catastrophe*. Both plays were produced on a double bill at the Stockholm Stadsteater on November 29, 1983.

D: . . . Good. There's our catastrophe. In the bag. Once more and I'm off.

A (*To* L): Once more and he's off.

(*Fade-up of light on* P's body. Pause. Fade-up of general light.)

D: Stop! [*Pause.*] Now . . . let 'em have it. (*Fade-out of general light. Pause. Fade-out of light on body. Light on head alone. Long pause.*) Terrific! He'll have them on their feet. I can hear it from here.

(*Pause. Distant storm of applause.* P *raises his head, fixes the audience. The applause falters, dies.*

Long pause.

Fade out of light on face.)

(300–301)

Suppose, wanting to honor Beckett for honoring Václav Havel, or wanting (presuming you were so moved) to honor Havel himself for raising his head and "fixing" his audience in far-off Czechoslovakia— suppose that you rose to your feet, as the Director knew you would, and applauded, like the audience in the play. What are you applauding? The audience preceding you, we can only assume, was a group of fools or sheep. They have played into the Director's hands. They are, so to speak, applauding fibrous degeneration (interestingly enough, Beckett's own condition), though they doubtless think they are cheering the realism of the *effect* of fibrous degeneration. Certainly they are ignorant of the monstrous creation we have witnessed, for one must assume that, as characters in the play, they did not see our version of *Catastrophe* but the box office hit of the finished product. But what are we, the second audience, applauding: the performance of the outrage or, inadvertently, the outrage itself? The art or the fact? We knew the fact, in countless variations, before coming to the play, and the art has charmed us, as always, into this aesthetic mood, wherein we suffer the wonderful effect of painless pain that has such a brief duration. And the Director—except for the "fixing"—knew exactly how to produce the effect, for it was he, this confusion of Reinhardt and Mengele, who perfected the object of our sympathy.

In short, we have been subtly groomed to play our role: to be ourselves, the complacent ones, at the theater. Somewhere, Havel is in a cell—a real catastrophe. We may, in sincere response, wish to write a check to Charter

77 or the Committee for the Defense of the Unjustly Prosecuted.[3] If nothing else, *Catastrophe* has reminded us of a horror: it has made us uneasy, if only in its trick ending. And finally, *we* are free, in this part of the world, to make plays about Havel and his kind. These are all things that justify the means of political theater. For I have not been insinuating here that Beckett is cynical of a hypocrisy in his audience or critical of a deficiency in the making and reception of art. Ultimately, *Catastrophe* is that rarest of things: an unpolemic polemic. It is finally Beckett's play because it does not fall into the easy self-congratulation of so many plays that begin and end on the right side. In fact, it is about the old Beckett dilemma. Of all moderns, Beckett knows that the artist's instrument of expression is flawed at the source—not in bad faith but simply, unavoidably, because it is a thing made of words and not the thing itself. There is simply no way to speak Havel, any more than one can speak the self. The voice that speaks, the Unnamable, says, knows that in some deep sense it lies. Still, one is "obliged to speak": "You must go on . . . you must say words, as long as there are any," though you know they don't "say you" (1965, 414). The other side of this same dilemma is the audience's: there is no way to react appropriately to the attempt to say "how it is" with Havel. You have got him in art but not in fact, and art is an illusion, what you have been dreaming for perhaps fifteen minutes. The irony of theater, particularly this kind of "inverted" theater, is that it is always at bottom either a pleasure or a bore. You expect your Protagonist, however relevant his fate, to be well done, and applause is our almost automatic gift to the actors for giving us such splendid emotions.

It is the look that "fixes" us, of course, that dots the "i" of the play. You might want to argue that the fixing occurs outside the control and design of the Director's illusion, in which case the Director has been outwitted by his own creation. Then too, we know that the real director and actor have rehearsed the look for the real audience (us) and that the look will occur on cue in the same way every night of the run. So there it is, built into the play as part of the fiction, and we are therefore free to applaud the act of refusal it represents rather than the act of outrage that built up to it. But we are not really off the hook. It was Beckett who slyly put the

[3] Charter 77 and VONS (Committee for the Defence of the Unjustly Prosecuted) are organizations to which Havel belonged, his membership being partly the cause of his imprisonment.

gesture there in the first place, squarely against the applause he knew would come, if only out of conventional respect for the players who have worked their art in your behalf. However you look at the matter, P is looking at *us*, and the logic of the play is that catastrophes are possible because there are people to see them, to report them to the world (like the Teton cowboy), or to read about them in the papers. We now know that the world is literally a theater in which the most brutal acts are political performances or private statements directed at the consumer public. This is the grim symbiosis of a media society, and I think the look that fixes us must be taken as a mischievous gesture through which Beckett writes us into the play, where we belong, somewhat as Havel puts the system inside the cell.[4]

A common instance suggests itself from everyday life. Every highway accident will produce what traffic reporters call a gawkers' block, in which traffic backs up for miles. You can scarcely blame this on a sudden decision in every driver to proceed more cautiously in order to avoid the fate of the unfortunate car. Perhaps caution is a factor in many cases, but there seems something more basic at work here—indeed, the very thing that led Ray Bradbury to write his story about the same ghostly crowd that always shows up at the scene of a disaster. For at least part of the cause of the gawkers' block is that people slow down in order to see *better*. No doubt the need to see is much too complex for a single explanation. Certainly it is more than morbidity or a simple curiosity about details. But it surely has something to do as well with what Heidegger calls the "tranquilliza-tion of everydayness." "Death is understood," he says, "as an indefinite something which, above all, must duly arrive from somewhere or other, but which is proximately *not yet present-at-hand* for oneself, and is there-fore no threat." Normally, one's thought on the death of others runs, "One of these days one will die too, in the end; but right now it has nothing to do with us" (1962, 297–98).

The highway accident is an abrupt detranquilizer. It suddenly an-nounces the invisible indifference of the causal series to human value, an unbearable thought to a culture that disapproves, as ours does, of talk about death. From the natural point of view (if there could be such a

---

[4] For a pertinent discussion of our "existential complicity in the theatre event," see Paul Hernadi (1985).

thing), accident is simply continuity, a nonevent, nothing but a momentum of molecules; accident is reality taking, so to speak, the path of least resistance through a loose bolt in some unfortunate person's left front wheel. But—after slowing down *to see*, one drives on: "it has nothing to do with us." One is a spectator, with nothing at stake. One is not the fisherman in the river gorge. And yet, on the following morning, one will search the newspaper to find out "what happened." For along with all the rest, we crave the confirmation of what we have seen.

Now it seems to me that this paradox finds its way into art as well. The simple explanation is that art addresses the paradox and offers a kind of triumph over it, and this I personally believe to be true. But, do the great catastrophes of the theater tranquilize or detranquilize one? Surely Aristotle is correct in saying that one learns from tragedy: one learns to name things and what categories things belong in ("This individual is a so-and-so."). And these are not simple lessons, for surely the great stories of the world are repeated over and over for purposes that psychology is only beginning to understand. But this particular paradox remains, and we've never resolved it. Theater detranquilizes by showing monstrous catastrophes brought on with and without human help. But finally one does applaud and drive home. Finally, the art in what one has seen overcomes the reality that was only an imitation. One of the functions of the curtain is to return us to tranquilized everydayness.

On this general theme, I like what Adorno says about Beckett's negativity as "the true form of objectivity": "Art ends up taking a stand that ceases to be one. For there is simply no conceivable standpoint from which the disaster might be named or articulated. *Endgame* is neither a play about nuclear war nor [is it] devoid of content: the determinate negation of content becomes its principle of form. What is more, it negates content as such" (1984, 354). So too *Catastrophe*. If I am at all right about the "fixing" of the audience as a critique of art's presumed mission and the tranquilization of its audience, I must add that the fixing was finally done *within the art* by an artist who "tak[es] a stand that ceases to be one"—that is, the stand ceases to be a "message" intended for an audience's edification. There is simply "nothing to be done," within art, through art, or beyond art, about the "thing" Beckett is describing in the *look*. It is of the same cut as Beckett's endless ruminations about the frustration of words in the trilogy. The problem hasn't been put to rest by the art, but the art isn't fooled into thinking it has: art simply negates the problem, as best it can, or stops the wound, as Hamm does with his stauncher.[5]

If I may allude once more to that slight *conceivable* taint of obscenity lurking in the theater experience: imagine the possibility that characters in a play (like our flying Peter Pan in Chapter 1) did not entirely condense themselves into the actors playing them, that somehow, in an additional sensory dimension, the ghost of the *real* Lear—the Lear idea, the Lear fact, from which Shakespeare only drew his great creation—imagine that it hovered in the vicinity of the catastrophic last scene of Shakespeare's play. Further, imagine that during the agony of Lear portrayed so movingly by the actor—during, say, the incomparable line, "Thou'lt come no more, / Never, never, never, never, never!"—that this ghost or idea or fact should suddenly crystallize into a face, much like Lear's own, and fix us, in effect, ask in a look of deep admonishment why we are there, we "men of stones," painlessly feeling his pain, how we can sit still during *that*, and why, if we have tongues and eyes, we do not use them to crack open heaven's vault.

This is what I think the fixing means in *Catastrophe*—again, mischievously, for there is a glint in Beckett's eye, not a sermon. And the shame felt by the first audience as its applause falters and dies is the double shame of being caught mistaking someone else's pain for our pleasure, as we often do during television newscasts, and of allowing pain to be aesthetically inflicted in our presence. That rough patron of realism who stopped Othello from strangling Desdemona was not of our breed, but the fact that we invented the joke about him suggests that he has some basis in the psychology of theater and that there is something lingering in our voyeurism that does not quite make moral sense. Of course, this something (whatever it is) is not the full measure of theater's appeal and it is outweighed, as I have said (perhaps too tranquilly), by a dozen virtues. But in

---

[5] I think offhand of the humble oyster on the sea bottom. What an irritation it must be to be invaded by a grain of sand. The oyster deals with the problem by surrounding the grain with nacreous material that forms a pearl—a thing of beauty to us, but a homemade solution to a problem for the oyster. Maybe art's primary motive is to manufacture a nacreous covering for the poet's irritations, which are also our own irritations insofar as the poet is one of us. And this allows us to put up with the enemy at one glistening remove. But isn't this another tranquilization from within the supposed detranquilization? Lord, another paradox! I think the oyster is better off.

the Theater of the Real, or the Now, where the Lears are still alive and unwell, agony doesn't settle into images very comfortably, and theater comes face to face with its double, the thing it can never be, which Lear called the thing itself.

Works Cited

Abel, Lionel. 1963. *Metatheatre: A New View of Dramatic Form*. New York: Hill and Wang.

Adorno, Theodor W. 1984. *Aesthetic Theory*. Trans. C. Lenhardt. London: Routledge and Kegan Paul.

Alter, Robert. 1984. *Motives for Fiction*. Cambridge: Harvard University Press.

Anderson, Maxwell. 1947. *Off Broadway: Essays about the Theater*. New York: William Sloane.

Aristotle. 1967. *Poetics*. Trans. Gerald F. Else. Ann Arbor: University of Michigan Press.

———. 1981. *Aristotle's Poetics: A Translation and Commentary for Students of Literature*. Trans. Leon Golden, commentary by O. B. Hardison, Jr. Tallahassee: Florida State University Press.

Arnheim, Rudolf. 1974. *Entropy and Art: An Essay of Disorder and Order*. Berkeley: University of California Press.

Augustine, Saint. 1973. From "The Confessions." In *An Augustine Reader*. Ed. John J. O'Meara. Garden City, N.Y.: Doubleday.

Bachelard, Gaston. 1969. *The Poetics of Space*. Trans. Maria Jolas. Boston: Beacon Press.

Bakhtin, M. M. 1986. *Speech Genres and Other Late Essays*. Trans. Vern W. McGee. Austin: University of Texas Press.

Barthes, Roland. 1972a. *Critical Essays*. Trans. Richard Howard. Evanston: Northwestern University Press.

———. 1972b. *Mythologies*. Trans. Annette Lavers. New York: Hill and Wang.

Barthes, Roland. 1975. *The Pleasure of the Text*. Trans. Richard Miller. New York: Hill and Wang.

Beckett, Samuel. 1931. *Proust*. New York: Grove Press.

———. 1965. *Three Novels*. New York: Grove Press.

———. 1984. *Collected Shorter Plays*. New York: Grove Press.

Benjamin, Walter. 1977. *The Origin of German Tragic Drama*. Trans. John Osborne. London: NLB.

Bentley, Eric. 1965. *The Life of the Drama*. New York: Atheneum.

Berkoff, Steven. 1989. *I Am Hamlet*. New York: Grove Weidenfeld.

Berlin, Normand. 1986. "The Tragic Pleasure of *Waiting for Godot*." In *Beckett at 80/Beckett in Context*, ed. Enoch Brater, pp. 46–63. New York: Oxford University Press.

Blau, Herbert. 1990. *The Audience*. Baltimore: Johns Hopkins University Press.

Bohannan, Laura. 1966. "Shakespeare in the Bush." *Natural History* 75 (August/September): 28–33.

Booth, Stephen. 1983. *"King Lear," "Macbeth," Indefinition, and Tragedy*. New Haven: Yale University Press.

Boyd, Richard. 1979. "Metaphor and Theory Change: What Is a 'Metaphor' For?" In *Metaphor and Thought*, ed. Andrew Ortony, pp. 356–408. Cambridge: Cambridge University Press.

Brecht, Bertolt. 1961. *Seven Plays by Bertolt Brecht*. Ed. Eric Bentley. New York: Grove Press.

——. 1966. *Brecht on Theatre: The Development of an Aesthetic*. Ed. and trans. John Willett. New York: Hill and Wang.

Bregman, Albert S. 1977. "Perception and Behavior as Compositions of Ideals." *Cognitive Psychology* 9: 250–92.

Burke, Kenneth. 1953. *Counter-Statement*. Los Altos, Calif.: Hermes.

——. 1957. *Philosophy of Literary Form: Studies in Symbolic Action*. Rev. ed. New York: Random House.

——. 1962. *A Grammar of Motives and A Rhetoric of Motives*. Cleveland: World Publishing.

——. 1970. *The Rhetoric of Religion: Studies in Logology*. Berkeley: University of California Press.

——. 1984. *Attitudes toward History*. 3d ed. Berkeley: University of California Press.

Carlson, Marvin. 1993. *Deathtraps: The Postmodern Comedy Thriller*. Bloomington: Indiana University Press.

Changeux, Jean-Pierre. 1985. *Neuronal Man: The Biology of Mind*. Trans. Laurence Garey. New York: Pantheon.

Chatman, Seymour. 1978. *Story and Discourse: Narrative Structure in Fiction and Film*. Ithaca: Cornell University Press.

Chekhov, Anton. 1977. *Anton Chekhov's Plays*. Trans. Eugene K. Bristow. New York: W. W. Norton.

Churchill, Caryl. 1991. *Cloud 9*. Rev. American ed. New York: Routledge.

Culler, Jonathan. 1985. *On Deconstruction: Theory and Criticism after Structuralism*. Ithaca: Cornell University Press.

Darwin, Charles. 1897. *The Origin of Species by Means of Natural Selection*. New York: Appleton.

Dufrenne, Mikel. 1973. *The Phenomenology of Aesthetic Experience*. Trans. Edward Casey, Albert A. Anderson, Willis Domingo, and Leon Jacobson. Evanston: Northwestern University Press.

Dürrenmatt, Friedrich. 1982. "Problems of the Theatre." In *Plays and Essays*, ed. Volkmar Sander. New York: Continuum.

———. 1984. "21 Points to the Physicists." In *The Physicists*. Trans. James Kirkup. New York: Grove Press.

Eco, Umberto. 1984. *The Role of the Reader: Explorations in the Semiotics of Texts*. Bloomington: Indiana University Press.

Eliot, T. S. 1954. *The Three Voices of Poetry*. New York: Cambridge University Press.

Else, Gerald F. 1967. *Aristotle's Poetics: The Argument*. Cambridge: Harvard University Press.

Eshleman, Clayton. 1981. *Hades in Manganese*. Santa Barbara, Calif.: Black Sparrow Press.

———. 1983. *Fracture*. Santa Barbara, Calif.: Black Swallow Press.

Fergusson, Francis. 1949. *The Idea of a Theater: The Art of Drama in Changing Perspective*. Garden City, N.Y.: Doubleday.

Field, Joanna. 1983. *On Not Being Able to Paint*. Los Angeles: Jeremy P. Tarcher.

Figes, Eva. 1976. *Tragedy and Social Evolution*. London: John Calder.

Freud, Sigmund. 1965. *The Interpretation of Dreams*. Trans. James Strachey. New York: Avon.

Frye, Northrop. 1957. *The Anatomy of Criticism: Four Essays*. Princeton: Princeton University Press.

———. 1967. *Fools of Time*. Toronto: University of Toronto Press.

Gadamer, Hans-Georg. 1985. *Truth and Method*. New York: Crossroad.

Gleick, James. 1988. *Chaos: Making a New Science*. New York: Penguin.

Goffman, Erving. 1986. *Frame Analysis: An Essay on the Organization of Experience*. Boston: Northeastern University Press.

Goodman, Nelson. 1978. *Ways of Worldmaking*. Indianapolis: Hackett.

Grene, David, and Richmond Lattimore, eds. 1960. *Greek Tragedies*. Vol. 1. Chicago: University of Chicago Press.

Handke, Peter. 1978. *Kaspar and Other Plays*. Trans. Michael Roloff. New York: Farrar, Straus and Giroux.

Harrop, John. 1992. *Acting*. London: Routledge.

Hayles, N. Katherine. 1990. *Chaos Bound: Orderly Disorder in Contemporary Literature and Science*. Ithaca: Cornell University Press.

———, ed. 1991. *Chaos and Order: Complex Dynamics in Literature and Science*. Chicago: University of Chicago Press.

Hegel, G. W. F. 1975. *Hegel on Tragedy*. Ed. Anne Paolucci and Henry Paolucci. New York: Harper and Row.

Heidegger, Martin. 1962. *Being and Time*. Trans. John Macquarrie and Edward Robinson. New York: Harper and Row.

———. 1975. *Poetry, Language, Thought*. Trans. Albert Hofstadter. New York: Harper and Row.

Hernadi, Paul. 1976. "The Actor's Face as the Author's Mask: On the Paradox of Brechtian Staging." In *Literary Criticism and Psychology*, vol. 7 of *Yearbook of Comparative Criticism*, ed. Joseph P. Strelka, pp. 125–36. University Park: Pennsylvania State University Press.

———. 1985. *Interpreting Events: Tragicomedies of History on the Modern Stage*. Ithaca: Cornell University Press.

Hofstadter, Douglas R. 1980. *Gödel, Escher, Bach: An Eternal Golden Braid*. New York: Vintage.

Holmes, Rupert. 1991. *Accomplice: A Comedy Thriller*. New York: Samuel French.

Ibsen, Henrik. 1957. *Six Plays by Henrik Ibsen*. Trans. Eva Le Gallienne. New York: Modern Library.

Ionesco, Eugène. 1958. *Amédée, The New Tenant, Victims of Duty*. Trans. Donald Watson. New York: Grove Press.

Iser, Wolfgang. 1993. *The Fictive and the Imaginary: Charting Literary Anthropology*. Baltimore: Johns Hopkins University Press.

Jackson, Shannon. 1992. "Performing the Performance of Power in Beckett's *Catastrophe*." *Journal of Dramatic Theory and Criticism* 6 (Spring): 23–41.

James, Henry. 1948. *The Art of Fiction*. New York: Oxford University Press.

Johnson, Samuel. 1986. *Selections from Johnson on Shakespeare*. Ed. Bertrand H. Bronson. New Haven: Yale University Press.

Jones, John. 1968. *On Aristotle and Greek Tragedy*. New York: Oxford University Press.

Kern, Stephen. 1983. *The Culture of Time and Space, 1880–1918*. Cambridge: Harvard University Press.

Kierkegaard, Søren. 1954. *Fear and Trembling and The Sickness unto Death*. Trans. Walter Lowrie. Garden City, N.Y.: Doubleday.

Koestler, Arthur. 1969. *The Act of Creation*. N.p.: Macmillan.

Krieger, Murray. 1960. *The Tragic Vision: Variations on a Theme in Literary Interpretation*. New York: Holt, Rinehart and Winston.

Lakoff, George, and Mark Johnson. 1980. *Metaphors We Live By*. Chicago: University of Chicago Press.

Langer, Susanne K. 1953. *Feeling and Form: A Theory of Art*. New York: Charles Scribner.

Leiris, Michel. 1987. *Nights as Day, Days as Night*. Trans. Richard Sieburth. Foreword by Maurice Blanchot. Hygiene, Colo.: Eridanos Press.

Libera, Antoni. 1985. "Beckett's *Catastrophe*." *Modern Drama* 28 (September): 341ff.

Lucas, F. L. 1962. *Tragedy: Serious Drama in Relation to Aristotle's Poetics*. New York: Collier.

Lukács, Georg. 1965. "The Sociology of Modern Drama." *Tulane Drama Review* 9 (Summer): 147–70.

———. 1974. *Soul and Form*. Trans. Anna Bostock. Cambridge: MIT Press.

Magarshack, David. 1960. *Chekhov the Dramatist*. New York: Hill and Wang.

Marranca, Bonnie. 1981. "The Politics of Performance." *Performing Arts Journal* 16: 54–67.

Mason, H. A. 1985. *The Tragic Plane*. Oxford: Clarendon Press.

Matte Blanco, Ignacio. 1975. *The Unconscious as Infinite Sets: An Essay in Bi-logic.* London: Duckworth.

Mehta, Xerxes. 1984. "Some Versions of Performance Art." *Theatre Journal* 36 (May): 165–98.

Merleau-Ponty, Maurice. 1964. *The Primacy of Perception and Other Essays on Phenomenological Psychology, the Philosophy of Art, History and Politics.* Ed. James M. Edie. Evanston: Northwestern University Press.

——. 1978. *Phenomenology of Perception.* Trans. Colin Smith. London: Routledge and Kegan Paul.

Metz, Christian. 1975. "The Imaginary Signifier." Trans. Ben Brewster. *Screen* 16 (Summer): 14–76.

Miller, J. Hillis. 1992. *Ariadne's Thread: Story Lines.* New Haven: Yale University Press.

Napier, A. David. 1986. *Masks, Transformation, and Paradox.* Berkeley: University of California Press.

Nietzsche, Friedrich. 1956. *The Birth of Tragedy and The Genealogy of Morals.* Trans. Francis Golffing. Garden City, N.J.: Doubleday.

——. 1968. *The Will to Power.* Trans. Walter Kaufmann and R. J. Hollingdale. New York: Random House.

Olson, Elder. 1966. *Tragedy and the Theory of Drama.* Detroit: Wayne State University Press.

Pavel, Thomas G. 1986. *Fictional Worlds.* Cambridge: Harvard University Press.

Pavis, Patrice. 1982. *Languages of the Stage: Essays in the Semiology of Theatre.* New York: Performing Arts Journal Publications.

Pinter, Harold. 1968. *Landscape.* London: Pendragon Press.

Poulet, Georges. 1981. "Criticism and the Experience of Interiority." In *Reader-Response Criticism from Formalism to Post-Structuralism,* ed. Jane P. Tompkins. Baltimore: Johns Hopkins University Press.

Quigley, Austin E. 1975. *The Pinter Problem.* Princeton: Princeton University Press.

Rayner, Alice. 1993. "The Audience: Subjectivity, Community, and the Ethics of Listening." *Journal of Dramatic Theory and Criticism* 7 (Spring): 3–24.

Richards, I. A. 1961. *Principles of Literary Criticism.* New York: Harcourt, Brace, and World.

Sartre, Jean-Paul. 1956. *Being and Nothingness: A Phenomenological Essay on Ontology.* Trans. Hazel E. Barnes. New York: Washington Square Press.

——. 1976. *Sartre on Theater.* Trans. Frank Jellinek. New York: Pantheon.

Scheler, Max. 1954. "On the Tragic." Trans. Bernard Stambler. *Crosscurrents* 4 (Winter): 179–91.

Schiller, Friedrich von. 1877. *The Correspondence between Schiller and Goethe.* 3 vols. Trans. Dora Schmitz. London: George Bell.

Shestov, Leon. 1966. *Chekhov and Other Essays.* Ann Arbor: University of Michigan Press.

Simmons, Ernest J. 1962. *Chekhov: A Biography.* Boston: Little, Brown.

Sparshott, Francis. 1983. "Preservation, Projection, and Presence: Preliminaries to a Consideration of Pictorial Representation." In *Essays in Aesthetics: Perspectives on the Work of Monroe C. Beardsley*, ed. John Fisher, pp. 131–46. Philadelphia: Temple University Press.

Starobinski, Jean. 1975 "The Inside and the Outside." *Hudson Review* 28 (Autumn):

States, Bert O. 1971. *Irony and Drama: A Poetics*. Ithaca: Cornell University Press.

———. 1985. *Great Reckonings in Little Rooms: On the Phenomenology of Theater*. Berkeley: University of California Press.

———. 1992. *Hamlet and the Concept of Character*. Baltimore: Johns Hopkins University Press.

———. 1993. *Dreaming and Storytelling*. Ithaca: Cornell University Press.

Steiner, George. 1968. *The Death of Tragedy*. New York: Knopf.

———. 1979. *Martin Heidegger*. New York: Viking Press.

Stoppard, Tom. 1973. *The Real Inspector Hound*. London: Faber and Faber.

Szondi, Peter. 1987. *The Theory of Modern Drama*. Ed. and trans. Michael Hays. Minneapolis: University of Minnesota Press.

Taussig, Michael. 1993. *Mimesis and Alterity: A Particular History of the Senses*. New York: Routledge.

Todorov, Tzvetan. 1977. *The Poetics of Prose*. Trans. Richard Howard. Ithaca: Cornell University Press.

———. 1980. *The Fantastic: A Structural Approach to a Literary Genre*. Trans. Richard Howard. Ithaca: Cornell University Press.

Turner, Victor. 1982. *From Ritual to Theatre: The Human Seriousness of Play*. New York: Performing Arts Journal Publications.

Van Laan, Thomas. 1991. "The Death-of-Tragedy Myth." *Journal of Dramatic Theory and Criticism* 5 (Spring): 5–31.

Vernant, Jean-Pierre, and Pierre Vidal-Naquet. 1981. *Tragedy and Myth in Ancient Greece*. Trans. Janet Lloyd. Sussex: Harvester Press; New Jersey: Humanities Press.

Walton, Kendall L. 1993. *Mimesis as Make-Believe: On the Foundations of the Representational Arts*. Cambridge: Harvard University Press.

Weitz, Morris. 1962. "The Role of Theory in Aesthetics." In *Philosophy Looks at the Arts*, ed. Joseph Margolis, pp. 48–60. New York: Scribner. Originally in *Journal of Aesthetics and Art Criticism* 15 (September): 27–35. The essay also appears in *A Modern Book of Aesthetics*, ed. Melvin Rader, pp. 199–208. New York: Holt, Rinehart and Winston, 1973.

Wellek, René, and Austin Warren. 1956. *Theory of Literature*. New York: Harcourt, Brace, and World.

Wilson, Edward O. 1978. *On Human Nature*. Cambridge: Harvard University Press.

Index

Abel, Lionel, 181; on Chekhov, 100
Accident, and the causal order, 61–64
Action: and accident, 61–64; in novel and theater, 75–76. *See also* Aristotle; Plot
Actor, the, 25–41; Aristotle on, 25; in Brecht, 110–11; cinema and stage compared, 30–31; as composite figure, 2; Harrop on, 25; Plato on, 26; Rousseau on, 26; Sartre on, 27
Adam, as tragic archetype, 129–30
Adorno, Theodor W.: on aesthetic feeling, 82–83; on the art work, 121; on Beckett, 197, 211; on catharsis, 81–82; on the enigma of art, 18, 20–21, 23
Aeschylus, *The Oresteia*, 154. *See also* Greek tragedy; Hegel, G. W. F.; Tragedy
Affirmation, in tragedy, 188–89
Alter, Robert, on Nabokov, 103
Anderson, Maxwell, on dramatic verse, 182
Aristotle, 178; on action (*praxis*), 57–73; on the actor, 25; Brecht on, 180; on catharsis, 82; on character (*ethos*), 123, 132, 143–44; on character and thought (*dianoia*), 147; comedy treatise of, 56; function of tragedy, 211; on hamartia, 124–35; on imitation (mimesis), 12–14, 20, 50–52, 158; influence of, 42–44, 180–81; on magnitude (wholeness), 49–52, 70, 83; on the marvelous, 64, 68, 100; on metabasis (reversal of fortune), 53; on the

mind, 154; "nested" effect in *Poetics*, 48–49; peripety, 22–23, 49, 53–56, 86–101. *Physics*, 78; on plot (*mythos*), 5–6, 47, 57–73; *Poetics* as textbook, 3–7; on probability, 69; on recognition (*anagnorisis*), 22–23, 53–56, 86–101; on spectacle (*opsis*), 147; on thought, 123, 143–44, 157, 167; on tragic hero, 123–24, 132; on the wonderful, 117. *See also* Tragedy
Arnheim, Rudolf, 49; on entropy, 122, 195n
Augustine, Saint, on time, 74–85
Author-character relationship, 158–79. *See also* Ventriloquism

Bachelard, Gaston, on sight, 74
Bakhtin, M. M., on "double-voicedness," 161
Barthes, Roland, 36; on the *fait divers*, 65–66, 131; on mythical speech, 105–6, 119–21; *Pleasure of the Text*, 9
Baudelaire, Charles, on the absolute comic, 55
Beckett, Samuel, 133, 170; Adorno on, 197; *All That Fall*, 199; Billie Whitelaw in, 199; *Breath*, 59; *Catastrophe*, 200–213; *Endgame*, 6, 135, 212; *Krapp's Last Tape*, 197–99; as lyric dramatist, 46; *Not I*, 197, 199; on Proustian time, 80; *Rockaby*, 197, 199; as tragic visionary, 197–99; *The Unnamable*, 198, 209; ventriloquism in, 177; *Waiting for Godot*, 72, 81, 154

Index

Index